Marketing: Principles and Practice

A management-oriented approach

Second Edition

Copyright © 2018 Svend Hollensen and Marc Oliver Opresnik

Texts:	© Copyright by Svend Hollensen and Marc Oliver Opresnik
Cover:	Linda Hartmann, panopticum design und kommunikation
Publisher:	Opresnik Management Consulting
Series:	Opresnik Management Guides, Book 8
Print:	createspace, an Amazon company

ISBN	9781720275244

Bibliografische Information der Deutschen Nationalbibliothek

Die Deutsche Nationalbibliothek verzeichnet diese Publikation in der Deutschen Nationalbibliografie; detaillierte bibliografische Daten sind im Internet über http://dnb.d-nb.de abrufbar

Marketing: Principles and Practice

A management-oriented approach

Second Edition

by

Prof. Svend Hollensen, Ph.D., University of Southern Denmark,

and

Prof. Marc Oliver Opresnik, Ph.D., Technische Hochschule Lübeck, Germany

To Jonna, Nanna and Julie

Svend Hollensen

To Charlie, Christine and Simon

Marc Opresnik

Preface

Books on marketing can inevitably be called into question as there are so many relevant works on the subject. However, many of them are either too difficult to understand, to lengthy and exhaustive or not related to practical decision making. Against this background, the aim of this book is to deal with marketing in such a way that covers as few pages and is as accessible as possible, while communicating the fundamental, most important theoretical aspects and facilitating the transfer of this knowledge to real-life decision situations. It concentrates on the essential marketing know-how for both, practitioners and students.

Target audience

This book is aimed primarily at students, MBA/graduate students and advanced undergraduates who wish to go into business. It will provide the information, perspectives, and tools necessary to get the job done. Our aim is to enable them to make better marketing decisions.

A second audience for this book is the large group of practitioners who want to build on the existing skills and knowledge already possessed.

A final target audience is the large group of students of marketing who want to effectively prepare for an examination and pass a test or the final exam.

Reading and learning outcomes

Having read this book:

- You will have a basic understanding of marketing and the process of marketing management.

- You will know the most important marketing instruments and how they interact.

- You can develop your own marketing plan.

Unique feature of this book

Most introductory texts deal solely with the marketing mix as the operational aspect of marketing or the strategic part. This marketing text not only integrates all relevant aspects of marketing but also structures them in such a way, that both practitioners and students acquire a comprehensive and holistic overview, how it all fits together. This is achieved by the structure of the book which follows the marketing planning and decision making process inside the company.

Outline

After outlining the fundamentals of marketing in the first chapter, the book is based on the main phases involved in marketing management, i.e. the decision-making process regarding formulating, implementing, and controlling a marketing plan:

- Phase 1: Situational analysis in the Marketing Planning Process (Chapter 2)
- Phase 2: Strategy formulation in the Marketing Planning Process (Chapter 3)
- Phase 3: Marketing Mix in the Marketing Planning Process (Chapter 4)
- Phase 4: Implementation and controlling in the Marketing Planning Process (Chapter 5)

Consequently, the book has a clear structure according to the **marketing planning process** of the firm (Figure I).

Figure I: Structure of the Book According to the Marketing Planning Process

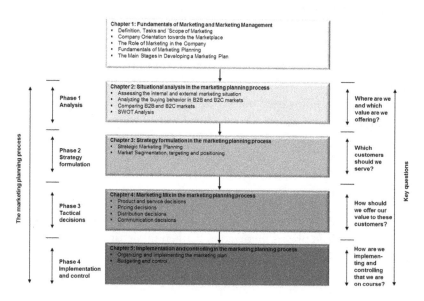

Throughout the writing period there has only been one constant in our lives – our families. Without them, nothing would have been possible. Thus, Professor Svend Hollensen and Professor Marc Oliver Opresnik dedicate this book to their families.

Svend Hollensen

University of Southern Denmark

Marc Oliver Opresnik

Technische Hochschule Lübeck, Germany

September 2018

Brief Contents

PREFACE...6

BRIEF CONTENTS 1

DETAILED CONTENTS...2

1. FUNDAMENTALS OF MARKETING AND MARKETING MANAGEMENT..........1

2. SITUATIONAL ANALYSIS IN THE MARKETING PLANNING PROCESS 28

3. STRATEGY FORMULATION IN THE MARKETING PLANNING PROCESS.........74

4. MARKETING MIX IN THE MARKETING PLANNING PROCESS 113

5. IMPLEMENTATION AND CONTROLLING IN THE MARKETING PLANNING PROCESS 215

6. CONCLUSION...233

REFERENCES...235

ABOUT THE AUTHORS 255

INDEX...258

Detailed Contents

1. FUNDAMENTALS OF MARKETING AND MARKETING MANAGEMENT 1

1.1 DEFINITIONS, TASKS AND SCOPE OF MARKETING 1
1.2 COMPANY ORIENTATION TOWARDS THE MARKETPLACE 7
1.3 THE ROLE OF MARKETING IN THE COMPANY 11
1.4 FUNDAMENTALS OF MARKETING PLANNING 12
1.5 THE MAIN STAGES IN DEVELOPING A MARKETING PLAN 16

2. SITUATIONAL ANALYSIS IN THE MARKETING PLANNING PROCESS 28

2.1 MARKETING RESEARCH 28
    2.1.1 Definition of Marketing Research 28
    2.1.2 Categories of Research 30
    2.1.3 Secondary Research 30
        2.1.3.1 Advantages of Secondary Research 31
        2.1.3.2 Disadvantages of Secondary Research 31
    2.1.4 Primary Research 33
        2.1.4.1 Qualitative and Quantitative Research 33
        2.1.4.2 Research Design 34
            2.1.4.2.1 Research Problem and Objectives 36
            2.1.4.2.2 Research Approaches 36
            2.1.4.2.3 Contact Methods 38
            2.1.4.2.4 Sampling Plan 40
            2.1.4.2.5 Contact Medium 42
            2.1.4.2.6 Pretesting, Data Collection and Analysis 43
        2.1.4.2 Problems with Using Primary Research 44
2.2 ASSESSING THE INTERNAL MARKETING SITUATION 46
    2.2.1 Market Orientation View (MOV) 47
    2.2.2 Resource Based View (RBV) 48
    2.2.3 Major Sources of Competitive Advantage 54
2.3 ASSESSING THE EXTERNAL MARKETING SITUATION 55
    2.3.1 PEST Analysis 57
    2.3.2 External Relationships to Stakeholders in the Value Net 58
        2.3.2.1 Relationships with Suppliers 58
        2.3.2.2 Relationships with Customers 60
        2.3.2.3 Relationships with Partners 61
        2.3.2.4 Relationships with Competitors 62
2.4 ANALYSING BUYING BEHAVIOUR IN THE B2C MARKET 63

2.5 ANALYSING BUYING BEHAVIOUR IN THE B2B MARKET 67

2.6 SWOT ANALYSIS 69

  2.6.1 Elements of a SWOT Analysis 70

  2.6.2 Matching and Converging in the SWOT Matrix 71

  2.6.3 Application of the SWOT Analysis 72

3. STRATEGY FORMULATION IN THE MARKETING PLANNING PROCESS 74

3.1 STRATEGIC MARKETING PLANNING 74

  3.1.1 Vision and Mission Statement 75

  3.1.2 Strategic Objectives 77

  3.1.3 Estimation of the Planning Gap and Problem Diagnosis 77

  3.1.4 The Search for Strategy Alternatives for Closing Planning Gap 80

  3.1.5 Ansoff's Generic Strategies for Growth 80

  3.1.6 Porter's Generic Strategies 84

  3.1.7 The BCG Portfolio Matrix Model 87

  3.1.8 The GE-Matrix Multifactor Portfolio Matrix 93

3.2 MARKET SEGMENTATION, TARGETING AND POSITIONING 95

  3.2.1 The Underlying Premises of Market Segmentation 96

  3.2.2 The Segmentation, Targeting and Positioning Approach 97

  3.2.3 Segmenting Consumer Markets (B2C) 99

    3.2.3.1 Profile Segmentation 100

      3.2.3.1.1 Demographic Variables 100

      3.2.3.1.2 Socio-Demographic Variables 101

      3.2.3.1.3 Geographic Variables 102

    3.2.3.2 Psychographic Segmentation 102

    3.2.3.3 Behavioural Segmentation 104

      3.2.3.3.1 Benefits sought 104

      3.2.3.3.2 Purchase occasion 104

      3.2.3.3.3 Purchase behaviour 105

      3.2.3.3.4 Usage 105

      3.2.3.3.5 Perceptions, Beliefs and Values 106

    3.2.3.4 Combining Segmentation Variables 106

  3.2.4 Segmenting the Business Markets (B2B) 106

  3.2.5 Target Marketing 107

  3.2.6 Positioning Strategy 110

4. MARKETING MIX IN THE MARKETING PLANNING PROCESS 113

4.1 PRODUCT AND SERVICE DECISIONS 113

4.1.1 Different Product Levels 114

4.1.2 Product Line Decisions 116

4.1.3 Product Mix Decisions 117

4.1.4 Services Marketing 119

    4.1.4.1 Characteristics of Services 119

    4.1.4.2 Categories of Service 120

    4.1.4.3 The 7Ps Model of Service Marketing 121

4.1.5 New Product Development (NPD) 124

4.1.6 The Product Life Cycle 125

4.1.7 Branding 127

    4.1.7.1 Brand Equity 128

    4.1.7.2 Brand Sponsorship 128

    4.1.7.3 Brand Development 129

4.2 PRICING DECISIONS 132

4.2.1 A Pricing Framework 132

    4.2.1.1 Internal Factors Affecting Pricing Decisions 132

    4.2.1.2 External Factors Affecting Pricing Decisions 134

4.2.2 General Pricing Approaches 138

    4.2.2.1 Cost-Based Pricing and Break-Even-Pricing 138

    4.2.2.2 Value-Based Pricing 141

    4.2.2.3 Competition-Based Pricing 142

4.2.3 Pricing new Products 143

4.2.4 Price Bundling 145

4.3 DISTRIBUTION DECISIONS 145

4.3.1 Types of Distribution Channel 146

4.3.2 Strategies for Market Coverage 147

4.3.3 Vertical Integration in the Distribution Channel 149

4.3.4 Multichannel Distribution Systems 152

4.3.5 Marketing Logistics and Supply Chain Management 152

4.3.6 Logistics Value Chain 153

4.4 COMMUNICATION DECISIONS 154

4.4.1 Key Opinion Leader Management 155

4.4.2 The Promotional Mix 155

4.4.3 Advertising 156

    4.4.3.1 Theories of How Advertising Works 157

    4.4.3.2 Developing an Advertising Strategy 159

4.4.4 Sales Promotion 169

    4.4.4.1 Major Sales Promotion Tools 170

4.4.4.1.1 Consumer Promotion Tools 170

4.4.4.1.2 Trade Promotion Tools 172

4.4.4.1.3 Business Promotion Tools.............................173

4.4.4.2 Developing the Sales Promotion Program....................174

4.4.5 Public Relations 174

4.4.6 Sponsorship..176

4.4.6.1 Principle Sponsorship Objectives.....................176

4.4.6.2 Components of Assessing a Sponsorship Property........177

4.4.6.3 Sponsorship Evaluation....................................180

4.4.7 Digital and Social Media Marketing 181

4.4.7.1 Evolution 181

4.4.7.2 Definition of Social Media Marketing 185

4.4.7.3 Extended Model of Social Media Marketing
Communication..187

4.4.7.4 The 6C Model of Social Media Marketing....................192

4.4.7.5 Effective Online Advertising Strategy 195

4.4.7.5.1 Who to Advertise to?....................................196

4.4.7.5.2 How to Advertise? 196

4.4.7.5.3 What to Advertise? 197

4.4.7.5.4 When to Advertise? 197

4.4.7.5.5 Where to Advertise?.....................................198

4.4.7.6 Online Performance Tracking 199

4.4.7.7 Building Buyer Loyalty 200

4.4.7.8 Smartphone Marketing....................................201

4.4.7.9 App Marketing 202

4.4.8 Direct Marketing 204

4.4.8.1 Benefits of Direct Marketing...........................205

4.4.8.2 Major Direct Marketing Tools.........................205

4.4.8.2.1 Direct Mail Marketing 206

4.4.8.2.2 Telemarketing 206

4.4.8.2.3 Catalogue Marketing 207

4.4.8.2.4 Direct Response Advertising 207

4.4.8.2.5 Online Marketing 208

4.4.9 Personal Selling 208

4.4.9.1 Sales Management 209

4.4.9.2 The Personal Selling Process...........................211

4.4.10 Product Placement...213

5. IMPLEMENTATION AND CONTROLLING IN THE MARKETING PLANNING PROCESS...**215**

5.1 ORGANIZING AND IMPLEMENTING THE MARKETING PLAN 215
    5.1.1 The Process of Developing the International Marketing Plan 215
    5.1.2 Deciding on the International Marketing Mix............................ 215
    5.1.3 Writing the Marketing Plan Document...................................... 216
        5.1.3.1 Title Page 218
        5.1.3.2 Table of Contents 219
        5.1.3.3 Executive Summary 219
        5.1.3.4 Introduction and Problem Statement 219
        5.1.3.5 Situational Analysis... 219
        5.1.3.6 Marketing Objectives 221
        5.1.3.7 Marketing Strategies 222
        5.1.3.8 Marketing Programs and Action Plans 222
        5.1.3.9 Budgets.. 222
        5.1.3.10 Implementation and Control...................................... 223
        5.1.3.11 Conclusion 224
    5.1.4 Implementing the Marketing Plan 224
    5.1.5 Deciding on the Marketing Organisation.............................. 225
5.2 BUDGETING AND CONTROL.. 226
    5.2.1 Marketing Productivity and Economic Results 227
    5.2.2 Marketing Budgeting 229
    5.2.3 Controlling the Marketing Programme................................. 231

6. CONCLUSION **233**

REFERENCES **235**

ABOUT THE AUTHORS **255**

INDEX...**258**

1. Fundamentals of Marketing and Marketing Management

1.1 Definitions, Tasks and Scope of Marketing

Peter Drucker, an Austrian-born American management consultant, educator, and author, whose writings contributed to the philosophical and practical foundations of the modern business corporation once stated: 'A business has two, and only two, basic functions: marketing and innovation. Marketing and innovation produce results; all the rest are costs.' In the future, marketing will play an increasingly important role for companies in order to achieve a sustainable competitive advantage and sustainable business growth (Bickhoff, Hollensen and Opresnik, 2014).

But what actually is marketing? Many people think of marketing as only sales and advertising! Every day we are bombarded with TV commercials, flyers, catalogues, sales calls, and commercial e-mail. However, selling and advertising are only one element of marketing. Today, marketing must be understood not in the old sense of making a sale but in a contemporary and holistic sense of satisfying customer needs. Marketing guru Philip Kotler defines marketing as societal and managerial process by which individuals and organizations obtain what they need and want through creating and exchanging value with others (Kotler, Armstrong and Opresnik, 2016).

To put in into a nutshell, Marketing is the achievement of corporate goals through meeting and exceeding customer needs and expectations better than the competition.

To apply this concept, three conditions must be met (Ellis-Chadwick and Jobber, 2016):

- First, company activities should be focused on providing customer satisfaction.
- Second, the achievement of customer satisfaction relies on an integrated effort. In the framework of a holistic and integrative approach to marketing today's marketers have to work closely with a variety of marketing partners when it comes to creating customer

lifetime value and building strong customer relationships. The responsibility for the implementation of the concept lies not just within the marketing department. As the late David Packard of Hewlett-Packard observed: 'Marketing is too important to leave it to the marketing organization.' Consequently, the belief that customer needs are instrumental to the operation of an enterprise should be internalized right through production, finance, research and development, engineering and all other departments. It is paramount to emphasize that marketing must affect every aspect of the customer experience. Every employee has an impact on the customer and must regard the customer as the source of the company's success and sustainable development. This concept of marketing implies it to be not just a function in the organization but a business philosophy which affects the entire company.

- Finally, management must be convinced that corporate goals can be achieved through satisfied customers.

Marketing has to be considered as a process by which companies create value for customers and build sustainable relationships in order to capture value from customers in return. Thus, marketing is the central driver of corporate profit and growth. The marketer' s role is to choose target markets, to build superior customer value and a sustainable competitive advantage by integrating all the activities in the company that affect the value offered to the customer.

A marketer is someone who seeks a response (attention, a purchase, a vote, a donation) from another party, called the prospect. If two parties are seeking to sell something to each other, they are both called marketers. Marketers are skilled at stimulating demand for their products, but that is merely a very limited view of what they actually do. Just as production and logistics professionals are responsible for supply management, marketers are responsible for demand management. They seek to influence the level, timing and composition of demand to meet the organization's objectives. Depending on a company's specific situation, there are different states of demand, which confront the marketer with challenges.

Eight demand states are possible (Kotler, Keller and Opresnik, 2017):

- *Negative demand*: Consumers dislike the product and may even pay to avoid it.

- *No demand*: Target customers are unaware of, or uninterested in, the product, e.g. farmers may not be interested in a new farming method. The marketing task would be to find ways to connect consumers' needs and interests with the benefits of the products and services.

- *Latent demand*: Consumers share a strong need that cannot be satisfied by any existing product, e.g. there is a strong latent demand for electric cars. The subsequent marketing task is to measure the size of the potential market and develop products and services to satisfy the respective demand.

- *Declining demand*: This is the biggest challenge facing most companies today. Due to rapid advances in technology and strong competitive pressure many companies are in danger of losing their competitive advantage and customer base. Against this background, the marketing task is to analyse the reasons for this decline and determine whether demand can be restored by opening up new target markets, by changing product benefits or by designing entirely new business models.

- *Irregular demand*: Customers purchases vary on a seasonal, monthly, weekly, daily, or even hourly basis.

- *Full demand*: Consumers are adequately buying all products put into the market.

- *Overfull demand*: More customers would like to buy the product than can be satisfied.

- *Unwholesome demand*: Consumers may be attracted to products that have undesirable social consequences.

Against the background of a holistic marketing philosophy, you can identify a specific set of tasks that make up successful marketing management (Kotler, Keller and Opresnik, 2017):

- *Developing marketing strategies and plans:* A key task is to identify potential opportunities and core competencies. You have to develop concrete marketing plans that specify the marketing strategy and tactics going forward.

- *Capturing marketing insights:* You need a reliable marketing information system to monitor their marketing environment so they can continually assess market potential and forecast demand. To transform strategy into programs, marketers must make basic decisions about their expenditures, activities, and budget allocations.

- *Connecting with customers:* As a marketer you have the task to consider how to best create value for its chosen target markets and develop strong, profitable, long-term relationships with customers. In order to accomplish these tasks, companies need to understand consumer markets as well as organizational buying behaviour: Who buys which products, and why? What features and prices is the customer looking for, and where do they shop? In this respect, companies need a sales force well trained in presenting product benefits. They must divide the market into major market segments, evaluate each one, and target those it can serve best.

- *Building strong brands:* You must understand the strengths and weaknesses of their brands as perceived by customers. They have to decide how to position them and must also pay attention to competitors, anticipating their strategies and knowing how to react adequately.

- *Shaping the market offerings:* The product is at the hearts of the marketing program and includes the product quality, design, features, and packaging. A critical marketing decision relates to the price. Marketers must decide on wholesale and retail prices, discounts, allowances, and credit terms.

- *Delivering value:* You must also determine how to deliver to the target market the value embodied in its products and services. Channel activities include those the company undertakes to make the product accessible and available to target customers. Marketers have to understand the various types of retailers, wholesalers, and physical-distribution firms and how they make their decisions.

- *Communicating value:* You must also communicate to the target market the value of their products and services. They need and integrated marketing communication program consisting of advertising, sales promotion, events, public relations, and personal communications. Companies also need to hire, train, and motivate salespeople.

- *Creating successful long-term growth:* Based on its product positioning, you must initiate new-product development, testing, and launching. Furthermore, they must build a marketing organization capable of implementing the marketing plan. Finally, a company needs feedback and control to understand the efficiency and effectiveness of its marketing activities.

While marketing originally concentrated on physical goods (especially consumer goods), today many more types of 'goods' are marketed. Marketers market 10 main types of entities (Kotler, Keller and Opresnik, 2017):

- *Goods:* Physical goods constitute the bulk of most countries' production and marketing efforts. Companies market diverse goods such as food products, cars, refrigerators, machines, televisions and other articles.

- *Services:* As economies advance, there is more focus on the production of services. Services include the work of hotels, car rental companies, barbers, maintenance and repair people, accountants, software programmers, management consultants and other market offerings. Many merchandises mix goods and services, such as a fast-food meal.

- *Events*: Marketers also promote events, such as trade shows, artistic performances, company anniversaries and global sporting events such as the Olympics and the World Cup.

- *Experiences*: By combining several services and goods, a company can create, stage, and market experiences. Examples includes parks like Disney World or Sea World.

- *Persons*: Artists like Madonna, musicians like the Rolling Stones, sport stars like David Beckham and other professionals get support from celebrity marketers.

- *Places*: Place marketers include economic development specialists, real estate agents, commercial banks, local business associations, and advertising and public relations agencies. In this respect, cities, states, regions, and whole nations compete to attract tourists, residents, factories, and company headquarters and consequently are marketed.

- *Properties*: Properties are intangible rights of ownership to either real property or financial property. They are bought and sold, and these exchanges require marketing. Examples include real estate agents marketing houses, or investment companies marketing securities to both institutional and individual investors.

- *Organizations*: Organizations work to build a strong, favourable, and unique image in the minds of their target groups. Companies, museums, universities and non-profits all use marketing to enhance their public images and compete for audiences and funds.

- *Information*: The production, packaging, and distribution of information are major industries. Information is ultimately what books, schools and universities produce, market, and distribute at a price to their customers.

- *Ideas*: Every market offering includes some basic idea. Products and services are platforms for delivering ideas or benefits.

1.2 Company Orientation Towards the Marketplace

A company has to decide which philosophy should guide their marketing efforts. There is no guarantee that all companies will adopt a holistic marketing orientation. In fact, there are five alternative concepts (Kotler, Keller and Opresnik, 2017):

- *The production concept*: It is one of the oldest concepts in business and holds that customers prefer products that are widely available and inexpensive. Managers of production-oriented businesses focus on achieving high production efficiency, low costs, and mass distribution. It believes that the central focus of the job is to attain economies of scale by producing a limited range of products in a form that minimizes production costs.

  This concept is still an applicable philosophy in some situations. For example, computer manufacturer Lenovo dominates the highly competitive, price-sensitive Chinese PC market through low labour costs, high production efficiency, and mass distribution. Possessing the lowest cost is seen as the major source of competitive advantage. The danger is that, in rapidly changing markets, an internal focus on production can lead to so-called *marketing myopia* in which implies that companies make the mistake of paying more attention to the specific products they offer than to the benefits and experiences produced by these products. Companies adopting this orientation run a major risk of focusing too narrowly on their own operations and losing sight of the real objective - satisfying customer needs and building customer relationships.

- *The product concept*: This philosophy holds that customers will favour products that offer the most in quality, performance, and innovative features. Under this concept, marketing strategy focuses on making continuous product improvements. Product quality and continuous improvement are important parts of most marketing strategies. However, focusing predominantly on the company's products can also lead to marketing myopia. A new or improved product will not necessarily be successful unless it is being priced, distributed, advertised, and sold adequately.

- *The selling concept*: Production-orientated businesses often make the transition to a sales orientation. Many companies actually follow the selling concept, which states that customers will not buy enough of the firm's products unless it undertakes a large-scale selling and promotion effort. This philosophy is typically practised with unsought goods and companies regard aggressive selling, advertising and sales promotion as means to penetrate the market. But selling is not marketing – in fact it can be just the opposite. As Theodore Levitt put in his famous 'Marketing myopia' article: ‚Selling tries to get the customer to want what the company has, marketing on the other hand, tries to get the company to produce what the customer wants.' Aggressive selling focuses on creating sales transactions rather than on building long-term, profitable customer relationships. This concept assumes customers coaxed into buying a product not only will not return or bad-mouth it or complain to consumer organizations but might even buy again which, in fact, are usually poor assumptions.

- *The marketing concept*: This philosophy holds that achieving organizational goals depends on knowing the needs and wants of target markets and delivering the desired satisfactions better than the competition do. Figure 1.1 contrasts the selling concept and the marketing concept.

The selling concept takes and inside-out perspective. It starts with the existing products of the company, and calls for aggressive selling and promotion to obtain profitable sales. It focuses predominantly on getting short-term sales with little concern about who buys or why.

In contrast, the marketing concept takes an outside-in perspective. It focuses on customer needs and wants, and integrates all the marketing activities that affect customers. In turn, it yields profits by creating lasting customer satisfaction.

Figure 1.1: Selling and Marketing Concepts Contrasted

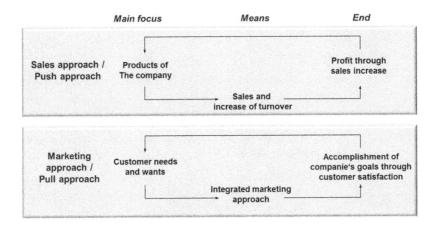

Source: Adapted from Bickhoff, Hollensen and Opresnik, 2014, modified

- *Relationship marketing concept*: In recent years, marketing has been undergoing extensive self-examination and internal debate. The overriding emphasis in the 'traditional' marketing approach is on acquiring as many customers as possible. Evidence is mounting, however, that traditional marketing is becoming too expensive and is less effective given changes in the micro and macro environment of firms. Many leading marketing academics and practitioners have concluded that many of the long-standing practices and operating modes in marketing need to be re-modelled, and we need to move towards an integrated relationship approach that is based on repeated market transactions and mutual sustainable gain for buyers and sellers. Relationship marketing reflects a strategy and process that integrate customers, suppliers, and other partners into the company's design, development, manufacturing, and sales processes. In the framework of this integrated and holistic concept, marketing exists to efficiently meet the satisfaction of customer needs, as well as those of the marketing organization. Marketing exchange seeks to achieve satisfaction for the consumer and the marketing organization (or company). In this latter group we include employees, shareholders, and managers. Other stakeholders like

9

competitors, financial and governmental institutions are also important. While recognizing that customer acquisition is, and will still remain, part of marketer's responsibilities this viewpoint emphasizes that a relationship view of marketing implies that maintenance and development are of equal or perhaps even greater importance to the company in the long run than customer acquisition. By differentiating between customer types the concept further suggests, that not all customers or potential customers should be treated in the same way. Relationship marketing, in contrast, sees the need to communicate in different ways dependent on customer's status and value.

This view of marketing also implies that suppliers were not alone in creating or benefiting from the value created by the corporation. Rather this philosophy can be seen as an on-going process of identifying and creating new value with individual consumers and then sharing the value benefits with them over the lifetime of the association.

This is due the *'lifetime value' concept* which concludes that a higher customer value will raise customer satisfaction; thereby customer loyalty will be instilling, which, in turn, creates higher profit due to increased volume resulting from positive word-of-mouth and repeat purchases.

Consequently, an enterprise should restrict taking a short-term view but rather should consider the income derived from that company's lifetime association with the consumer (see Figure 1.2).

Figure 1.2: Profit Growth over Time

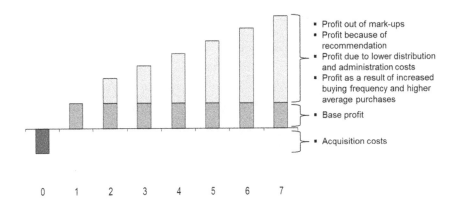

Source: Adapted from Hollensen and Opresnik, 2015, modified

In the framework of an integrative customer retention strategy a company should consequently project the value of individual customers over time rather than focus on customer numbers only. Thus, the overall objective of the relationship marketing concept is to facilitate and maintain long-term customer relationships, which leads to changed focal points and modifications of the marketing management process. The familiar superior objectives of all strategies are enduring unique relationships with customers, which cannot be imitated by competitors and therefore provide sustainable competitive advantages (Hollensen and Opresnik, 2015).

1.3 The Role of Marketing in the Company

As outlined already, it is paramount that marketing must not be a function in the organization but moreover a business philosophy. Marketing must affect every aspect of the customer experience. Consequently, every employee has an impact on the customer and must regard the customer as the source of the company's success.

Against this background, the **concept of internal marketing** is of key importance: It originates primarily from service organizations where it was first practiced as a strategy for making all employees aware of the need for customer satisfaction. In general, internal marketing refers to the managerial actions necessary to make all members of the organization understand and accept their individual roles in implementing marketing strategy. This means that all employees, from the chief executive officer to frontline marketing personnel, must realize how each individual job assists in implementing the marketing strategy. Under this approach, every employee has two sets of customers: external and internal. Ultimately, successful marketing implementation results from an accumulation of individual actions where all employees are responsible for implementing the marketing strategy. Ensuring that all staff, whatever their status, deliver a service of the highest quality to both internal and external customers is a key issue for all organizations. Essentially, this is what an integrative marketing management really implies, namely to direct each and every activity towards the customer, making formerly product-focused companies fully customer-centric. In this framework, the holistic and integrated relationship marketing approach can help imbue companies to rethink marketing and develop a more inclusive approach directing all departments, functions and staff towards the customer. Although this requires organizational transformation and a change in mindset, we suggest it to be an inevitable way to focus on customers need and wants and ensure a sustainable growth of companies (Hollensen and Opresnik, 2015).

1.4 Fundamentals of Marketing Planning

Marketing is the organisation function charged with defining customer targets and the best way to satisfy their needs and wants competitively and profitably. Because consumers and business buyers face an abundance of suppliers seeking to satisfy their every need, companies and not-for-profit organisations cannot survive today by simply doing a good job. They must do an excellent job if they are to remain in the increasingly competitive global marketplace. Many studies have demonstrated that the key to profitable performance is knowing and satisfying target customers with competitively superior offers. This process takes place today in an increasingly global, technical, and competitive environment.

There are some key reasons why marketing planning has become so important.

Recent years have witnessed an intensifying of competition in many markets. Many factors have contributed to this, but amongst some of the more significant are the following:

- A growth of global competition, as barriers to trade have been lowered and global communications improved significantly.
- the role of the multinational conglomerate has increased. This ignores geographical and other boundaries and looks for profit opportunities on a global scale.
- In some economies, legislation and political ideologies have aimed at fostering entrepreneurial and 'free market' values.
- Continual technological innovation, giving rise to new sources of competition for established products, services and markets.

The importance of competition and competitor analysis in contemporary strategic marketing cannot be overemphasized. Indeed, because of this we shall be looking at this aspect in more depth in later chapters. This importance is now widely accepted amongst both marketing academics and practitioners. Successful marketing in a competitive economy is about competitive success and that in addition to a customer focus a true marketing orientation also combines competitive positioning.

The Marketing concept holds that the key to achieving organisational goals lies in determining the needs and wants of target markets, and delivering the desired 'satisfaction' more effectively and resourcefully than competitors.

Marketing planning is an approach adopted by many successful, market-focused companies. While it is by no means a new tool, the degree of objectivity and thoroughness with which it is applied varies significantly.

Marketing planning can be defined as the structured process of researching and analysing the marketing situations, developing and documenting marketing objectives, strategies, and programs, and implementing, evaluating, and controlling activities to achieve the goals. This systematic process of marketing planning involves analyzing the environment and the company's capabilities, and deciding on courses of action and ways to implement those decisions. As the marketing environment is so changeable that paths to new opportunities can open in an instant, even as others become obscured or completely blocked, marketing planning must be approached as an adaptable, ongoing process rather than a rigid, static annual event.

The outcome of this structured process is the marketing plan, a document that summarizes what the marketer has learned about the marketplace and outlines how the firm plans to reach its marketing objectives. In addition, the marketing plan not only documents the organisation's marketing strategies and displays the activities that employees will implement to reach the marketing objectives, but it entails the mechanisms that will measure progress toward the objectives and allows for adjustments if actual results take the organisation off course.

Marketing plans generally cover a 1-year-period, although some may project activities and financial performance further into the future. Marketers must start the marketing planning process at least several months before the marketing plan is scheduled to go into operation; this allows sufficient time for thorough research and analysis, management review and revision, and coordination of resources among functions and business units.

Marketing planning inevitably involves change. It is a process that includes deciding currently what to do in the future with a full appreciation of the resource position; the need to set clear, communicable, measurable objectives; the development of alternative courses of action; and a means of assessing the best route towards the achievement of specified objectives. Marketing planning is designed to assist the process of marketing decision making under prevailing conditions of risk and uncertainty.

Above all the process of marketing planning has a number of benefits (Hollensen, 2006):

- **Consistency**: The individual marketing action plans must be consistent with the overall corporate plan and with the other departmental or functional plans.

- **Responsibility**: Those who have responsibility for implementing the individual parts of the marketing plan will know what their responsibilities are and can have their performance assessed against these plans. Marketing planning requires management staff to make clear judgmental statements about assumptions, and it enables a control system to be designed and established whereby performance can be assessed against pre-defined criteria.

- **Communication**: Those implementing the plans will also know that the overall objectives are and how they personally may contribute in this respect.

- **Commitment**: Assuming that the plans are agreed upon by those involved in their implementation, as well as by those who will provide the resources, the plans do stimulate a group commitment to their implementation, and ultimately lead to better strategy-implementation.

Plans must be specific to the organisation and its current situation. There is not one system of planning but many systems, and a planning process must be tailor-made for a particular firm in a specific set of conditions.

Marketing planning as a functional activity has to be set in a corporate planning framework. There is an underlying obligation for any organisation adopting marketing planning systems to set a clearly defined business mission as the basis from which the organisational direction can develop.

Without marketing planning, it is more difficult to guide research and development (R&D) and new product development (NPD); set required standards for suppliers; guide the sales force in terms of what to emphasize, set realistic, achievable targets, avoid competitor actions or changes in the marketplace. Above all, businesses which fail to incorporate marketing planning into their marketing activities may therefore not be in a position to develop a sustainable competitive advantage in their markets (Hollensen, 2006).

1.5 The Main Stages in Developing a Marketing Plan

Marketing planning is a methodical process involving assessing marketing opportunities and resources, determining marketing objectives, and developing a plan for implementation and control.

Marketing planning is an ongoing analysis/planning/control process or cycle (see Figure 1.3). Many organisations update their marketing plans annually as new information becomes accessible.

Once built-in, the key recommendations can then be presented to key stakeholders within the organisation. The final task of marketing planning is to summarize the relevant findings from the marketing analysis, the strategic recommendations and the required marketing programs in a report: the written marketing plan. This document needs to be concise, yet complete in terms of presenting a summary of the marketplace and the business's position, explaining thoroughly the recommended strategy and containing the detail of marketing mix activities. The plan should be informative, to the point, while mapping out a clear set of marketing activities designed to satisfactorily implement the desired target market strategy (Hollensen, 2006).

Figure 1.3 illustrates the several stages that have to be gone through in order to arrive at a marketing plan. Each of the stages illustrated here will be discussed in more detail later in this chapter and in later sections of the book.

As illustrated in Figure 1.3 the development of a marketing plan is a process, and each step in the process has a structure that enables the marketing plan to evolve from abstract information and ideas into a tangible document that can easily be understood, evaluated, and implemented. The following section is devoted to an in-depth discussion of each step in this process (Gilmore et al., 2001; Day, 2002).

Step 1: Mission, Corporate Goals and Objectives

An organisation's **mission** can be described as a broadly defined, enduring statement of purpose that distinguishes a company from others of its type. It is enduring and specific to the individual organisation and tells what the organisation hopes to accomplish and how it plans to achieve this goal. This expression of purpose provides management with a clear sense of direction.

Figure 1.3: The Stages of Building a Marketing Plan

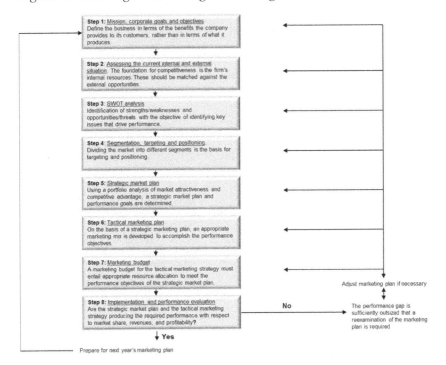

Source: Adapted from Hollensen and Opresnik, 2015, modified

The corporate **mission statement** needs comprehensive considerations by top management to establish the business, which the company is really in and to relate this consideration to future business intentions. It is a general statement that provides an integrating function for the business, from which a clear sense of business definition and direction can be derived.

This stage is often overlooked in marketing planning, and yet without it the plan will lack a sense of contribution to the development of the entire enterprise. By deriving a clear mission statement, boundaries for the 'corporate entity' can be conceived in the context of environmental trends that influence the company (Hollensen, 2006).

It is useful to establish the distinctive competences of the organisation and to focus upon what customers are buying rather than upon what the company is selling. This will assist in the development of a marketing oriented mission statement. A clear mission statement should include the customer groups to be served the consumer needs to be served and the technologies to be utilized.

Essentially, four characteristics are associated with an effective mission statement (Day, 1999):

- First, it must be based on a solid comprehension of the business, and the vision to foresee how the forces influencing its operations with alter in the future.
- Second, the mission should be based upon the deep personal conviction and motivation of the founder or leader, who has the ability to make his or her vision transmittable. An example is Google's mission to organize all the world's information and make it universally accessible and useful. Consequently, the mission must be shared throughout the organisation.
- Third, effective mission statements should instil the strategic intent of winning throughout the organisation. This helps to create a sense of common and shared purpose.
- Finally, mission statements should be enabling. Managers should believe they have the freedom to make decisions about the strategy. The mission statement provides a framework within which managers decide which opportunities and threats to address, and which to disregard.

The general purpose expressed in the organisation's mission statement must be translated into more specific guidelines as to how these general intentions will operate. Organisations and the people who manage them tend to be more productive when they have established standards to motivate them, specific directions to guide them, and stated achievements levels against which to assess their performance.

Step 2: Assessing the Current Internal and External Situation

The situation analysis attempts to provide answers to the following questions:

- 'Where are we now?'
- 'How did we get here?'
- 'Where are we heading?'

Answers to these key questions depend upon an analysis of the internal and external environment of a business. Thus, the situation analysis encompasses the forces that shape market attractiveness, competitive position, and present performance (Ellis-Chadwick and Jobber, 2016).

The basis for competitiveness is the firm's internal resources, capabilities and competences. These should be matched with the external opportunities, and altogether it sums up to step 3 – the SWOT analysis.

Step 3: SWOT analysis

A SWOT analysis is a structured tool to evaluating the strategic position of a company by identifying its strengths, weaknesses, opportunities and threats. The subsequent steps will be only as good as the situation analysis and key performance issues that are uncovered in the situation and SWOT analysis.

In assessing current situations, SWOT analysis attempts to identify one or more strategic relationships or match-ups between strategic business units

(SBU) current strengths or weaknesses and its present or future opportunities and threats. Corporations face strategic windows in which key requirements of a market and the particular competencies of the organisation best fit together. Identifying these limited time periods is a rationale for employing a SWOT analysis.

The tool provides a simple method of synthesizing the results of the internal and external analysis undertaken in step 2.

Strengths are the bases for building company competences and finally competitiveness. An internal organisational check attempts to ascertain the type and degree of each SBU's strengths and weaknesses. By recognising their special capabilities and limitations, firms are better able to adjust to the external environmental conditions of the marketplace. In this respect, it is of key importance to always question the strengths identified for their impact on customer satisfaction.

'Know yourself and your competence' is the basic tenet that guides this assessment of the abilities and deficiencies of the organisation's internal operations. It is also the basic tenet in the so-called Resource Based View (RBV), which will be further discussed in Chapter 2.

All businesses do have **weaknesses**. Successful businesses try to minimise their shortcomings. A weakness can be any business function or operation that is not able to resist external forces or withstand attack. A weak business function or operation is one that is deficient or inferior in its ability to reap the benefits presented by an external opportunity. Weaknesses are most viewed in comparative terms; a company has a weakness when it is unable to perform a business function or conduct a business operation as effectively and efficiently as its competitors (Hollensen, 2006).

The internal factors that may be viewed as strengths or weaknesses depending upon their impact on the organisation's positions (they may represent a strength for one organisation but a weakness, in relative terms, for another), may include all of the four elements of the marketing mix, as well as other functions such as personnel, finance etc.

The second part of a SWOT analysis involves the organisation's external environments. This environmental scanning process involves the opportunities and threats that are part of a SWOT analysis. The external factors, which again may be threats to one organisation whereas they offer opportunities to another, may include factors such as technological change, legislation, and socio-cultural changes, as well as changes in the marketplace or competitive position.

Opportunities are unsatisfied customer needs that the organisation has a good chance of meeting successfully. For an environmental occurrence to be considered an opportunity by a particular business, a favourable juncture of circumstances must exist. A unique business strength must fit an attractive environmental need in order to create a high probability of a successful match, as when a low-cost producer identifies an unserved market of low-income consumers. Good opportunities are needs that the company can satisfy in a more complete fashion than can existing competitors. In this context it has to emphasized that these opportunities are indeed external factors which are not controllable by the company such as demographic change, the fitness trend etc..

Threats are finally aspects of the external environment that create challenges posed by an unfavourable trend or development that would lead, in the absence of defensive marketing action, to lower sales or profit.

Once a SWOT analysis has been completed management has to evaluate how to turn weaknesses into strengths and threats into opportunities. For example, a perceived weakness in customer focus might suggest the need for extensive staff training to create a new strength. Because these activities are designed to convert weaknesses into strengths and threats into opportunities they are called **conversion strategies**.

Another option provided is to match strengths with opportunities. An example of a company that successfully matched strengths with opportunities in the UK clothing retailer Next, which identified an opportunity in the growing demand for telemarketing services. One of the company's strengths was the fact that it had run its own call centres for more than a decade to service its own home shopping operation. As a result, Next has created a profitable business running call centres for other organisations (Ellis-Chadwick and Jobber, 2016). These activities are called **matching strategies**.

The SWOT-analysis is just one tool to assess the current situation. It has its own weaknesses in that it tends to persuade companies to compile lists rather than to think about what is really important to their business. It also presents the resulting lists without clear prioritization, so that, for example, weak opportunities may appear to balance strong threats.

The aim of any SWOT analysis should be to identify potential 'strategic windows' and isolate what will be important to the future of the organisation and that subsequent marketing planning will address.

Step 4: Segmentation, Targeting and Positioning

In addition to analyzing the environment, marketers need to analyze their markets and their customers, whether consumers or businesses. This means looking closely at market trends, changing customer behaviour, product demand and future projections, buying habits, needs and wants, customer attitudes, and customer satisfaction.

Marketers have to apply their knowledge of the market and customers – acquired through research – to determine which parts of the market, known as segments, should be targeted for marketing activities as marketing is not about chasing any customer at any price. A decision has to be made regarding those groups of customers respectively segments that are attractive to the business (Ellis-Chadwick and Jobber, 2016). This implies dividing the overall market into separate groupings of customers, based on characteristics such as age, gender, geography, needs, behaviour, or other variables.

The purpose of **segmentation** is to group customers with similar needs, wants, behaviour, or other characteristics that affect their demand for or usage of the good or service being marketed.

Once the market has been segmented, the next set of decisions focuses on **targeting**, including whether to market to one segment, to several segments, or to the entire market, and how to cover these segments. The company also needs to formulate a suitable **positioning**, which means using marketing to create a competitively distinctive place (position) for the brand or product in the mind of targeted customers. This positioning must effectively set the product apart from competing products in a way that is meaningful to customers.

Step 5: Strategic Market Plan (Marketing Strategy)

At this point in the marketing planning process, the company has examined its current situation, looked at markets and consumers, set objectives, and identified segments to be targeted and an appropriate positioning. Now management can create the marketing strategies, effectively combining the basic marketing mix tools of product, place, price, and promotion, enhanced by service strategies to build stronger customer relationships.

Marketing strategies must be consistent with the organisation's overall corporate goals and objectives. As marketing objectives are essentially about the match between products and markets they must be based on realistic customer behaviour in those markets.

To be most effective, objectives must be measurable. The measurement may be in terms of sales volume, turnover volume, market share, or percentage penetration of distribution outlets. As it is measured, it can, within limits, be unequivocally monitored and corrective action taken as appropriate. Usually marketing objectives must be based, above all, on the organisation's financial objectives; financial measurements are converted into the related marketing measurements. An example of a measurable marketing objective might be 'to enter market X with product Y and capture 15 percent of the market by value within the first three years.'

In principle, the strategic market plan describes how the firm's marketing objectives will be achieved. It is essentially a pattern or plan that integrates an organisation's major goals, policies, and action sequences into a cohesive whole. Marketing strategies are generally concerned with the 4Ps:

1. Product strategies
    - Developing new products, repositioning or re-launching existing ones, and scrapping old ones
    - Adding new features and benefits
    - Balancing product portfolios
    - Changing the design or packaging
2. Pricing strategies
    - Setting the price to skim or to penetrate
    - Pricing for different market segments
    - Deciding how to meet competitive pricing
3. Promotional strategies
    - Specifying the advertising platform and media
    - Deciding the public relations brief
    - Organizing the sales force to cover new products and services or markets
4. Place distribution strategies
    - Choosing the channels
    - Deciding levels of customer service

One often-overlooked aspect of the marketing strategy is timing. Choosing the best time for each element of the strategy is often vital. Sometimes, taking the right action at the wrong time can be almost as bad as taking the wrong action at the right time.

Timing is, therefore, an essential part of any plan and should normally appear as a schedule of planned activities (Hollensen, 2006).

Step 6: Tactical Marketing Plan

The next step in the marketing planning process is the development of a tactical marketing plan to put the strategic market plan into operation. Although the overall marketing strategy to protect, grow, harvest, enter, or exit a market position is set by the strategic market plan, more-specific tactical marketing strategies need to be developed. Marketing managers have at their disposal four marketing tools with which they can match their products and services to customer's requirements. These marketing mix decisions consist of evaluations about price levels, the blend of promotional techniques, the distribution channels and the types of products to manufacture (Ellis-Chadwick and Jobber, 2016).

Therefore, the firm's overall marketing strategies need to be developed into detailed plans and programs. Although these detailed plans may cover each of the 4Ps, the focus will vary, depending on your organisation's specific strategies. A product-oriented company will focus its plans for the 4Ps around each of its products. A market or geographically-oriented company will concentrate on each market or geographical area. Each will base its plans on the detailed needs of its customers and on the strategies chosen to satisfy these needs.

The most important element is the detailed plans, which spell out exactly what programs and individual activities will take place over the period of the plan (usually over the next year). Without these specified – and preferably quantified – activities the plan cannot be monitored, even in terms of success in meeting its objectives.

Step 7: Marketing Budget

The traditional quantification of a marketing plan appears in the form of budgets. The purpose of a marketing budget is to pull all the revenues and costs involved in marketing together into one comprehensive file. It is a managerial tool that balances what is needed to be spent against what can be afforded and helps make choices about priorities. It is then used in tracking the performance in practice.

Resources need to be allocated in a marketing budget based on the strategic and operational marketing plan. Without adequate resources, the tactical marketing strategies cannot succeed, and, as a consequence, performance objectives cannot be achieved.

Specifying a marketing budget is perhaps the most difficult part of the market planning process. Although specifying the budget is not a clear-cut process, there must be a logical connection between the strategy and performance objectives and the marketing budget.

Each area of marketing activity should be allocated to centres of responsibility. Indeed, as a key functional area of business the marketing budget is one of the key budgets to concentrate towards the total budgetary control system of the organisation.

In many organisations, budgeting is the transitional step between planning and implementation, because the budget, and allocated centres within it, will project the cost of each activity over the specified period of time, and also act as a guide for implementation and control (Hollensen, 2006).

Step 8: Implementation and Performance Evaluation

The best marketing plan is useless unless it 'degenerates into work' (Drucker, 1993, p. 128). Consequently, the business must design an organisation that has the capability of implementing the strategy and the tactical plan. Once strategies and plans are implemented, the company needs to plan for ways to determine effectiveness by identifying mechanisms and metrics to be used to measure progress toward objectives. Most companies use sales forecasts, schedules, and other tools, to set and record standards against which progress can be assessed. By comparing actual results against daily, weekly, monthly, quarterly, and yearly projections, management can see where the firm is ahead, where it is behind, and where it needs to make adjustments to get back on the right path.

In the course of reviewing progress, marketers also should look at what competitors are doing and what the markets are doing so they can put their own outcomes into context.

To control implementation, marketers should start with the objectives they have set, establish standards for measuring progress toward those targets, measure the performance of the marketing programs, diagnose the results, and then take corrective action if results fail to measure up. This is the marketing control process. The control process is iterative; managers should expect to retrace their steps as they systematically implement strategies, assess the results, and take action to bring performance in line with expectations. Companies use this control process to analyse their marketing implementation on the basis of such measures as market share, sales, profitability, and productivity.

There are three main marketing planning approaches, in terms of involvement of the organisation as a whole. They are:

- **Top-down planning**: Here top management sets both the goals and the plan for lower-level management. While decision making may be immediate at the top level, implementation of the plans may not be as swift because it takes time for various units (division, groups, and departments) to learn about the plans and to reorganize their tasks accordingly to accomplish the new goals.

- **Bottom-up planning**: In this approach, the various units of the organisation create their own goals and plans, which are then approved (or not) by higher management. This can lead to more creative approaches, but it can also pose problems for coordination. More pragmatically, strategy all too frequently emerges from a consolidation of tactics.

- **Goals-down-plans-up-planning**: This is the most common approach, at least among the organisations that invest in such sophisticated planning processes. Top management set the goals, but the various units create their own plans to meet these goals. These plans are then typically approved as part of the annual planning and budgetary process.

2. Situational Analysis in the Marketing Planning Process

2.1 Marketing Research

2.1.1 Definition of Marketing Research

As discussed in chapter one, the marketing concept is a business philosophy that puts the customer and customer satisfaction at the centre of things. Marketing research is an organisational activity that plays an important role in implementing this marketing philosophy. It helps in improving management decision making by providing relevant, accurate, and timely information. Every decision poses unique needs for information, and relevant strategies can be developed based on the information gathered through marketing research in action.

To find out a) if there is a market, b) how big the market is and c) what the competition is doing, a systematic and scientifically valid approach is required. This approach is called market research. Sometimes the term 'Marketing research' is used as well. When this distinction is made, 'market research' is defined more narrowly as the research of markets (excluding e. g. competitors and customers). 'Marketing research' goes beyond 'market research' and includes competitor and customer research as well as other sources of information like internal records and software-based marketing decision support systems. Thus, marketing research can be defined as the systematic collection, analysis and interpretation of data about markets, customers and competitors. It has to provide a reliable basis for marketing decision-making. However, marketing research is no guarantee for business success e.g. studies put the failure rate of new consumer products at 95 per cent in the United States and at 90 per cent in Europe. Especially in high-tech marketing, e. g. in telecommunications, computers, consumer electronics and biotech, failure risks are particularly high. The reasons are:

- High market uncertainty

- High competitive volatility

- High investment cost

- Short product life cycles

Nevertheless, there are also marketing success stories, which involve little or no market research at all e. g. the 'Sony Walkman' was based on the 'gut feeling' and vision of Sony's chairman, who allegedly pushed his idea through against the fierce resistance of his managers. In that case, Sony was 'market-driving', not 'market-driven'. It created a new market by launching a product that no consumer could even imagine!

Marketing research not only looks at the market in general, but that it also seeks to obtain sophisticated and detailed information about customers, market segments and the competition. In addition, if a company wants to assess the market position, it has to look inside the organisation in order to identify those parameters that determine its competitive strengths, e. g. the cost structure or innovation power.

Looking at approaches to conducting marketing research, the two main forms of market research are **ad-hoc research** and **continuous research**. Ad-hoc research, focuses on a specific problem and can take the form of custom designed surveys or omnibus studies. Continuous research involves interviewing the same sample of people repeatedly. Continuous research methods include: consumer panels, retail audits and television viewership panels. Marketing databases and website analysis are also means of collecting data on customers on an on-going basis. Regardless of which form of research is chosen the company must decide whether it should carry out the research using internal company resources or employ a market research agency.

This decision is likely to depend on the company resources: time, money, skills and experience available.

2.1.2 Categories of Research

The researcher can gather two types of data collection: secondary data and primary data:

- **Primary data:** These can be defined as information that is collected first-hand, generated by original research tailor-made to answer specific current research questions.

  The major advantage of primary data is that the information is specific ('fine grained'), relevant and up to date.

  The disadvantages of primary data are, however, the high costs and amount of time associated with its collection.

- **Secondary data:** These can be defined as information that has already been collected for other purposes and is thus readily available.

  The major disadvantage is that the data are often more general and 'coarse grained' in nature.

  The advantages of secondary data are the low costs and amount of time associated with its collection. For those who are unclear on the terminology, secondary research is frequently referred to as 'desk research'.

The two basic forms of research (primary and secondary research) are roughly characterized in Figure 2.1.

2.1.3 Secondary Research

With many international markets to consider, it is essential that firms begin their market research by seeking and utilising secondary data.

2.1.3.1 Advantages of Secondary Research

Secondary research conducted from the home base is less expensive and less time consuming than research conducted abroad. No contacts have to be made outside the home country, thus keeping commitment to possible future projects at a low level. Research undertaken in the home country about the foreign environment also has the benefit of objectivity. The researcher is not constrained by overseas customs. As a preliminary stage of a market-screening process, secondary research can quickly generate background information to eliminate many countries from the scope of enquiries.

Figure 2.1: Primary and Secondary Data Sources

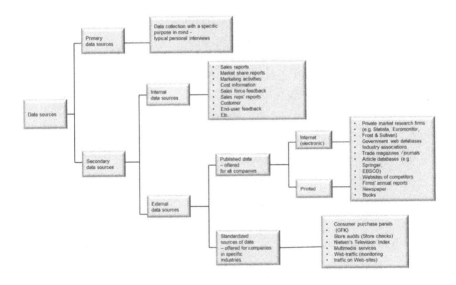

Source: Adapted from Hollensen and Opresnik, 2015, modified

2.1.3.2 Disadvantages of Secondary Research

Problems with secondary research are as follows.

Non-availability of data

In many developing countries, secondary data are very scarce. Weak economies have poor statistical services – many do not even carry out a population census. Information on retail and wholesale trade is especially difficult to obtain. In such cases, primary data collection becomes vital.

Reliability of data

Sometimes political considerations may affect the reliability of data. In some developing countries, governments may enhance the information to paint a rosy picture of the economic life in the country. In addition, due to the data collection procedures used, or the personnel who gathered the data, many data lack statistical accuracy. As a practical matter, the following questions should be asked to judge the reliability of data sources (Cateora, 1993, p. 346):

- Who collected the data? Would there be any reason for purposely misrepresenting the facts?
- For what purpose was the data collected?
- How was the data collected (methodology)?
- Are the data internally consistent and logical in the light of known data sources or market factors?

Data classification

In many countries, the data reported are too broadly classified for use at the micro level.

Comparability of data

International marketers often like to compare data from different countries. Unfortunately, the secondary data obtainable from different countries are not readily comparable because national definitions of statistical phenomena differ from one country to another.

Although the possibility of obtaining secondary data has increased dramatically, the international community has grown increasingly sensitive to the issue of data privacy. Readily accessible large-scale databases contain information valuable to marketers but they are considered sensitive by the individuals who have provided the data. The international marketer must therefore also pay careful attention to the privacy laws in different nations and to the possible consumer response to using such data. Neglecting these concerns may result in research backfiring and the corporate position being weakened.

In doing secondary research or building a decision support system, there are many information sources available. Generally, these secondary data sources can be divided into internal and external sources (Figure 2.1). The latter can be classified as either international/global or regional/country-based sources.

2.1.4 Primary Research

2.1.4.1 Qualitative and Quantitative Research

If a marketer's research questions are not adequately answered by secondary research it may be necessary to search for additional information in primary data. These data can be collected by quantitative research and qualitative research. Quantitative and qualitative techniques can be distinguished by the fact that quantitative techniques involve getting data from a large, representative group of respondents (Hollensen and Opresnik, 2015):

- **Quantitative research:** Data analysis based on questionnaires from a large group of respondents.
- **Qualitative research:** Provides a holistic view of a research problem by integrating a larger number of variables, but asking only a few respondents. The objective of qualitative research techniques is to give a holistic view of the research problem, and therefore these

techniques must have a large number of variables and few respondents. Choosing between quantitative and qualitative techniques is a question of trading off breadth and depth in the results of the analysis.

Data retrieval and analysis of qualitative data, however, are characterised by a high degree of flexibility and adaptation to the individual respondent and his or her special background. Another considerable difference between qualitative and quantitative surveys is the source of data (Hollensen and Opresnik, 2015):

- **Quantitative techniques** are characterised by a certain degree of distance as the construction of the questionnaire, data retrieval and data analysis take place in separate phases. Data retrieval is often done by people who have not had anything to do with the construction of the questionnaire. Here the measuring instrument (the questionnaire) is the critical element in the research process.
- **Qualitative techniques** are characterised by proximity to the source of data, where data retrieval and analysis are done by the same person, namely, the interviewer. Data retrieval is characterised by interaction between the interviewer and the respondent, where each new question is to a certain degree dependent on the previous question. Here it is the interviewer and his or her competence (or lack of the same) which is the critical element in the research process.

2.1.4.2 Research Design

Figure 2.2 shows that designing research for primary data collection calls for a number of decisions on research approaches, contact methods, sampling plan and research instruments. The following pages will look at the various elements of Figure 2.2 in further detail (Hollensen and Opresnik, 2015).

Figure 2.2: Research Design within Primary Data Collection

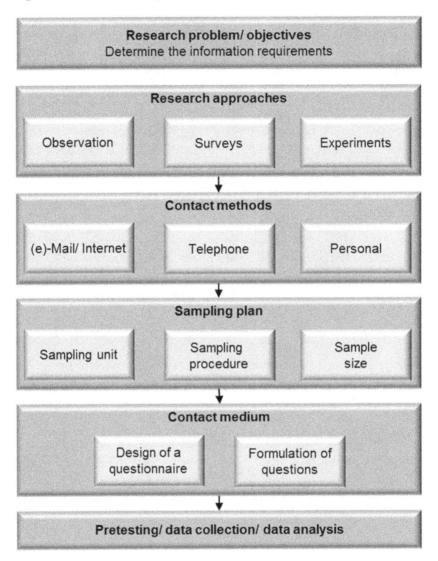

Source: Adapted from Hollensen and Opresnik, 2015, modified

2.1.4.2.1 Research Problem and Objectives

Companies are increasingly recognising the need for primary international research. As the extent of a firm's international involvement increases, so does the importance and complexity of its international research. The primary research process should begin with a definition of the research problem and the establishment of specific objectives. The major difficulty here is translating the business problem into a research problem with a set of specific researchable objectives. In this initial stage researchers often embark on the research process with only a vague grasp of the total problem. Symptoms are often mistaken for causes, and action determined by symptoms may be oriented in the wrong direction.

Research objectives may include obtaining detailed information for better penetrating the market, for designing and fine-tuning the marketing mix, or for monitoring the political climate of a country so that the firm can expand its operations successfully. The better defined the research objective is, the better the researcher will be able to determine the information requirement.

2.1.4.2.2 Research Approaches

In Figure 2.2 three possible research approaches are indicated: observation, surveys and experiments (Hollensen and Opresnik, 2015):

- **Observation** is an approach to the generation of primary data which is based on watching and sometimes recording market-related behaviour. Observational techniques are more suited to investigating what people do than why they do it. Here are some examples of this approach:

  Observational research can obtain information that people are unwilling or unable to provide. In some countries individuals may be reluctant to discuss personal habits or consumption. In such cases observation is the only way to obtain the necessary information. In contrast, some things are simply not observable, such as feelings, attitudes and motives, or private behaviour. Long-term or infrequent behaviour is also difficult to observe. Because of these limitations, researchers often use observation along with other data collection methods.

- **Experiments** gather casual information. They involve selecting matched groups of subjects, giving them different treatments, controlling unrelated factors and checking for differences in group responses. Thus, experimental research tries to explain cause-and-effect relationships.

The most used marketing research application of experiments is in test marketing. This is a research technique in which a product under study is placed on sale in one or more selected localities or areas, and its reception by consumers and the trade is observed, recorded and analysed. In order to isolate, for example, the sales effects of advertising campaigns, it is necessary to use relatively self-contained marketing areas as test markets.

Performance in these test markets gives some indication of the performance to be expected when the product goes into general distribution. However, experiments are difficult to implement in global marketing research. The researcher faces the task of designing an experiment in which most variables are held constant or are comparable across cultures. To do so represents a major challenge. For example, an experiment that intends to determine a casual effect within the distribution system of one country may be difficult to transfer to another country where the distribution system is different. As a result experiments are used only rarely, even though their potential value to the international market researcher is recognised.

- **Surveys** are based on the questioning of respondents and represents, both in volume and in value terms, perhaps the most important method of collecting data. Typically, the questioning is structured: a formal questionnaire is prepared and the questions are asked in a prearranged order. The questions may be asked verbally, in writing or via a computer.

2.1.4.2.3 Contact Methods

The method of contact chosen is usually a balance between speed, degree of accuracy and costs. In principle, there are four possibilities when choosing a contact method: mail, internet/e-mail, telephone interviews and personal (face-to-face) interviews (Hollensen and Opresnik, 2015):

- **Mail surveys** are among the least expensive. The questionnaire can include pictures – something that is not possible over the phone. Mail surveys allow the respondent to answer at their leisure, rather than at the often inconvenient moment they are contacted for a phone or personal interview. For this reason, they are not considered as intrusive as other kinds of interviews. However, mail surveys take longer than other kinds. You will need to wait several weeks after mailing out questionnaires before you can be sure that you have obtained most of the responses. In countries of lower educational and literacy levels, response rates to mail surveys are often too small to be useful.

- **Internet/e-mail surveys** can collect a large amount of data that can be quantified and coded into a computer. A low research budget combined with a widely dispersed population may mean that there is no alternative to the mail/Internet survey. E-mail surveys are both very economical and very fast. It is possible to attach pictures and sound files. However, many people dislike unsolicited e-mail even more than unsolicited regular mail. Furthermore, it is difficult to generalise findings from an e-mail survey to the whole population. People who have e-mail are different from those who do not, even when matched on demographic characteristics, such as age and gender. In section 7 the online research method will be further discussed.

- **Telephone interviews** are somewhere between personal and mail surveys. They generally have a response rate higher than mail questionnaires but lower than face-to-face interviews, their cost is usually less than with personal interviews, and they allow a degree of flexibility when interviewing. However, the use of visual aids is not possible and there are limits to the number of questions that can be asked before respondents either terminate the interview or give quick (invalid) answers to speed up the process. With computer-aided telephone interviewing (CATI), centrally located interviewers read questions from a computer monitor and input answers via the keyboard. Routing through the questionnaire is computer controlled, helping the process of interviewing. Some research firms set up terminals in shopping centres, where respondents sit down at a terminal, read questions from a screen and type their answers into the computer.

- **Personal interviews** take two forms – individual and group interviewing. **Individual interviewing** involves talking with people in their homes or offices, in the street or in shopping arcades. The interviewer must gain the cooperation of the respondents. **Group interviewing** (focus-group interviewing) consists of inviting six to ten people to gather for a few hours with a trained moderator to talk about a product, service or organisation. The moderator needs objectivity, knowledge of the subject and industry, and some understanding of group and consumer behaviour. The participants are normally paid a small sum for attending. Personal interviewing is quite flexible and can collect large amounts of information. Trained interviewers can hold a respondent's attention for a long time and can explain difficult questions. They can guide interviews, explore issues and probe as the situation requires. Interviewers can show subjects actual products, advertisements or packages, and observe reactions and behaviour. The main drawbacks of personal interviewing are the high costs and sampling problems. Group interview studies usually employ small sample sizes to keep time and costs down, but it may be hard to generalise from the results. Because interviewers have more freedom in personal interviews the problem of interviewer bias is greater.

There is no 'best' contact method – it all depends on the situation. Sometimes it may even be appropriate to combine the methods.

2.1.4.2.4 Sampling Plan

A sampling plan is a scheme outlining the group (or groups) to be surveyed in a marketing research study, how many individuals are to be chosen for the survey, and on what basis this choice is made.

Sampling unit: Except in very restricted markets it is both impractical and too expensive for a researcher to contact all the people who could have some relevance to the research problem. This total number is known statistically as the 'universe' or 'population'. In marketing terms, it comprises the total number of actual and potential users/customers of a particular product or service.

The population can also be defined in terms of elements and sampling units. Suppose that a lipstick manufacturer has a **sampling plan** to assess consumer response to a new line of lipsticks and wants to sample females over 15 years of age. It may be possible to sample females of this age directly, in which case a sampling unit would be the same as an element. Alternatively, households might be sampled and all females over 15 in each selected household interviewed. Here the sampling unit is the household, and the element is a female over 15 years old.

What is usually done in practice is to contact a selected group of consumers/customers to be representative of the entire population. The total number of consumers who could be interviewed is known as the 'sample frame', while the number of people who are actually interviewed is known as the 'sample' (Hollensen and Opresnik, 2015).

Sampling procedure: There are several kinds of sampling procedure, with probability and non-probability sampling being the two major categories:

- **Probability sampling:** here it is possible to specify in advance the chance that each element in the population will have of being included in a sample, although there is not necessarily an equal probability for each element. Examples are simple random sampling, systematic sampling, stratified sampling and cluster sampling.
- **Non-probability sampling:** here it is not possible to determine the above-mentioned probability or to estimate the sampling error.

These procedures rely on the personal judgement of the researcher. Examples are convenience sampling, quota sampling and snowball sampling.

Sample size: Once we have chosen the sampling procedure the next step is to determine the appropriate sample size. Determining the sample size is a complex decision and involves financial, statistical and managerial considerations. Other things being equal the larger the sample, the less the sampling error. However, larger samples cost more money, and the resources (money and time) available for a particular research project are always limited.

In addition, the cost of larger samples tends to increase on a linear basis, whereas the level of sampling error decreases at a rate only equal to the square root of the relative increase in sample size. For example, if sample size is quadrupled data collection costs will be quadrupled too, but the level of sampling error will be reduced by only one-half. Among the methods for determining the sample size are the following:

- Traditional statistical techniques (assuming the standard normal distribution).
- Budget available: although seemingly unscientific this is a fact of life in a business environment, based on the budgeting of financial resources. This approach forces the researcher to consider carefully the value of information in relation to its cost.
- Rules of thumb: the justification for a specified sample size may boil down to a 'gut feeling' that this is an appropriate sample size, or it may be a result of common practice in the particular industry.
- Number of subgroups to be analysed: generally speaking, the more subgroups that need to be analysed, the larger the required total sample size.

In transnational market research, sampling procedures become a rather complicated matter. Ideally a researcher wants to use the same sampling method for all countries in order to maintain consistency. Sampling desirability, however, often gives way to practicality and flexibility. Sampling procedures may have to vary across countries to ensure reasonable comparability of national groups. Thus, the relevance of a sampling method depends on whether it will yield a sample that is representative of a target group in a certain country, and on whether comparable samples can be obtained from similar groups in different countries (Hollensen and Opresnik, 2015).

2.1.4.2.5 Contact Medium

Designing the questionnaire: A good questionnaire cannot be designed until the precise information requirements are known. It is the vehicle whereby the research objectives are translated into specific questions. The types of information sought, and the types of respondent to be researched, will have a bearing upon the contact method to be used, and this in turn will influence whether the questionnaire is relatively unstructured (with open-ended questions), aimed at depth interviewing, or relatively structured (with closed-ended questions) for 'on the street' interviews (Hollensen and Opresnik, 2015).

Formulation (wording) of questions: Once the researcher has decided on specific types of questions the next task is the actual writing of the questions. Four general guidelines are useful to bear in mind during the wording and sequencing of each question:

- The wording must be clear: for example, try to avoid two questions in one.
- Select words so as to avoid biasing the respondent: for example, try to avoid leading questions.
- Consider the ability of the respondent to answer the question: for example, asking respondents about a brand or store that they have never encountered creates a problem. Since respondents may be forgetful, time periods should be relatively short. For example: 'Did you purchase one or more cola(s) within the last week?'
- Consider the willingness of the respondent to answer the question: 'embarrassing' topics that deal with things such as borrowing

money, sexual activities and criminal records must be dealt with carefully. One technique is to ask the question in the third person or to state that the behaviour or attitude is not unusual prior to asking the question. For example: 'Millions of people suffer from haemorrhoids. Do you or does any member of your family suffer from this problem?' It is also a feasible solution to ask about 'embarrassing' topics at the end of the interview.

When finally evaluating the questionnaire, the following items should be considered:

- Is a certain question necessary? The phrase 'It would be nice to know' is often heard, but each question should either serve a purpose or be omitted.
- Is the questionnaire too long?
- Will the questions achieve the survey objectives?

2.1.4.2.6 Pretesting, Data Collection and Analysis

Pretesting: No matter how comfortable and experienced the researcher is in international research activities, an instrument should always be pretested. Ideally such a pre-test is carried out with a subset of the population under study, but a pre-test should at least be conducted with knowledgeable experts and/or individuals. The pre-test should also be conducted in the same mode as the final interview. If the study is to be 'on the street' or in the shopping arcade, then the pre-test should be the same. Even though a pre-test may mean time delays and additional cost the risks of poor research are simply too great for this process to be omitted.

Data collection: The global marketing researcher must check that the data are gathered correctly, efficiently and at a reasonable cost. The market researcher has to establish the parameters under which the research is conducted. Without clear instructions, the interviews may be conducted in different ways by different interviewers. Therefore, the interviewers have to be instructed about the nature of the study, start and completion time, and sampling methodology. Sometimes a sample interview is included with detailed information on probing and quotas. Spot checks on these administration procedures are vital to ensure reasonable data quality.

Data analysis and interpretation: Once data have been collected the final steps are the analysis and interpretation of findings in the light of the stated problem. Analysing data from cross-country studies calls for substantial creativity as well as scepticism. Not only are data often limited, but frequently results are significantly influenced by cultural differences. This suggests that there is a need for properly trained local personnel to function as supervisors and interviewers; alternatively international market researchers require substantial advice from knowledgeable local research firms that can also take care of the actual collection of data. Although data in cross-country analyses are often of a qualitative nature the researcher should, of course, use the best and most appropriate tools available for analysis. On the other hand, international researchers should be cautioned against using overly sophisticated tools for unsophisticated data. Even the best of tools will not improve data quality. The quality of data must be matched with the quality of the research tools (Hollensen and Opresnik, 2015).

2.1.4.2 Problems with Using Primary Research

Most problems in collecting primary data in international marketing research stem from cultural differences among countries, and range from the inability of respondents to communicate their opinions to inadequacies in questionnaire translation (Cateora et al., 2000).

Sampling in field surveys

The greatest problem of sampling stems from the lack of adequate demographic data and available lists from which to draw meaningful samples. For example, in many South American and Asian cities street maps are unavailable, and streets are neither identified nor houses numbered. In Saudi Arabia, the difficulties with probability sampling is so acute that non-probabilistic sampling becomes a necessary evil. Some of the problems in drawing a random sample include:

- no officially recognised census of population;
- incomplete and out-of-date telephone directories;
- no accurate maps of population centres, therefore no area samples can be made.

Non-response

Non-response is the inability to reach selected elements in the sample frame. As a result, opinions of some sample elements are not obtained or properly represented. A good sampling method can only identify elements that should be selected; there is no guarantee that such elements will ever be included.

Language barriers

This problem area includes the difficulty of exact translation that creates problems in eliciting the specific information desired and in interpreting the respondents' answers. In some developing countries with low literacy rates written questionnaires are completely useless. Within some countries, the problem of dialects and different languages can make a national questionnaire survey impractical – this is the case in India, which has 25 official languages. The obvious solution of having questionnaires prepared or reviewed by someone fluent in the language of the country is frequently overlooked. In order to find possible translation errors marketers can use the technique of back translation, where the questionnaire is translated from one language to another, and then back again into the original language (Douglas and Craig, 2007). For example, if a questionnaire survey is going to be made in France, the English version is translated into French and then translated back to English by a different translator. The two English versions are then compared and, where there are differences, the translation is checked thoroughly.

Measurement

The best research design is useless without proper measurements. A measurement method that works satisfactorily in one culture may fail to achieve the intended purpose in another country. Special care must therefore be taken to ensure the reliability and validity of the measurement method.

2.2 Assessing the Internal Marketing Situation

The foundation of any marketing plan is the firm's **mission and vision statement,** which answers the question, 'What business are we in and where should we go?' Business mission definition profoundly affects the firm's long-run resource allocation, profitability and survival. The mission statement is a statement of the organization's purpose—what it wants to accomplish in the larger macro environment. A clear mission statement acts as an 'invisible hand' that guides people in the enterprise (Kotler, Armstrong and Opresnik, 2016). When examining internal strengths and weaknesses, the marketing manager should focus on organizational resources, company or brand image, employee capabilities and available technology.

When examining external opportunities and threats, the marketing managers must analyze aspects of the marketing environment. This process is called **environmental scanning** – the collection and interpretation of information about forces, events and relationships in the external environment that may affect the future of the organization or the implementation of the marketing plan. Environmental scanning helps identify market opportunities and threats, and provides guidelines for the design of marketing strategy. The six macro-environmental forces studied most often are social, demographic, economic, technological, political and legal, and competitive.

The matching of the internal strengths and weaknesses with external opportunities and threats automatically leads us to the two important views we will discuss in this chapter (Hollensen and Opresnik, 2015):

- Market Orientation View (MOV) – outside-in perspective
- Resource Based View (RBV) – inside-out perspective

2.2.1 Market Orientation View (MOV)

The term market (or marketing) orientation generally refers to the implementation of the marketing concept. A market orientation entails (1) one or more departments engaging in activities geared toward developing an understanding of customers' current and future needs and the factors affecting them, (2) sharing of this understanding across departments, and (3) the various departments engaging in activities designed to meet select customer needs. In other words, a market orientation refers to the organization-wide generation, dissemination and responsiveness to market intelligence (Kohli and Jaworski, 1990).

One key is achieving understanding of the market and the customer throughout the company, and building the capability for responsiveness to market changes. The real customer focus and responsiveness of the company is the context in which marketing strategy is built and implemented.

Another issue is that the marketing process should be seen as interfunctional and cross-disciplinary, and not simply the responsibility of the marketing department. This is the real value of adopting the process perspective on marketing, which is becoming more widely adopted by large organizations (Hollensen, 2006).

In MOV it is also clear that a deep understanding of the competition in the market from the customer's perspective is critical. Viewing the product or service from the customer's viewpoint is often difficult, but without such a perspective a marketing strategy is highly vulnerable to attack from unsuspected sources of competition.

In essence, market orientation refers to the way a firm implements the marketing concept. In principle, this three-component view of market orientation (generation of, dissemination of and responsiveness to market intelligence) makes it possible to diagnose an organization's level of market orientation, pinpoint specific deficiencies and design interventions tailored to the particular needs of an organization. It should be emphasized that a market orientation is not the exclusive responsibility of a marketing department but, rather, is a company-wide mode of operation.

2.2.2 Resource Based View (RBV)

The traditional market orientation literature emphasizes the superior performance of companies with high quality, organization-wide generation and sharing of market intelligence leading to responsiveness to market needs; the RBV suggests that high performance strategy is dependent primarily on historically developed resource endowments.

Resource-based marketing essentially seeks a long term fit between the requirements of the market and the abilities of the organization to compete in it.

This does not mean that the resources of the organization are seen as fixed and static. Far from it: market requirements evolve over time and the resource profile of the organization must be continuously developed to enable it to continue to compete and, indeed, to enable it to take advantage of new opportunities. The essential factor, however, is that opportunities are seized where the organization has an existing or potential advantage through its resource base, rather than just pursued ad hoc.

Why do organizations exist? The simple answer for commercial organizations may be to earn returns on their investments for shareholders and owners of those organizations. For non-commercial organizations, such as charities, faith-based organizations, public services and so on, the answer may lie in the desire to serve specific communities. However, organizations, both commercial and non-profit, are rarely driven by such simple goals. Often there are many demands, sometimes complementary, sometimes competing, that drive decisions.

In the context of commercial organizations a number of primary stakeholders can be identified. These include shareholders and owners, managers, employees, customers and suppliers. While the market-oriented culture (MOV) discussed above serves to place customers high in the priority ranking, the reality for most organizations will be a complex blend of considerations of all relevant stakeholders.

The RBV of the firm discussed above implies that the first stage in assessing strengths and weaknesses should be to conduct an audit of the resources available to the company, including both the tangible and intangible (Figure 2.3 bottom).

The types of resources and capabilities listed earlier can be simplified as follows (Hollensen and Opresnik, 2015):

- **Technical resources**: a key resource in many organizations, and one becoming increasingly important in a world of rapidly changing technology, is technical skill. This involves the ability of the organization to develop new processes and products through research and development, which can be utilized in the marketplace.
- **Financial standing**: a second important resource is the organization's financial standing. This will dictate, to a large extent, its scope for action and ability to put its strategies into operation. An organization of sound financial standing can raise capital from outside to finance ventures. In deciding marketing strategy, a major consideration is often what financial resources can or cannot be put into the programme.
- **Managerial skills**: managerial skills in the widest possible sense are a further resource of the organization. The experience of managers and the way in which they discharge their duties and motivate their staff, have a major impact on corporate performance.
- **Organization**: the very structure of the organization can be a valuable asset or resource. Some structures, such as the matrix organization, are designed to facilitate wide use of skills throughout the organization. The system has proved useful in focusing control at the brand level, encouraging a co-ordinated marketing mix and facilitating a flexible, rapid response to changing circumstances. It is not without its drawbacks, however. The product management system can lead to responsibility without authority, conflicts between product managers within the same organization and the 'galloping midget' syndrome – managers moving on to their next product management job having maximized short-term returns at the expense of longer-term market position.

- **Information systems**: the information and planning systems in operation also provide a valuable resource. For example, those organizations, such as banks dealing in foreign currency speculation, rely heavily on up-to-the minute and accurate information systems. New technological developments, such as electronic point-of-scale scanning, allow data to be collected and processed in a much shorter time than a few years ago. These companies with the systems in place to cope with the massive increases in data that such newer collection procedures are creating will be in a stronger position to take advantage of the opportunities afforded.

Figure 2.3: The Roots of Competition

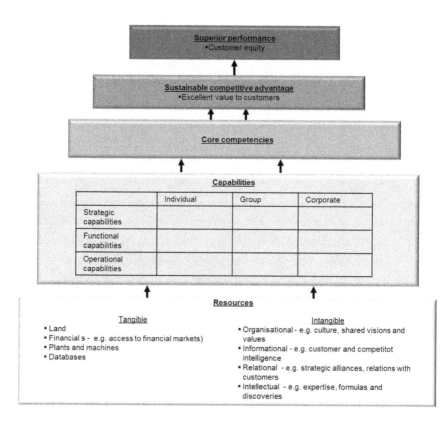

Source: Adapted from Hollensen and Opresnik, 2015, modified

Resources are broken down into two fundamental categories (Hollensen and Opresnik, 2015):

- **Tangible resources** include those factors containing financial or physical value as measured by the firm's balance sheet. Intangible resources, on the other hand, include those factors that are non-physical (or non-financial) in nature and are rarely, if at all, included in the firm's balance sheet.

- **Intangible resources** essentially fall into two categories: assets and skills (or capabilities). If the intangible resource is something that the firm 'has', it is an asset. If the intangible resource is something that the firm 'does', it is a skill and it is being turned into a capability. However, the distinction between assets and capabilities may not be so easy to make. Intangible assets such as copyrights, patents, registered designs and trademarks are all afforded legal protection through property rights. Such legal protection can create barriers to competitive duplication. Other forms of intellectual property include held-in-secret technology. Held-in-secret technology – technology specifically developed to fit the firm's unique strategy and particular business model – can lead to unique, socially complex and context specific assets that may be difficult for competitors to understand let alone duplicate. Given their legally enforceable protection or held-in-secret standing, intellectual property assets are argued to be more difficult to duplicate than tangible resources.

Capabilities can be seen as strategic, functional or operational:

- **Strategic capabilities** underpin the definition of direction for the firm. They include issues such as the dominant logic or orientation guiding management (which will strongly influence strategic direction), the ability of the organization to learn (to acquire, assimilate and act on information) and the ability of senior managers to manage the implementation of strategy.

- **Functional capabilities** lie in the execution of functional tasks. These include marketing capabilities, financial management capabilities and operations management capabilities.
- **Operational capabilities** are concerned with undertaking individual line tasks, such as operating machinery, the application of information systems and completion of order processing.

Second, capabilities may lie with individuals, with groups, or at the corporate level.

- **Individual competencies** are the skills and abilities of individuals within the organization. They include the ability of the individual to analyse critically and assess a given situation (whether this is a CEO assessing a strategic problem, or the shop-floor worker assessing the impact of a machine failure).
- **Group competencies** are where individual abilities come together in teams or ad hoc, informal, task-related teams. While the abilities of individuals are important, so too is their ability to work together constructively.
- **Corporate-level competencies** relate to the abilities of the firm as a whole to undertake strategic, functional or operational tasks. This could include the ability of the firm to internalize learning, so that critical information is not held just by individuals but is shared throughout the firm.

The need to identify the 'distinctive competence' of a company is underlined by a very influential analysis of successful international businesses by Prahalad and Hamel (1990), who argue that a company is likely to be genuinely world class at perhaps five or six activities, and superior performance will come from focusing on those to the exclusion of others. The late 1990s saw much effort to refocus major organizations on to their core activities. Prahalad and Hamel (1990) define core competencies as the underlying skills, technologies and competencies that can be combined in different ways to create the next generation of products and services.

Three tests are suggested by Prahalad and Hamel for identifying core competencies:

- A core competency should be difficult for competitors to copy. Clearly a competency that can be defended against competitors has greater value than a competency that other companies can share.
- A core competence provides potential access to a wide variety of markets. Competencies in display systems are needed, for example, to enable a company to compete in a number of different markets, including flat-screen TV sets, calculators, laptop or notebook computers, mobile phones, and so on.
- A core competency should make a significant contribution to the benefits the customer derives from using the ultimate product or service. In other words, the competency is important where it is a significant determinant of customer satisfaction and benefit.

These requirements are essentially the same as those emerging from the earlier RBV literature to define resources capable of creating sustainable competitive advantage. Added to these three characteristics a further useful test is whether the competency can be combined with other skills and capabilities to create unique value for customers – the grouping of competencies discussed earlier. It could be, for example, that a company does not fulfil the above criteria, but when combined with other competencies is an essential ingredient in defining the firm's uniqueness. Put another way: what would happen if we did not have that competency?

Prahalad and Hamel (1990) argue that the critical management ability for the future will be to identify, cultivate and exploit the core competencies that make growth possible. The argument about core competencies is compelling, and it is certainly driving major corporate changes, such as:

- the emergence of a network of strategic alliances, where each partner brings its core competency into play to build a market offering
- the demerger and sale of non-core activities and brands
- organizational changes away from SBUs to a new 'strategic architecture'.

2.2.3 Major Sources of Competitive Advantage

Companies producing offerings with a higher perceived value and/or lower relative costs (compared to competitors) are supposed to have a competitive advantage. The 'high perceived value' advantage can be considered as differentiation, but the elements of this must be evaluated from a customer perspective. The word 'perceived' is used to emphasize the fact that value is a subjective evaluation rather than a direct measure of utility. This involves an element of judgement, and is sometimes seen as irrational. It is how customers themselves rate the offering in relation to other competitive products or services that is critical in a purchase decision. The prime consideration of the value of any resource to an organisation lies in the answer to the following question: Does this resource contribute to creating value for customers? Value creation may be direct, such as through the benefits conveyed by superior technology, better service, meaningful brand differentiation and ready accessibility. The resources that contribute to these benefits (technology deployed, skilled and motivated personnel, brand name and reputation, and distribution coverage) create value for consumers as soon as they are employed. Other resources may, however, have an indirect impact on value for customers. Effective cost control systems, for example, are not valuable to customers in and of themselves. They only add value for customers when they translate into lower prices charged, or by the ability of the organisation to offer additional customer benefits through the cost savings achieved (Hollensen and Opresnik, 2015).

The value of a resource in creating customer value must be evaluated relative to the resources of competitors. For example, a strong brand name such as Nike on sports-wear may convey more value than a less well-known brand. In other words, for the resource to contribute to sustainable competitive advantage it must serve to distinguish the organisation's offerings from those of competitors.

The 'value' of a product or service should be seen in relation to the customer's cost of obtaining the product/service and the cost of ownership. These costs will include such issues as the buying price of an offering compared to the price of a competitive offering. These elements might be modified by the perceived cost of obtaining and cost of ownership. The way components are assessed and compared could vary from one customer to another. It is often possible to 'delight' customers by exceeding their expectations. The 'perceived value' (compared to price) together with the relative cost is illustrated in Figure 2.4.

Figure 2.4: The Competitive Triangle

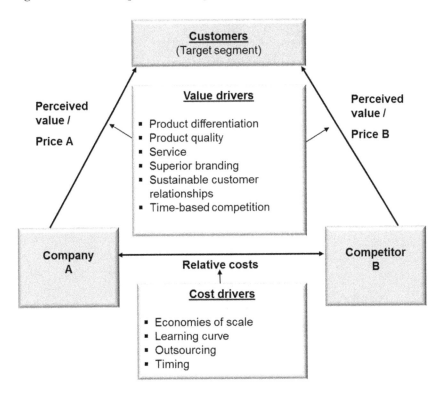

Source: Adapted from Hollensen and Opresnik, 2015, modified

2.3 Assessing the External Marketing Situation

A marketing-oriented company continually analyses the environment in which it operates, adapting to take advantage of emerging opportunities and to minimise eventual threats.

At its simplest, the whole marketing system can be divided into three levels (see Figure 2.5):

- **The focal company**: Understanding and analysing the internal situation was dealt with already within this chapter
- **Industry level/value net/micro level**: The focal company's most important actors/ stakeholders at this level are suppliers, partners/complementors, competitors and of course the customers.
- **Macro level**: The most important changes taking place in the macroenvironment can be summarized in the so-called PEST analysis:

P: Political and legal factors

E: Economic factors

S: Social/cultural factors

T: Technological factors

Figure 2.5: The three Levels in the Marketing System/Value Net

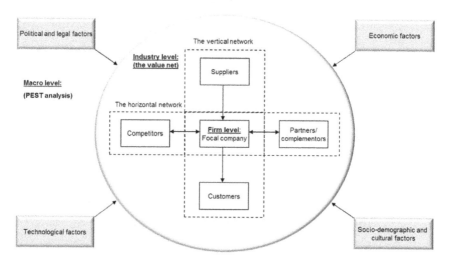

Source: Adapted from Hollensen and Opresnik, 2015, modified

In the following we will discuss each of the four elements in the PEST analysis. Later in the chapter, the dimensions of the microenvironment will be introduced and examined (Hollensen and Opresnik, 2015).

2.3.1 PEST Analysis

The macroenvironment consists of a number of broad forces that influence not only the company but also the other stakeholders and actors in the microenvironment. Traditionally, four forces – political/legal, economic, social/cultural and technological – have been the focus of attention, with the result that the term PEST analysis has been used to describe the macro environmental analysis (Ellis-Chadwick and Jobber, 2016).

- **Political and Legal Factors:** The political environment consists of laws, government agencies, and pressure groups that influence and limit various companies and individuals in a given society. Political and legal forces can highly influence marketing decisions by setting the rules by which business can be conducted. For example, smoking bans in public places do have substantial effects on the demand for cigarettes.

- **Economic Factors:** The economic environment consists of factors that affect consumer buying power and spending patterns. Nations vary vastly in their levels and distribution of income and rates of economic growth.

- **Social/Cultural Factors:** The social and cultural environment is made up of institutions and other forces that affect a society's basic values, perceptions, preferences, behaviours as well as population growth, age distribution and other elements, which in turn can affect marketing decision making.

- **Technological Factors:** The technological environment involves forces that create new technologies, generating new product and market opportunities. It is perhaps the most dramatic force now shaping company's future. The latter part of the twentieth century saw technological change and development impact on virtually every industry.

2.3.2 External Relationships to Stakeholders in the Value Net

The value net or microenvironment consists of the stakeholders in the company's immediate environment that influences its capabilities to operate successfully in its chosen markets. Marketing success requires building relationships with those actors, specifically customers, competitors, distributors, suppliers and other stakeholders. Since the company has relationships with different types of interdependencies, with different objective for the development of the relationship, etc., it is imperative to differentiate between how different relationships are handled.

In particular, the relationships and interactions are typically established with the following actors (see Figure 2.5):

- Suppliers
- Customers
- Complementors/partners
- Competitors

These relationships will now be introduced and analyzed in more depth (Hollensen and Opresnik, 2015).

2.3.2.1 Relationships with Suppliers

Suppliers form an important link in the company's overall customer value proposition system as they provide the resources needs by the firm to produce its goods and services.

The first strategic issue is to decide what items to procure. This is defined by the range of the operations that are undertaken in-house by the buying organisation. This determines the degree of **vertical integration**, which in purchasing terms has been addressed as the make-or-buy issue. What to produce internally and what to buy from external suppliers has been an issue in manufacturing firms for a very long time, despite the fact that it was actually not identified as a matter of strategic importance until the 1980s. It is obvious that buying firms over time have come to rely more on 'buy' than 'make'. Consequently, outsourcing to external suppliers has increased noticeably over time. Having suppliers that compete with one another is one way of increasing efficiency in the purchasing operations. A buying company can switch from one supplier to the other and thus influence the vendors towards improving their efforts. The prospect to play off suppliers against each other in terms of price conditions has been a particularly recommended purchasing policy. The core of this strategy is to avoid becoming too integrated with suppliers, because integration leads to dependence. Customer relationships based on this reason are characterized by low involvement from both parties. The tendency in the overall industrial system towards increasing specialization has called for more coordination between the individual companies. Sequentially, this leads to more adaptation between buyer and seller in terms of activities and resources. These adaptations are made because they improve efficiency and effectiveness. They also create interdependencies between consumer and supplier. Such relationships are characterized by a high involvement approach.

Against this background, buyers and suppliers can join forces to improve supply relationship, or even supply network, performance and consequently allow the supply chain to deliver better value to the customer. Lean supply techniques aim to eliminate redundancies in all areas of the business, from the shop-floor to manufacturing processes, and from new product development to supply chain management. Agile supply techniques, on the other hand, are directed towards plummeting the time it takes for a supply chain to deliver a good or service to the end customer and are aimed at supply chains that have to respond to unpredictable demand patterns. Both the 'lean' and 'agile' supply schools have provided a great deal of case evidence that demonstrates that collaboration, in the cause of lean or agile goals, can be effective in reducing costs and/or increasing productivity and functionality. For example, the lean school has referred to the Japanese automobile industry, especially the Toyota Motor Corporation, as an excellent example of lean practice. The agile school has pointed to the production of the Smart Car, a car that offers entire customization, backed up by a service that offers responsiveness to customer demands.

There are two basic ways of working in the context of supplier relationship management: arm's length and collaborative. An arm's length way of working involves a low level of contact between the buyer and supplier. By low contact, we mean the absence of initiatives that are aimed at cost reduction or functionality improvement. In arm's length exchanges, the buyer and supplier simply exchange the contractual information that is required for the transaction to occur. For example, information about the placing of the order, the recording of the fulfilment and the settlement of the invoice. Most companies today treat their suppliers as partners in creating and delivering customer value. Walt-Mart goes to large lengths to work with its suppliers. For example, it helps them to test new products in its outlets. In addition, its Supplier Development Department publishes a Supplier Proposal Guide and maintains a supplier Web site, both of which support suppliers to navigate the complex Wal-Mart procurement process. Wal-Mart is aware of the fact, that good partnership relationship management results in success for the company, suppliers, and, ultimately, its customers (Kotler, Armstrong and Opresnik, 2016).

2.3.2.2 Relationships with Customers

As we have outlined before, customers are at the centre of the marketing philosophy and effort, and it is the task of marketing management to satisfy their needs and wants better than the competition.

In the relationship approach a specific transaction between the focal company and a customer is not a secluded event but takes place within an exchange relationship characterized by mutual dependency and interaction over time between the parties involved. An analysis could not break off at the individual relationship as in the network approach such relationships are seen as interrelated. Thus, the various actors on a market are connected to each other, directly or indirectly. A specific market can then be described and analyzed as one or more networks.

An exchange relationship implies that there is an individual specific dependency between the seller and the consumer. The relationship develops through interaction over time and signifies a joint orientation of the two parties towards each other. In the interaction, the buyer is equally as active as the seller. The interaction consists of social, business and information exchange and an adaptation of products, processes and routines to better reach the economic objectives of the parties. Consequently, marketing planning should start at the relationship level. Interaction with the buyers and potential buyers is an important aspect of the planning process. The planning should include objectives and activities regarding the development of the relationships. The objectives should not only be formulated for the business exchange, such as sales volume and type of products, but also for social and information exchange, and for adaptation processes for products and processes (Hollensen, 2006).

Although marketing authors acknowledge the benefits of a 'broadened view of marketing' there is no doubt that 'customer markets' should remain the most important focus. RM focuses not on what you can do to your customer but on what you can do for your customer and what you can do with your customer, to ensure customer satisfaction. The goal is to treat your customers as valued partners, to establish their needs and develop their loyalty.

2.3.2.3 Relationships with Partners

This kind of relationship is based on cooperation between manufacturers of complimentary functions and or products/services. In such an affiliation, each partner has a strategic resource that the other needs and in this way each partner is motivated to develop some kind of exchange process between supplier and customer.

For example, partners segregate the value chain activities between themselves. One partner develops and produces a good while letting the other partner market it. The focal company, A, may want to enter a foreign market, but lacks local market knowledge and does not know how to get admittance to foreign distribution channels for its products. Therefore, A seeks and find a partner, B, which has its competencies in the downstream functions, but is rather feeble in the upstream function. In this way, A and B can create a coalition where B can help A with distribution and selling in a foreign market, and A can help B with R&D or production.

2.3.2.4 Relationships with Competitors

As the marketing concepts states that to be successful, a company must provide greater customer value than its competitors do, marketers must gain strategic advantages by positioning their offerings strongly against competitor's offerings in the minds of the consumers. Therefore, marketing-oriented companies not only monitor and seek to understand customers but also research competitors and their brands to understand their strengths, weaknesses, strategies, and response patterns.

In analyzing competition, a number of factors need to be well thought-out. These range from the number and size of competitors, their capabilities (strengths and weaknesses), their international marketing strategies, their sales volume and relative market share, to the type of competitor, i.e. multi-national versus local and their relative resources. The major international competitors, such as Microsoft or Procter&Gamble, have access to extensive financial and other resources. But local competitors should not be ignored, as they have less administrative overhead, lower operating costs, greater flexibility and most likely sophisticated local market knowledge. When competitors are involved in resource exchange alliances, competition implies some issues. The dilemma is that in creating an alliance with a competitor, a company is, in fact making them more competitive. Interaction among competitors has been treated traditionally within economic theory, and has been explained in terms of the structure of an industry within it operates. It is further argued that intensity in competition is dependent on the degree of symmetry between companies, while the degree of concentration determines whether competitors act in collusion or competition with each other. Based on the motives for interaction and the intensity of the relationship concerned, five types of interaction are distinguished: conflict, competition, co-existence, co-operation, and collusion. Conflict and competition are described as active vis-à-vis competitors, although they differ in terms of the motives for specific interaction. Conflict represents object-oriented competition, geared towards destroying the opposing counterpart. Competition is goal-oriented, directed towards achieving one's own goals even though this may have a negative effect on other competitors. Co-existent competition occurs when actors do not see one another as competitors and therefore act independently of each other. Tacit collusion arises from implicit agreements among the actors to avoid active competition. Finally, in co-operation, the companies involved strive towards the same goals, for example by working together in strategic alliances or projects. The interaction between competitors is variable and can involve both co-operative and competitive interaction (Hollensen, 2006).

2.4 Analysing Buying Behaviour in the B2C Market

Customer buying behaviour refers to the buying behaviour of final consumers - individuals and households who buy goods and services for personal consumption. All of these final consumers combine to make up the consumer market. Organizational buying, on the other hand, focuses on the purchase of products and services for use in an organization's activities. Sometimes, it is difficult to classify a product as either a consumer or an organizational good. Cars sell to customers for personal consumption and organizations for use in carrying out their activities e.g. to provide transport for a sales executive.

For both types of buyers, an understanding of customers can be gained by answering the following questions (Ellis-Chadwick and Jobber, 2016):

- Who is important in the buying decision?
- How do they buy?
- What are their choice criteria?
- Where do they buy?
- When do they buy?

Buyer behaviour as it relates to customers will now be examined based upon the first three questions as these are often the most intractable aspects of buyer behaviour.

Who is important in the buying decision?

Consumers around the world vary vastly in age, income, education level, and tastes. They can also buy an enormous variety of goods and services.

How these diverse customers connect with each other and with other elements of their surroundings impacts their choices among products, services and companies (Kotler, Armstrong and Opresnik, 2016).

The marketing implications of understanding who buys mainly lie within the areas of marketing communications and segmentation. An identification of the roles played within the buying centre is a prerequisite for targeting effective communications.

The person, who actually uses or consumes the product may not be the most influential member of the buying centre, nor the decision-maker. Even when the user does play the predominant role, communication with other members of the buying centre can be useful when their knowledge may function as persuasive forces during the decision-making process. The second implication is that the changing roles and influences within the family buying centre are providing new opportunities to segment hitherto stable markets.

How do they buy?

The central question for marketers is: How do customers respond to the various marketing efforts of the company? The company actively has a strong role to play in designing and providing appropriate stimulation to the purchase decisions.

The customer buying process is a dynamic interaction between the consumer and the environment. The consumer actively participates in the process by searching for information on alternatives available, by providing evaluations of products and services, and by expressions of risk.

In this process, the company also plays an active role by manipulating the variables under its control. The company modifies the marketing mix to accommodate the demands expressed by consumers. The more successful it is in matching its marketing mix with expressed and latent demands in the market, the greater is the possibility that consumers will patronize the company's products now and in the future. Consumer behaviour is determined by a host of variables studied in different disciplines (Hollensen and Opresnik, 2015).

Consumer behaviour may be described with the help of the **stimulus-organisms-response model (S-O-R model)** as a relationship between a stimulus of some sort, such as a new product, the way information about the innovation is processed by the consumer, and the response the consumer makes having evaluated the alternatives (Figure 2.6).

Figure 2.6: The S-O-R Model

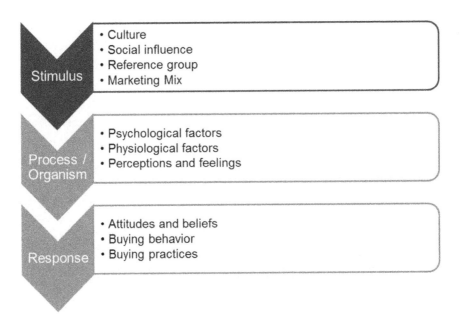

Source: Adapted from Hollensen and Opresnik, 2015, modified

The stimulus is driven by the range of elements in the marketing mix, which the company can manipulate to achieve its corporate objectives. These stimuli derive from the product or service itself, or from the marketing programme developed by the company to support its products and services. A number of symbolic stimuli derive from the use of media such as television. Stimuli also include many of the conditioning variables discussed above. Chief among these are the cultural and social influences on consumer behaviour and the role of reference groups. As cultural factors exert a broad and deep influence on consumer behavior marketers need to understand the role played by the buyer's culture, subculture, and social class.

Process refers to the sequence of stages used in the internal process of these influences by the consumer. This sequence highlights the cause-and-effect relationships involved in making decisions. The processes include the perceptual, physiological and inner feelings and dispositions of consumers towards the product or service being evaluated.

The third component refers to the consumer's response in terms of changes in behaviour, awareness and attention, brand comprehension, attitudes, intentions and actual purchase. This response may indicate a change in the consumer's psychological reaction to the product or service. As a result of some change in a stimulus, the consumer may be better disposed to the product, has formed a better attitude towards it, or believes it can solve a particular consumption-related problem. Alternatively, the response may be in the form of an actual change in purchasing activity. The consumer may switch from one brand to another, or from one product category to another. Consumer responses may also take the form of a change in consumption practices, whereby the pattern of consumer behaviour is changed. Supermarkets frequently offer incentives to get people to shop during slack periods of the week, which involves a change in shopping practice.

Generally speaking, a great deal of interest is focused on responses that involve buying or the disposition to buy. Manufacturers spend considerable sums of money in developing and promoting their products, creating brands and otherwise designing marketing effort to influence consumer behaviour in a particular way. At the same time, consumers may be more or less disposed to these efforts. Through the influence of external stimuli and internal processing mechanisms, a convergence may occur between consumer needs and wants, and the products and services provided. On other occasions, no such convergence occurs.

A key determinant of the extent to which consumers evaluate a brand is their **level of involvement**. Different buyers may engage in different types of decision-making processes depending on how highly involved they are with the product. High-involvement products for one buyer may be low-involvement products for another.

The level of involvement with any product depends on its perceived importance to the consumer's self-image. High-involvement products tend to be tied to self-image, whereas low-involvement products are not. A middle-aged consumer who feels (and wants to look) youthful may invest a great deal of time in her decision to buy a sport-utility vehicle instead of a station wagon. When purchasing an ordinary light bulb, however, she buys almost without thinking, because the purchase has nothing to do with self-image. The more visible, risky, or costly the product, the higher the level of involvement (Hollensen and Opresnik, 2015).

2.5 Analysing Buying Behaviour in the B2B Market

In one way or another, most large enterprises sell to other organizations. Companies such as Boeing, DuPont, IBM, Caterpillar, and countless other firms sell most of their products to other organizations. Even large consumer-products companies, which make products used by final consumers, must first sell their products to other enterprises. The business buying process can be described as the decision process by which business buyers determine which products and services their organizations need to purchase, and then find, evaluate, and choose among alternative suppliers and products. Consumer behaviour relates to the buying behaviour of individuals (or families) when purchasing products for their own use. Organizations buy to enable them to provide goods and services to the final customer. This has implications for marketing management, as we shall see later. Organizational buying behaviour has many similarities to consumer behaviour. Both encompass the behaviour of human beings, whether individually or in groups. Organizational buyers do not necessarily act in a more rational manner than individual consumers. Organizational buyers are affected by environmental and individual factors, as outlined in the previous section. One of the main differences from consumer buying is that organizational buying usually involves group decision making (known as the **'decision-making unit' (DMU)** and sometimes referred to as the **buying centre**). In such a group, individuals may have different roles in the purchase process.

These can be categorized as (Anderson and Narus, 2004):

- **Initiator**: the person who first suggests making a purchase.

- **Influencers / evaluators**: people who influence the buying decision. They often help define specifications and provide information for evaluating options. Technical personnel are especially important as influencers.
- **Gatekeepers**: group members who regulate the flow of information. Frequently, the purchasing agent views the gatekeeping role as a source of his or her power. A secretary may also act as a gatekeeper by determining which vendors get an appointment with a buyer.
- **Decider**: the person who has the formal or informal power to choose or approve the selection of the supplier or brand. In complex situations, it is often difficult to determine who makes the final decision.
- **Purchaser**: the person who actually negotiates the purchase. It could be anyone from the president of the company to the purchasing agent, depending on the importance of the decision.
- **Users**: members of the organization who will actually use the product. Users often initiate the buying process and help define product specifications.

One person may play all the above roles in the purchase decision or each role may be represented by a number of personnel. The sales person trying to sell to an organization should be aware of the roles people assume in the buying centre. Another difference in organizational buying is that many products are more complex and require specialist knowledge to purchase. As many products are changed according to the specifications of the buyer there is more communication and negotiation between buyer and sellers. After-sales service is also very important in organizational buying and suppliers are often evaluated quite rigorously after purchase. In general, organizational markets have fewer, larger buyers who are geographically concentrated. Another aspect of organizational buying is the nature of derived demand. That is, demand for organizational (especially industrial) goods is derived from consumer markets. If demand for the end product consumer good falls then this has an effect along the production line to all the inputs. So, in organizational marketing the end consumers should not be ignored and trends should be monitored (Hollensen and Opresnik, 2015).

2.6 SWOT Analysis

Successful SWOT analysis is basically a process of finding the optimum fit between the firm's controllable strengths and weaknesses and uncontrollable opportunities and threats of the firm's environment in which it operates; and not just today's environment, but also that of the predictable future. This explains why charting a SWOT profile (strengths, weaknesses, opportunities and threats) is by one of the most popular marketing planning tools. It provides a means by which all the key internal (company-related) and external (environment-related) issues can be summarized at a glance. A sophisticated SWOT profile facilitates the development of a strategy that capitalizes on a company's strengths, minimises any weaknesses, exploits emerging opportunities and avoids, as far as possible, any threats. By carefully matching environmental trends to the firm's own distinctive competences the strategic market planner is able to develop strategies that build on the company's strengths, whilst at the same time minimising its weaknesses. By doing so, the marketer aims to achieve what is called a '**strategic fit**' (Hollensen, 2006).

The SWOT framework became popular during the 1970s because of its inherent assumption that managers can plan the alignment of a firm's resources with its environment. Subsequently, during the decade of the 1980s, Porter's (1980) introduction of the industrial organisation paradigm with his five forces /diamond models gave dominance to a firm's external environment, overshadowing the popularity of SWOT. In the 1990s, Barney (1991) reinvented SWOT as the foundation framework linking firm resources to sustained competitive advantage (Barney, 1991).

Figure 2.7 illustrates the 'roots' back to the beginning of this book's chapter 2, in which there was a comprehensive discussion of roots of the Resource Based View RBC (inside-out) based on the firm's strengths and weaknesses and Market Orientation View MOV (outside-in based on the opportunities and threats in the environment). These roots in Chapter 2 now end up in this section where everything is concluded in form of the SWOT-analysis (Hollensen and Opresnik, 2015).

2.6.1 Elements of a SWOT Analysis

When implementing a SWOT analysis to devise a set of strategies, the following guidelines should be taken into account (Hollensen, 2006):

- **Strengths**: Determine your organisation's well-built points, from an internal perspective as well as from the perspective of the external customer. Key questions are as follows: Are there any unique or distinct advantages, which make the organisation stand out in the crowd? What makes the customers choose the organisation over the competition? Are there any products or services which the competition cannot imitate (both now and in the future)?

- **Weaknesses**: Determine the organisation's weaknesses, not only from an internal point of view, but also more importantly, from the external view of the customers. Key questions include: Are there any operations or procedures that can be streamlined? How and why do competitors operate more effective and efficient? Does the competition have a certain market segment occupied?

- **Opportunities**: Another key factor is to determine how the organisation can continue to grow within the marketplace. After all, opportunities are everywhere, such as changes in technology, government policy, social patterns, and so on. The most basic questions are as follows: Where and what are the attractive opportunities within the marketplace? Are there any new emerging trends within the market? What does the organisation predict in the future that may depict new opportunities?

- **Threats**: Threats are external factors and per definition uncontrollable. However, they are instrumental in the design of a sophisticated analysis. It is vital to be prepared and face threats even during unstable situations. Central questions with respect to threats include the following: What is the competition doing that is offsetting the organisational development? Are there any changes in consumer demand, which call for new requirements of products or services? Is the changing technology hurting the organisation's position within the marketplace?

Figure 2.7: SWOT Analysis and the Structure of Chapter 2

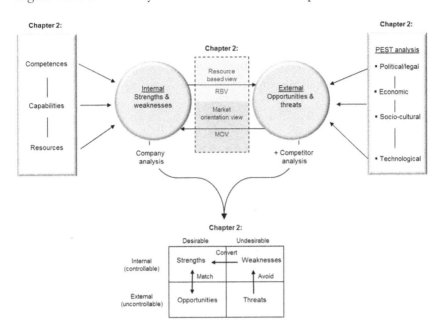

Source: Adapted from Hollensen and Opresnik, 2015, modified

2.6.2 Matching and Converging in the SWOT Matrix

SWOT analysis should function as a catalyst to facilitate and guide the creation of marketing strategies that will produce the preferred results. The process of organizing information within the SWOT analysis enables the company to discern new opportunities. In many ways, good marketing is the art of finding, developing and profiting from opportunities. A **marketing opportunity** is an area of customer need and interest in which there is a high probability that a company can profitably satisfy that need (Hollensen and Opresnik, 2015).

To address these opportunities properly, the marketing manager should appraise every strength, weakness, opportunity, and threat to determine its total impact on the firm's marketing efforts. This assessment will also give the manager an idea of the basic strategic options available.

The following actions are those suggested by the SWOT matrix:

1. Make a match between strengths and opportunities
2. Convert weaknesses to strengths
3. Convert threats to opportunities
4. Minimise, if not avoid, weaknesses, and threats

2.6.3 Application of the SWOT Analysis

The application of SWOT analysis is the matching of specific internal and external factors, which creates a strategic matrix. It is essential to emphasize that the internal factors are within the control of the organisation, such as operations, finance, marketing, and in other areas (See Figure 2.8). The external factors are out of the company's control, such as political and economic factors, technology, and competition. The four combinations are called the Maxi-Maxi (Strengths/Opportunities), Maxi-Mini (Strengths/Threats), Mini-Maxi (Weakness/Opportunities), and Mini-Mini (Weaknesses/Threats).

Figure 2.8: The Application of the SWOT-Matrix

	Strengths (S)	Weaknesses (W)
Opportunities (O)	S / O	W / O
Threats (T)	S / T	W / T

Source: Adapted from Hollensen and Opresnik, 2015, modified

1. **Maxi-Maxi (S/O):**

This combination shows the organisation's strengths and opportunities. In essence, an organisation should strive to maximise its strengths to take advantage of new opportunities.

2. **Maxi-Mini (S/T):**

This combination shows the organisation's strengths in consideration of threats, e.g. from competitors. In essence, an organisation should strive to use its strengths to evade or minimise threats.

3. **Mini-Maxi (W/O):**

This grouping displays the organisation's weaknesses in tandem with opportunities. It is an exertion to conquer the organisation's weaknesses by making the most out of new opportunities and challenges.

4. **Mini-Mini (W/T):**

This combination shows the company's weaknesses by comparison with the existing external threats. This is most definitely a protective strategy, to minimise an organisation's internal weaknesses and avoid external threats.

As mentioned earlier the SWOT analysis is the matching of specific internal and external factors. However, what about the matching items within internal factors and items within external factors. The primary reason this is not applied is that matching these factors will create strategies that do not make sense as strategies must have an external factor as a trigger in order for it to be feasible (Lee et al., 2000).

3. Strategy Formulation in the Marketing Planning Process

The word '**strategy**' is derived from the Greek term 'strategós' and when it appeared in use during the 18th century, it was seen in its narrow sense as the 'art of the general' and 'the art of arrangement' of troops. Military strategy deals with the planning and conduct of campaigns, the movement and disposition of forces, and the deception of the enemy. Thus, strategy originally referred to the skills and decision making process of the general (executive), while 'stratagem', translated as 'an operation or act of generalship', and referred to a specific decision made by the executive (Hollensen and Opresnik, 2015).

3.1 Strategic Marketing Planning

Strategic planning is the process of developing and maintaining a strategic fit between the company's goals and capabilities and its changing marketing opportunities. Planning is a complex process which consists of several inter-related stages. However, with time there is change and hence planning is and should be a continuous process, where each stage needs to be reconsidered for relevancy and in relation to the other stages. The plan is the stages 'frozen' in time; the process is a continuous assessment of the relevancy of each of these stages with changes in time.

In planning, we look ahead to decide what to do. The planning process itself is a systematic way of approaching the following questions and they will be used as guidance for the rest of the chapter (Hollensen and Opresnik, 2015):

- What business are we in? (Mission statement – section 3.1.1)
- Where are we today (situation analysis – chapter 2)
- Where do we want to go (strategic objectives – section 3.1.2)
- How do we get there?
- Estimation of planning gap and problem diagnosis (section 3.1.3)
- The search for strategic alternatives (Ansoff's growth matrix, Porter's three generic strategies, the BCG and GE mode – section 3.1.4 – 3.1.8)

3.1.1 Vision and Mission Statement

The **vision and mission concepts** are often interlinked but generally there is a difference (Hollensen and Opresnik, 2015):

- A **business mission statement** describes 'Who we are and what is the overall purpose of our business'. It is a company's reason for being and reflects people's idealistic motivations for doing the company's work by capturing the soul of the organisation. The core purpose or mission of a company is like a 'guiding star' on the horizon continuously providing direction and inspiring change. It is important to state that mission statements should not only be defined in technology terms ('We make and sell furniture') but with respect to the market and in terms of customer needs as products and technologies eventually become outdated, but basic market needs may last forever. For example, Nike's mission is not simply to sell shoes but to 'Help people experience the emotion of competition, winning and crushing competitors'.

- A **business vision statement** describes 'Where we wish to go,' 'What do we wish to become?' It provides a mental image of the successful accomplishment of the mission. It is typically:
  - Short
  - Idealistic and imaginative
  - Inspires enthusiasm
  - Ambitious

The rest of this section will primarily be about the mission: Mission reflects unique qualities of the program.

Whether the organisation is a large corporation or a small non-profit agency, its mission statement visibly articulates its strategic scope. The mission statement should answer fundamental questions such as, 'What is our business?', 'Who are our constituencies?', 'What value do we provide customers, employees, suppliers, and other constituent groups?' and 'What should our business be in the future?' Senior management in all businesses needs to answer such questions. The responsibility for developing and articulating a mission statement is at the corporate level.

Mission statements should be driven by three factors: heritage, resources, and environment (Hollensen, 2006):

- The organisation's heritage is its history – where it has been, what it has done well, and what it has done poorly. A superior mission statement cannot ignore previous events and how they shaped the organisation. It also must be sensitive to the organisation's image in the minds of its constituencies. Past successes should be extended, past failures avoided, and the organisation's current image must be addressed realistically

- Resources refer to everything the organisation can manage, such as cash reserves, recognized brands, unique technologies, and talented employees. Resources can also include borrowing power, existing relationships with distributors, and excess plant capacity. A good mission statement notes the organisation's resources and sets paths that are compatible with what the organisation has at its disposal. As in the case of heritage, mission statements that are out of touch with organisation's resources elicit scepticism and can do more harm than good. If a minor regional brand were to include 'penetrating Asian markets' in its mission statement, it would be met with substantial scepticism.

- The environment is everything happening currently that affects the company's ability to achieve objectives or implement strategies, both inside and outside the organisation. Some environmental factors are temporary, such as a hurricane. Most temporary factors are too short-sighted to be considered in a mission statement. Other factors, however, such as changes in the political system of the Russian Republic, terror acts, rise or fall of oil prices may have a longer life and should be considered in the mission statement if they affect the organisation's ability to survive and prosper.

At the corporate level, the mission statement defines the organisation's business and reflects fundamental beliefs about its strengths and weaknesses, as well as its environment.

3.1.2 Strategic Objectives

Strategic management also requires that firms set strategic objectives-specific and measurable performance standards for strategically important areas. The company's mission needs to be turned into detailed supporting objectives for each level of management. Each manager should have objectives and be responsible for reaching them (Kotler, Armstrong and Opresnik, 2016).

An organisation cannot set realistic, realizable objectives until it has the requisite information but, on the basis of experience, marketing management will nonetheless have tentative on sales volume, market share or whatever indicators represent progress towards accomplishing the firm's vision. What exactly these tentative will be influenced by subjective estimates of what is considered reasonable at the time in relation to what resources are likely to be available.

For a manager to be able to direct an activity towards the achievement of some objectives it must be possible to imagine the goal in a way that is meaningful for guiding the activity. This is why objective objectives purely in terms of profit are inadequate; they offer too little direction (Hollensen and Opresnik, 2015).

Strategic objectives can be stated in terms of different criteria, such as sales, market share or return on investment, or they can be stated in absolute or relative terms. To be effective, objectives must be specific in terms of:

- the performance dimension being measured
- the measures most appropriate for the performance dimension
- the target value for each measure
- the time by which the target should be achieved

3.1.3 Estimation of the Planning Gap and Problem Diagnosis

What do the' facts' suggest will be the future if the firm takes no action to change current strategies? Such a prediction is known as a 'reference projection'. A reference projection is the future that can be expected in the absence of planned change. The reference projection is compared with some 'target projection' or the set of tentative goals, which the company sets for itself. The **planning gap (performance gap)** is the difference between the target and the reference projections (see Figure 3.1).

Figure 3.1: Illustration of the 'planning gap'

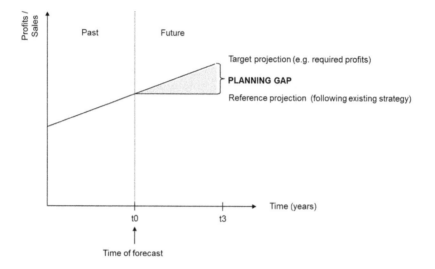

Source: Adapted from Hollensen and Opresnik, 2015, modified

The gap may stem from the difference between future desired profit objectives and a forecast of expected profit based on past performance and following existing strategy.

In the face of such a planning gap, a number of options are available; the intention, however is to close the gap. For example, the gap could be closed by revising objectives in a downward way. Such a step might be taken where the initial objectives are unrealistic. Alternatively, or in addition, the gap could be closed by actions designed to move the company off the projection curve and towards the desired curve.

The planning gaps identified will depend on which performances are of interest. At the highest level, it could be cash flow projections, economic value added, earnings per share, sales and market share or various financial indices like return on investment (ROI). At the marketing level, it would be in terms of sales, market share, costs or various behavioural indices like buyer attitudes (Hollensen and Opresnik, 2015).

Problem Diagnosis

If a company has a large planning gap, we speak freely of its being the problem. More accurately, the planning gap is not the problem but the symptom of one. The recognition of a problem situation is not in itself the identification of the actual problem. We do not discover a problem but diagnose one. Problem diagnosis aims at identifying the type of solution that applies which is the first step on the road to developing an actual solution, just as diagnosing a failure to start the car as being due to some electrical fault, is the first step towards getting the car started again. Unfortunately, different people will make different diagnosis, depending on their experience, professional expertise and their concerns.

We cannot recognize a problem without understanding what would count as a solution, just as we cannot comprehend an objective without accepting what would count as the achievement of it. The actual problem that is addressed depends somewhat on which individual or group can make the problem, as they see it, count. But all management stakeholders in a company are influenced by believable arguments and so true technical expertise usually succeeds. Hopefully, it must for if the wrong problem is addressed, the wrong decisions are made and this can be more wasteful of resources than solving the right problem in an inefficient way. Although we hesitate to acknowledge it, the fact is that once we move away from some pure deductive system like mathematics, we are in the realm of persuasion where persuasive rhetoric is crucial so that a dramatic description of what is considered to be the problem can emotionally compel attention and often our assent (Hollensen, 2006).

3.1.4 The Search for Strategy Alternatives for Closing Planning Gap

The strategic options for closing the planning gap should not only fit the challenging situation and take account of trends and competition but should also take advantage of the firm's core competencies and strengths.

The strategy search process should always allow for the possibility of inspiration, which may beat anything arrived at by systematic analysis. It is not uncommon for someone to come up with an idea that is instantly recognizable as being the right answer.

The inspired solution is thus accepted, not because it saves time but because it is perceived to be advanced and effective. This said, the identification of appropriate strategies rests on having the requisite experience and the content of the strategy, not procedure, is all-important. Where the requisite experience is lacking, the search for strategies becomes opaque (Hollensen, 2006).

3.1.5 Ansoff's Generic Strategies for Growth

One aspect of strategic management is the development of precise strategies for achieving company objectives. Strategies must respond to the environment and provide specific guidelines for decision-making. Because companies face unique combinations of internal and external factors, the strategies developed by any one organisation are unlikely to be entirely adaptable to any other organisation.

At a more general level, however, it is possible to discern recurring patterns in the strategies adopted by organisations. These recurring patterns are called generic strategies. So if we elaborate on the 'planning' gap in Figure 3.1 we get what is illustrated in Figure 3.2 where the 'gap' is filled up with **Ansoff's expansion-strategies** (Hollensen and Opresnik, 2015).

Figure 3.2: Filling the 'planning gap' with Ansoff's strategies

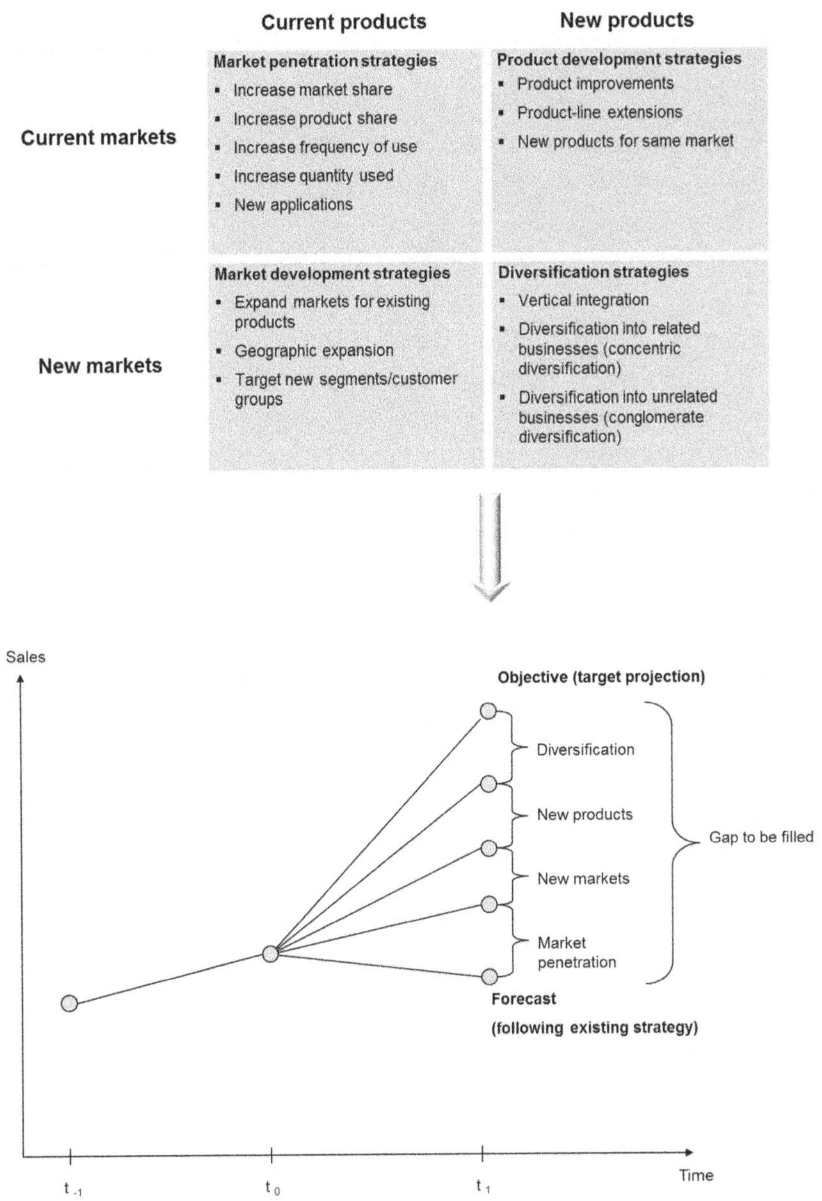

	Current products	**New products**
Current markets	**Market penetration strategies** • Increase market share • Increase product share • Increase frequency of use • Increase quantity used • New applications	**Product development strategies** • Product improvements • Product-line extensions • New products for same market
New markets	**Market development strategies** • Expand markets for existing products • Geographic expansion • Target new segments/customer groups	**Diversification strategies** • Vertical integration • Diversification into related businesses (concentric diversification) • Diversification into unrelated businesses (conglomerate diversification)

Source: Adapted from Hollensen and Opresnik, 2015, modified

Market Penetration

Organisations seeking to grow by gaining a larger market share in their current industry or market follow a penetration strategy. Following alternatives are available:

- Increase market share on current markets with current products
- Increase product share (Increase frequency of use, increase quantity used, new applications)

The most basic method of gaining market penetration in existing markets with current products is by winning competitor's customers. This may be achieved by more effective use of the marketing mix, e.g. by more valuable promotion, distribution, or by cutting prices. Other strategic options in terms of market penetration involve buying competitors and to protect the penetration already gained by discouraging competitive entry. **Market entry barriers (MEB)** can be created by cost advantages (lower labour costs, access to raw materials, economies of scale), high switching costs (the costs of changing from an existing supplier to a new supplier, for example), high marketing expenditures and displaying aggressive tendencies to retaliate (Kotler, Armstrong and Opresnik, 2016).

Penetration strategies can be very successful when the company has a technological or production advantage that allows it to take market share away from competitors while still operating profitably. However, such strategies can also be very costly, if they rely primarily on setting prices below those of competing products.

Market Development Strategies

Market development entails the promotion of new uses of existing products to new customers, or the marketing of existing products and their current uses to new market segments. The strategy involves the following strategic possibilities:

- Geographic expansion (new countries/regions)
- New segments/customer groups

For example, Tesco the UK supermarket chain, practiced market development by marketing existing grocery products, which were sold in large out-of-town supermarkets and superstores, to a new market segment – convenience shoppers – by opening smaller shops in town centres and next to petrol stations.

Market development is also feasible through entering new segments by involving the search for overseas opportunities. The growth of markets in China, India, Russia and Eastern Europe is providing major market development opportunities for all sorts of business (Ellis-Chadwick and Jobber, 2016).

Product Development Strategies

Organisations can also remain within their established industries or markets and seek extension by introducing new products or services in current markets. This is also called a **technology development strategy**.

The strategy may take the following forms (Ellis-Chadwick and Jobber, 2016):

- In the case of **product-line extensions** customers are given greater choice. For example, the original iPod has been followed by the launches of the iPod nano, shuffle and touch, giving its target market of young music lovers greater choice in terms of size, price and capacity. When new features are added trading up may occur, with customers buying the enhanced-value product. However, when the new products are cheaper than the original (as in the case with the iPod) the danger is **cannibalization** of sales of the core offer.
- **Product replacement strategies** involve the replacement of old brands/products with new ones, often based on technology change. The company thus replaces an old product with an innovation although both may be marketed side by side for a time.

- **Product development strategies** are in peril if competitors can easily copy the new product being introduced by using lower manufacturing or delivery costs. They can be at risk if the products are not different enough from existing products to inspire demand.

Diversification Strategies

Pursuing a growth strategy by introducing new products or technologies in new markets or industries is called **diversification**. The following alternatives are available:

- **Vertical integration** (forward integration or backward integration)
- Diversification into related businesses (**concentric/horizontal diversification**)
- Diversification into unrelated businesses (**conglomerate/lateral diversification**)

The term 'diversification' is frequently associated with expansion into areas unrelated to the company's current operations in order to offset cyclical downturns in one area with cyclical growth in other areas. Diversification was popular with many large companies in the 1970s and gave rise to legendary conglomerates.

The entry into new markets is the most risky option, especially when the entry strategy is not based on the core competencies of the business. However, it can also be highly rewarding, as exemplified by Honda's move from motorcycles to cars based on its core competences in engines (Ellis-Chadwick and Jobber, 2016).

3.1.6 Porter's Generic Strategies

According to Porter (1985), forging successful strategy begins with understanding of what is happening in one's industry and deciding which of the available competitive niches one should attempt to dominate. For example, a company may discover that the largest competitor in an industry is aggressively pursuing cost leadership, that others are trying the differentiation route, and that no one is attempting to focus on some small specialty market. On the basis of this information, the firm might sharpen its efforts to distinguish its product from others or switch to a focus approach. As Porter states, the idea is to position the firm 'so it won't be slugging it out with everybody else in the industry; if it does it right, it won't be directly toe-to-toe with anyone'. The objective is to mark out a defensible competitive position – defensible not just against rival companies but also against the forces driving industry competition.

What it means is that the give-and-take between firms already in the business represents only one such force. Others are the bargaining power of suppliers, the bargaining power of buyers, the threat of substitute products or services, and the threat of new entrants (**Porter's five-forces model**).

Combining the dimensions of distinctive advantage and business cope (broad versus narrow) in a matrix, results in the strategic typology illustrated in Figure 3.3.: differentiation, cost leadership, differentiation focus, and cost focus.

A **cost leadership strategy** involves the achievement of the lowest cost position in an industry. The company serves segments in the industry and directs great importance to minimising costs on all fronts. Heinz is believed to be a cost leader in its industry. The firm markets acceptable products at reasonable prices, which implies that their low costs result in above-average profits. Wal-Mart is also a cost leader, which allows the company the option of charging lower prices than its competitors to achieve higher sales and yet achieve comparable profit margins, or to match competitor's prices and attain higher profit margins (Ellis-Chadwick and Jobber, 2016).

A **differentiation strategy** involves the selection of one or more choice criteria that are used by many customers in an industry. The company aims at uniquely positioning itself to meet these criteria better than the competition. The goal is usually to differentiate in a way that leads to a price premium in excess of the cost of differentiating. Differentiation gives customers a reason to prefer one product or service over another. Nokia, for example, became market leader in mobile phones by being the first to realize that they were fashion items and to design stylish phones to differentiate the brand from its competitors. Hewlett-Packard adopted this strategic orientation when the market for handheld calculators was in the early stages. Hewlett-Packard calculators were more expensive than Texas Instruments products, but their technology and performance were superior. In later years, Texas Instrument matched the performance and technological features of Hewlett- Packard calculators while retaining its cost leadership, forcing Hewlett-Packard to reduce its prices.

Figure 3.3: Porter's Generic Strategies

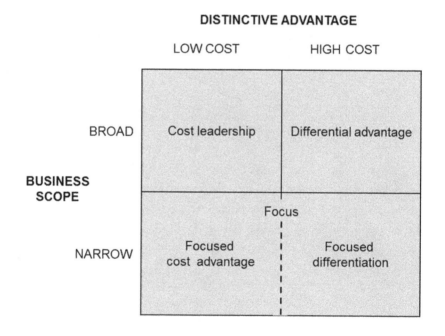

Source: Adapted from Hollensen and Opresnik, 2015, modified

Within the framework of a **cost focus strategy**, a company seeks a cost advantage with one or a small number of target market segments. Examples of cost focusers are easy Jet and Ryanair, who focus on short-haul flights with a basic product trimmed to reduce costs (Ellis-Chadwick and Jobber, 2016).

With the **focused differentiation strategy**, a company aims to differentiate within one or a small number of target segments. The specific needs of the particular segment suggest that there is an opportunity to differentiate the product offering from the competition's, which may be targeting a broader group of customers. For example, Ritz-Carlton focuses on the top 5 percent of corporate and leisure travellers. Company's pursuing this approach must ensure that the needs of their target group differ from those of the broader market in order to have a basis for differentiation (Ellis-Chadwick and Jobber, 2016).

The essence of corporate success, then, is to choose a generic strategy and pursue it consistently. Below-average performance results in a **stuck-in the-middle position**. Sears and Holiday Inn encountered difficult times because they did not stand out as the lowest in cost, highest in perceived value, or best in serving some specific market segment.

3.1.7 The BCG Portfolio Matrix Model

A major activity in strategic planning is business portfolio analysis, whereby management evaluates the products and business units making up the company. The firm aims at putting strong resources into its more profitable businesses and phase down or drop its weaker ones. The first step within the process is to identify the key strategic business units. A **strategic business unit (SBU)** is a unit of the company that has a separate mission and objectives and that can be planned independently from other company businesses. An SBU can be a company division, a product line within a division, or a single product, service or brand (Kotler, Armstrong and Opresnik, 2016).

The next step in business portfolio analysis is to assess the attractiveness of its various SBUs and decide how much support each one deserves. A good planning system must guide the development of strategic alternatives for each of the company's current businesses and new business possibilities. It must also provide for management's review of these strategic alternatives and for corresponding resource allocation decisions. The result is a set of approved business plans that, taken as a whole, represent the direction of the firm. This process starts with, and its success is largely determined by, the creation of sound strategic alternatives.

The top management of a multi-business firm cannot generate these strategic alternatives. It must rely on the managers of its business ventures and on its corporate development personnel. However, top management can and should establish a conceptual framework within which these alternatives can be developed. The best-known portfolio planning tool as such a framework is the portfolio matrix associated with the **Boston Consulting Group (BCG)**. Briefly, the portfolio matrix is used to establish the best mix of businesses in order to maximise the long-term earnings growth of the company. The portfolio matrix concept addresses the issue of the potential value of a particular business for the company. This value has two variables: first, the potential for generating attractive earnings levels now; second, the potential for growth or, in other words, for significantly increased earnings levels in the future. The portfolio matrix concept holds that these two variables can be quantified. Current earnings potential is measured by comparing the market position of the business relative to that of its competitors. Empirical studies have shown that profitability is directly determined by **relative market share**. Relative market share is shown on the horizontal axis and refers to the market share of each product relative to its largest competitor. It acts as a proxy for competitive strength. The division between high and low market share is usually 1. Above this figure a product line has a market share greater than its largest rival. Growth potential is measured by the **growth rate of the market** segment in which the business operates. Clearly, if the segment is in the decline stage of its life cycle, the only way the business can increase its market share is by taking volume away from competitors. Within this framework, market growth rate is used as a proxy for market attractiveness (Ellis-Chadwick and Jobber, 2016).

Figure 3.4 shows a matrix with its two sides labelled market growth rate and relative market share. The area of each circle represents sales. The market share position of each circle is determined by its horizontal position. Each circle's product sales growth rate (corrected for inflation) in the market in which it competes is shown by its vertical position.

Figure 3.4: The BCG-Model

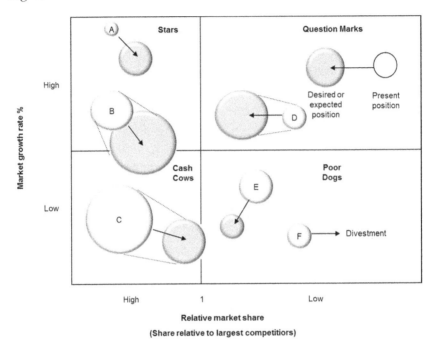

Source: Adapted from Hollensen and Opresnik, 2015, modified

With regard to the two axes of the matrix, relative market share is plotted on a logarithmic scale in order to be consistent with the **experience curve effect**, which implies that profit margin or rate of cash generation differences between two competitors tends to be proportionate to the ratio of their competitive positions. A linear axis is used for growth for which the most generally useful measure is volume growth of the business concerned; in general, rates of cash use should be directly proportional to growth (Hollensen, 2006).

Using the two dimensions discussed here in Figure 3.4, one can classify businesses and products into four basic categories. Businesses in each category, exhibit different financial characteristics and offer different strategic choices (Ellis-Chadwick and Jobber, 2016):

- **Question Marks**

  Question marks are low-share business units in high-growth markets. Because of growth, these products require more cash than they are able to generate on their own. If nothing is done to increase market share, a question mark will simply absorb large amounts of cash in the short run and later, as the growth slows down, become a – poor – dog. Thus, unless something is done to change its perspective, a question mark remains a cash loser throughout its existence and ultimately becomes a cash trap.

  Against this background, the company faces a fundamental choice: to increase investment (**building strategy**) to attempt to turn the question marks into stars. Because the business is growing, it can be funded to dominance. It may then become a star and later, when growth slows down, a cash cow. This strategy is a costly one in the short run. An abundance of cash must be poured into a question mark in order for it to win a major share of the market, but in the long run this strategy is the only way to develop a sound business from the question mark stage. Another strategy is to withdraw support by either **harvesting** (raising price while lowering marketing expenditure) or **divesting** (dropping or selling it). In a few cases it may be viable to find a small market segment (**niche strategy**) where dominance can be achieved. Unilever, for example, identified its specialty chemicals business as a question mark. It realized that it had to invest heavily or exit the market. Unilever's decision was to sell and invest the billions raised in predicted future winners such as personal care and dental products.

- **Stars**

  High-growth market leaders are called stars. They are likely to be profitable because they are market leaders but require substantial investment to finance growth and to meet competitive challenges. Overall, cash flow is therefore likely to be roughly in balance. Thus, star products represent probably the best profit opportunity available to a company, and their competitive position must be maintained. If a star is allowed to fall because of cutbacks in investment and rising prices (creating an umbrella for competitors) the star will ultimately become a – poor – dog.

The appropriate **strategic objective is to build** sales and/or market share. Resources should be invested to maintain/increase the leadership position and competitive challenges should be repelled. The ultimate value of any product or service is reflected in the stream of cash it generates net of its own reinvestment. For a star, this stream of cash lies in the future. To obtain real value, the stream of cash must be discounted back to the present at a rate equal to the return on alternative opportunities. It is the future pay-off of the star that counts, not the present reported profit. Stars are the cash cows of the future and need to be protected. For GE, the plastics business is a star in which it keeps investing. As a matter of fact, the company even acquired Thomson's plastics operations (a French company) to further strengthen its position in the business (Hollensen, 2006).

- **Cash Cows**

Cash cows are market leaders in mature (low-growth) markets. High market share leads to high profitability and low market growth means that investment – in new production facilities – is minimal. This leads to a large positive cash flow. As a result, these businesses generate cash surpluses that help to pay dividends and interest, provide debt capacity, supply funds for research and development, meet overheads, and also make cash available for investment in other products. Consequently, cash cows are the foundation on which everything else depends. These products must be protected. Technically speaking, a cash cow has a return on assets that exceeds its growth rate. Only if this is true will the cash cow generate more cash than it uses. Consequently, the appropriate **strategic objective is to hold** sales and market share. The excess cash that is generated should be used to fund stars, question marks that are being built, and research and development for new products.

- **Poor Dogs**

  Products with low market share positioned in low-growth situations are called – poor – dogs. Their insufficient competitive position condemns them to poor profits. Because growth is low, dogs have little potential for gaining sufficient share to achieve viable cost positions. Usually they are net users of cash. Their earnings are low, and the reinvestment required just to keep the business together consumes cash inflow. The business, therefore, is likely to regularly absorb cash unless further investment is rigorously avoided. For those products that achieve second or third position in the market place (cash dogs) a small positive cash flow may result, and for a few others it may be possible to reposition the product into a **defendable niche**. But for the bulk of dogs the appropriate strategic objective is to **harvest** to generate positive cash flow for a time, or to **divest**, which allows resources to be allocated elsewhere. GE's consumer electronics business had been in the dog category, maintaining only a small percentage of the available market in a period of slow growth, when the company decided to unload the business (including the RCA brand acquired in late 1985) to Thomson, France's state-owned, leading electronics manufacturer (Hollensen, 2006).

In summary, the portfolio matrix approach provides for the simultaneous comparison of different products. It also underlines the importance of cash flow as a strategic variable. Thus, when continuous long-term growth in earnings is the objective, it is necessary to identify high-growth product/market segments early, develop businesses, and pre-empt the growth in these segments. If necessary, short-term profitability in these segments may be forgone to ensure achievement of the dominant share. Costs must be managed to meet scale-effect standards. The appropriate point at which to shift from an earnings focus to a cash flow focus must be determined and a liquidation plan for cash flow maximisation established. A **cash-balanced mix** of businesses should be maintained (Hollensen, 2006).

3.1.8 The GE-Matrix Multifactor Portfolio Matrix

The BCG-model discussed above provides a useful approach for reviewing the roles of different products in a company. As stated above, however, the matrix approach leads to many difficulties. Stimulated by this success and some of the weaknesses of the model (particularly the criticism of its over simplicity) McKinsey & Co developed a more wide-ranging Market Attractiveness-Competitive Position (MA-CP) model in conjunction with General Electric (GE) in the USA.

Instead of using market growth rare alone, a range of market attractiveness criteria were used, such as market size, market growth rate, beatable rivals, market entry barriers, social, political and legal factors. Similarly, instead of using only the relative market share as a measure for competitive strength, a number of factors were used, such as relative market share, reputation, distribution capability, market knowledge, service quality, innovation capability and cost advantages. The framework discussed here may be applied to either a product/market or an SBU. As a matter of fact, it may be equally applicable to a much higher level of aggregation in the organisation, such as a division or a group. Management is permitted to decide which criteria are applicable for their products. After depicting the criteria, management's next task is to agree upon a weighting system for each set of criteria, with those factors that are most important having a higher weighting, for example ten points to be shared. Next management assesses the particular market for the product under examination on each of the factors, for example, on a scale from 1-10. By multiplying each weighting by its corresponding rating, and then summing, a total score indicating the overall attractiveness of the particular market for the product under examination is obtained. The same kind of process is then applied in the framework of the competitive strength assessment. Finally, the market attractiveness and competitive strength scores for the product under appraisal can now be plotted on the MA-CP matrix. The process is repeated for each product under investigation. Each product position is given by a circle, the size of which is in proportion to its sales (Hollensen and Opresnik, 2015).

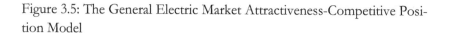

Figure 3.5: The General Electric Market Attractiveness-Competitive Position Model

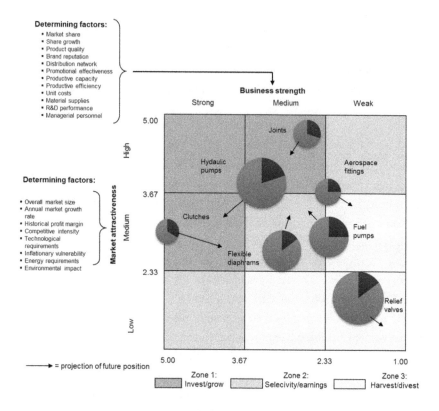

Source: Adapted from Hollensen and Opresnik, 2015, modified

Like in the BCG model, for an individual business, the recommendations for setting strategic objectives are dependent on the product's position.

Figure 3.6 provides an overview of the appropriate strategies.

Figure 3.6: The generic strategies of the General Electric Market Attractiveness-Competitive Position Model

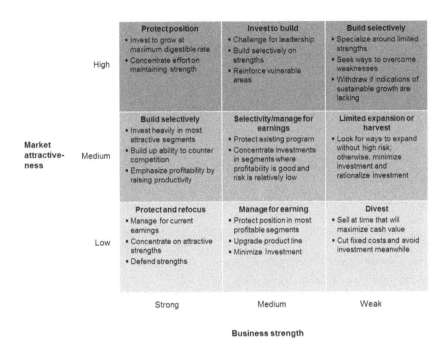

Source: Adapted from Hollensen and Opresnik, 2015, modified

3.2 Market Segmentation, Targeting and Positioning

Markets consist of buyers, who differ in one or more ways, for example, in their wants, resources, buying attitudes, and locations. The technique that is used by marketers to get grips with the diverse nature of markets is called **market segmentation**. Through market segmentation, companies divide large, heterogeneous markets into smaller homogenous segments that can be targeted more efficiently and effectively with products and services that match their unique needs and wants. The objective is to identify groups of customers with similar requirements so that they can be served effectively while being of a sufficient size for the product or service to be supplied efficiently. Usually, especially in consumer markets, it is not possible to create a marketing mix that satisfies every individual's specific requirements precisely. Market segmentation, by grouping together customers with similar needs, provides a commercially viable way of serving these consumers (Ellis-Chadwick and Jobber, 2016).

The first step within the process of market segmentation involves the identification of the best ways to segment a market and then pin down the characteristics of each group (this second step is called **profiling**). Next, the company must evaluate the attractiveness of the segments and select the most appropriate target markets. Finally, the business organisation needs to **position** the product or service relative to competitive offerings within the chosen market segments.

3.2.1 The Underlying Premises of Market Segmentation

In order to get an overview of segmentation issues it is important to first consider the underlying requirements for market segmentation. To be useful, market segments have to be (Hooley et al., 2004):

- **Measurable**: The size, purchasing power, and profiles of the segments can be measured. The operational use of segmentation usually requires that segment targets can be identified by measurable characteristics to enable their potential value as a market target to be estimated and for the segment to be identified. Fundamental to utilizing a segmentation scheme to make better marketing decisions is the ability of the marketing strategist to evaluate segment attractiveness and the current or potential strengths the company has in serving a particular segment. Depending on the level of segmentation analysis, this may require internal company analysis or external market appraisal.

- **Accessible**: The market segments can be effectively reached and served. A fragrance company, for example, finds that heavy users of its brand are single men and women who stay out late and socialize a lot. Unless this group lives or shops at certain places and is exposed to certain media, its members will be difficult to reach.

- **Substantial**: The market segments are large and profitable enough to serve. In this context, a segment could be the largest possible homogenous group worth pursuing with a tailored marketing program.

- **Differentiable**: The segments are conceptually distinguishable and respond differently to diverse marketing mix elements and programs. For segmentation to be useful customers must differ from one another in some important respect, which can be used to divide the large heterogeneous market. If they were not different in some significant way, if they were totally homogeneous, then there would be no basis on which to segment the market. However, in reality all customers differ in some respect as already stated above. The key to whether a particular difference is useful for segmentation purposes lies in the extent to which the variations are related to different behaviour patterns (e.g. different levels of demand for the product or service, or different use/benefit requirements) or susceptibility to different marketing mix combinations (e.g. different product/service offerings, different media, messages or distribution channels), i.e. whether the differences are important to how we develop a marketing strategy.

- **Actionable**: Effective programs can be designed for attracting and serving the segments. For example, although a small company might identify multiple target segments, its resources like staff and capital may be insufficient to develop and implement a separate marketing program for each segment.

3.2.2 The Segmentation, Targeting and Positioning Approach

Market segmentation provides a basis for the selection of target markets. A target market is a depicted segment of market that a company has decided to serve. As customers in the target market segment have similar characteristics, a single marketing mix can be developed to match those requirements.

The selection of a target market or markets is a three-step process, as shown in Figure 3.7: **Segmentation, Targeting and Positioning (STP)**.

Figure 3.7: The STP of market segmentation

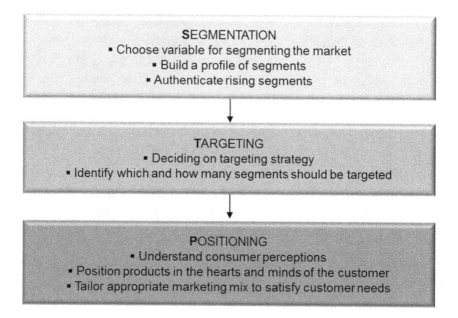

Source: Adapted from Hollensen and Opresnik, 2015, modified

According to this model, the process begins with the aggregation of customers into groups, to maximise homogeneity within, and heterogeneity between the segments (Hollensen and Opresnik, 2015).

The first step is **market segmentation** – dividing a market into smaller groups of buyers with distinct needs, characteristics, or behaviours who might require separate products or marketing mixes. The company identifies different ways to segment the market and develops profiles of the resulting market segments. It is important to state, that a given market can be segmented in various ways depending on the choice criteria at this stage. For example, the market for motor cars could be broken down according to the type of buyer (individual or organisational), by major benefit sought (e.g. functionality or status) or by family size (empty nesters versus family with children). Extremely small groups of customers identified through the segmentation process are called **niche markets**. The second step is **target marketing** – evaluating each market segment's attractiveness and selecting one or more of the market segments to target with an appropriate marketing strategy. The final step is **market positioning** – setting the competitive positioning for the products and services and creating a tailored marketing mix in order to achieve a sustainable competitive advantage and to create a unique spot in customers' minds (Kotler, Armstrong and Opresnik, 2016).

The implicit goal of all STP is to improve marketing performance. Thus, an organisation may aim to use STP to increase customer satisfaction, competitive differentiation, and profitability. The STP process offers additional benefits when used accurately. It significantly increases marketers' ability to develop a thorough understanding of the needs of their well-defined customer segments, and it improves their ability to respond to changing segment needs. Marketing efficiency is improved as resources are targeted at segments that offer the most potential for the organisation. Because the marketing program is better matched with segment requirements, effectiveness of the marketing approach is improved. Specifically, STP analysis aid marketing managers design a product line to meet market demand, determine advertising messages that will have most appeal, select media that will have greatest impact for each segment and time product and advertising launches to capitalize on market responsiveness.

In the following sections, we discuss each of the steps in the STP process, segmenting, targeting, and positioning, in more detail (Hollensen and Opresnik, 2015).

3.2.3 Segmenting Consumer Markets (B2C)

As mentioned already, a market may be segmented in many ways. Segmentation variables are the criteria that are used for dividing a market into segments. When examining criteria, the marketer must try to identify good predictors of differences in buyer behaviour. There is an array of options and no single, prescribed way of segmenting a market (Wind, 1978). A marketer has to try different segmentation variables, alone and in combination, to find the best way to view the market structure. In addition, the bases selected must fulfil the criteria outlined earlier for effective segmentation.

The major groups of consumer segmentation criteria are **profile, psycho-graphic and behavioural.**

3.2.3.1 Profile Segmentation

Profile segmentation variables allow customer groups to be classified in such a way that they can be reached by communications media (e.g. advertising, direct mail). Even if behaviour and/or psychographic segmentation have successfully separated between consumer preferences there is often an urge to analyse the resulting segments in terms of profile variables such as age and socio-economic group in order to communicate to them. The reason is that readership and viewership profiles of newspapers and television programmes tend to be expressed in that way (Ellis-Chadwick and Jobber, 2016).

We shall now examine a number of the most common **demographic, so-cio-economic and geographic segmentation variables.**

3.2.3.1.1 Demographic Variables

Demographic variables are the most popular bases for segmenting customer groups. One reason is that customer needs, wants and usage rates often vary closely with these variables. Another is that demographic variables are easier to measure than most other types of variables described hereafter. Even if market segments are first defined using other bases, such as behaviour, their demographic characteristics must be known and analyzed in order to assess the size of the target market and to reach it efficiently. We shall look at the demographic variables **age, gender and life cycle:**

- **Age** has been used as a basic segmentation variable in many markets. The market for holidays is a classic example, with holiday companies tailoring their products to particular age groups such as 'under 30s' or 'senior citizens'. Another example includes Procter & Gamble selling Crest spin brushes featuring favourite children's characters. For adults, it sells more serious models, promising 'a dentist-clean feeling twice a day' (Kotler, Armstrong and Opresnik, 2016). In these segmentation schemes it is rational that there are significant differences in behaviour and product/service requirements between the demographic segments identified.

- **Gender** segmentation is a basic approach has long been used in clothing, cosmetics, and magazines. Many segmentation schemes use gender as a first step in the segmentation process, but then further refine their targets within the chosen gender category, e.g. by social class. In some markets the most relevant variable is gender preference as marketers have noticed opportunities for targeting women. Citibank, for example, launched Women & Co., a financial program created around the distinct financial needs of women.

- **Life cycle segmentation** centres on the idea that consumers pass through a series of quite distinct phases in their lives, with each phase being associated with different purchasing patterns and needs. The unmarried person living at home may have very different purchasing patterns from a chronological counterpart who has left home and recently married. It is also recognized that the purchasing pattern of adults often changes as they approach and move into retirement. Producers of baby products, for example, build mailing lists of households with new-born babies on the basis of free gifts given to mothers in maternity hospitals (Hollensen, 2006).

3.2.3.1.2 Socio-Demographic Variables

Socio-demographic variables include social class and income. Here we shall look at **social class** as a predictor of buyer behaviour. Like the demographic variables discussed above, social class has the advantage of being fairly easy to measure, and is used for media readership and viewership profiles.

In many cases, occupation and social class are linked together because, in numerous developed economies, official socio-economic group (social class) categorizations are based upon occupation. The extent to which social class is a predictor of buyer behaviour, however, has been open to question as many people who hold similar occupations have dissimilar lifestyles, values and purchasing patterns. Nevertheless, social class has proved useful in discriminating between owing a dishwasher and having central heating, for example, and therefore should not be discounted as a segmentation variable (O'Brian and Ford, 1988).

3.2.3.1.3 Geographic Variables

Geographic variables facilitate the division of markets into different geographical units such as nations, regions, states, countries, cities, or even neighbourhoods. The geographic segmentation method is useful where there are geographic locational differences in consumption patterns and preferences. For example, in the UK beer drinkers in the north of England prefer a frothy head on their beer, whereas in some parts of the south, local taste dictates that beer should not have a head (Ellis-Chadwick and Jobber, 2016). Geographic segmentation is still widely used, at least as one element in a combination of segmentation bases. Undoubtedly, geographic segmentation is potentially at its most powerful and useful when considering international markets, and therefore is considered in more detail in the framework of segmenting international markets and countries.

The increasing concern regarding the poor predictive power of many of the above stated 'conventional' bases for segmenting consumer markets, coupled with improvements in data collection and analysis methods, has led to the development in recent years of more contemporary and, some would suggest more powerful, bases for segmenting consumer markets like **psychographic and behavioural segmentation** which shall be discussed in more detail now.

3.2.3.2 Psychographic Segmentation

Psychographic segmentation involves grouping customers according to their **lifestyle and personality characteristics**:

- **Lifestyle characteristics**: This research attempts to isolate market segments on the basis
  of the style of life adopted by their members. At one stage these

approaches were seen as alternatives to the social class categories discussed above. Lifestyle segmentation is based upon the fact that individuals have characteristic modes and patterns of living, which may influence their motive to purchase selected products and brands. For example, some individuals may prefer a 'homely' lifestyle, whereas others may see themselves as living a 'sophisticated' lifestyle. Lifestyle segmentation is concerned with three main elements: activities (such as leisure activities, sports, hobbies, entertainment, home activities, work activities, professional work, shopping behaviour, house work and repairs, travel and miscellaneous activities, daily travel, holidays, charitable work); interaction with others (such as self-perception, personality and self-ideal, role perceptions, as mother, wife, husband, father, son, daughter, etc., and social interaction, communication with others, opinion leadership); and opinions (on topics such as politics, social and moral issues, economic and business-industry issues and technological and environmental issues).

- **Personality characteristics** are more difficult to measure than demographics or socio-economics. They are generally inferred from large sets of questions often involving detailed computational (multivariate) analysis techniques. Although the idea that brand choice may be related to personality is intuitively appealing, the usefulness of personality as a segmentation variable is likely to depend on the product category. Buyer and brand personalities are likely to match where brand choice is a direct manifestation of personal values but for the majority of fast-moving consumers goods, such as detergents and tea, the reality is that people buy a repertoire of different brands (Lannon, 1991).

The approaches to consumer market segmentation that have been described so far have all been associative segmentation. That is to say, they are used where differences in purchasing behaviour/customer are perceived as being associated with them. If a company uses social class, for example, to segment a market it is assuming that purchasing behaviour is a function of social class. Most of the problems with using such associative bases tend to be related to the issue of the extent to which they are in fact associated with, or are a reflection of, actual purchasing behaviour.

Because of this, numerous marketers believe that it is more sensible to use direct bases for segmenting markets. Such bases take actual consumer behaviour as the starting point for identifying different segments. They are often referred to as **behavioural segmentation bases** and shall be described in more detail now (Hollensen and Opresnik, 2015).

3.2.3.3 Behavioural Segmentation

The key behavioural bases for segmenting consumer markets are benefits sought, purchase occasion, purchase behaviour, usage, and perceptions, beliefs and values. Each will now be discussed.

3.2.3.3.1 Benefits sought

A powerful form of segmentation is to group buyers according to the different benefits that they seek from the product or service. Benefit segmentation takes the basis of segmentation right back to the underlying reasons why customers are attracted to various product offerings. As such it is perhaps the closest means yet to identifying segments on bases directly relevant to marketing decisions. Developments in techniques such as conjoint analysis make them particularly suitable for identifying benefit segments. The total market for a product or service is broken down into segments distinguished by the principal benefits sought by each segment. A 'benefits sought' basis for segmentation can provide useful insights into the nature and extent of competition and the possible existence of gaps in the market.

3.2.3.3.2 Purchase occasion

Customers can be distinguished according to the occasions when they purchase a product. Attitudinal characteristics attempt to draw a causal link between customer characteristics and marketing behaviour and occasion segmentation can help companies build up product usage. For example, orange

juice is most often consumed at breakfast, but orange growers have pro-
moted drinking orange juice as a cool and refreshing drink at other times
during the day. In contrast, Coca-Cola's 'Coke in the Morning' campaign attempts to increase Coke consumption by promoting the beverage as an
early morning pick-me-up.

3.2.3.3.3 Purchase behaviour

The most direct method of segmenting markets is on the basis of the behaviour of the consumers in those markets. Study of purchasing behaviour
has centred on such issues as the time of purchase (early or late in the product's overall life cycle) and patterns of purchase (the identification of brand-
loyal customers). Differences in purchase behaviour can be based on the
time of purchase relative to the launch of the product. When a product is
launched, a key task is to identify the innovator segment which consists of
customers who purchase a product when it is still new. Evidently during the
launch of new products isolation of innovators as the initial target segment
could significantly improve the product's or service's chances of acceptance
on\the market. However, attempts to seek out generalized innovators have
been less successful than looking separately for innovators in a specific
field. Generalizations seem most relevant when the fields of study are of
similar interest. Opinion leaders can be particularly influential in the early
stages of the product life cycle. Recording companies, for example, recognize the influence that disc jockeys have on the record-buying public and attempt to influence them with free records and other inducements to play
their records.

3.2.3.3.4 Usage

Customers may also be segmented on the basis of being 'heavy', 'light' and
'non-users' of a product or service category. The profiling of heavy users allows this group to receive most marketing focus on the assumption that
creating brand loyalty among these people will pay large dividends. Consequently, brands are sometimes developed to target heavy users. Noticeably,
the usage segmentation concept is more useful in some markets than in others.

3.2.3.3.5 Perceptions, Beliefs and Values

The final behavioural base for segmenting consumer markets is by studying perceptions, beliefs and values. This is categorized as a behaviour variable because perceptions, beliefs and values are often linked to behaviour. Customers are grouped by identifying those people who view the products in a market in a similar way (perceptual segmentation) and have similar beliefs (belief segmentation). Car manufacturers use belief segmentation to segment the market and target specific groups. For example, Mazda targets car buyers who believe their car is their friend, with which they can have fun and enjoy new experiences (Bruce, 2005).

3.2.3.4 Combining Segmentation Variables

As stated above, marketers rarely limit their segmentation analysis to only one of a few variables. Rather, they are increasingly using multiple segmentation bases in an effort to identify smaller, yet better defined target groups. For example, Research Services Ltd, a UK marketing research company, has developed 'SAGACITY', a market segmentation scheme based upon a combination of occupation, life cycle and income. 12 distinct customer groupings are formed with different aspirations and behaviour patterns (Ellis-Chadwick and Jobber, 2016).

3.2.4 Segmenting the Business Markets (B2B)

The imperative to divide the market into different segments in order to offer products that match differing needs is at the very heart of both B2B and B2C marketing. The strength, width and depth of the segmentation demands will vary from industry to industry and from country to country depending on factors that often change, which will be discussed later in the section. Only if the varying and diverse benefits demanded by different industries and organisations are known can products and services be offered with benefits that will satisfy these many disparate needs.

The basic approach to segmentation, targeting and positioning does not differ greatly between consumer and organisational markets. As one might expect, segmenting industrial product markets introduces a number of additional bases for segmentation, whilst precluding some of the more frequently used ones in consumer product markets (Hollensen and Opresnik, 2015).

3.2.5 Target Marketing

Market segmentation reveals the company's market segment opportunities. The firm now has to evaluate the various segments and decide how many and which segments it can serve and apply distinct and appropriate marketing mix strategies. In evaluating different market segments, a company must look at three basic factors: **segment size, segment growth, segment structural attractiveness**, and **company objectives and resources** (Kotler, Armstrong and Opresnik, 2016).

The organisation must first collect and analyze data on current segment sales, growth rates, and expected profitability for various segments. In general, large-sized segments are more attractive than small ones since sales potential is greater, and the chance of achieving economies of scale is improved. However, the 'right size and growth' of segments is a relative matter as the largest, fastest-growing segments are not necessarily the most attractive ones for every company. Smaller companies, as already mentioned above, may lack the skills and resources needed to serve the larger segments or they may find these segments too competitive. Such enterprises may select segments that are smaller and less attractive, in an absolute dimension, but that are potentially more profitable for them (Hollensen and Opresnik, 2015).

The company also needs to examine the structural factors that affect long-term segment attractiveness. Michael **Porter's Five Forces Model** (Porter, 1985) provides a useful tool in this context. For example, a segment is less attractive if it already contains many strong and aggressive *competitors*. The existence of many actual or potential *substitutes* (products or services) may limit prices and the profits that can be gained in a specific segment. In addition, the *threat of new entrants* is another factor to be taken into account: a segment may seem superficially attractive because of the lack of current competition, but care must be taken to assess the dynamics of the market. A judgement must be made regarding the likelihood of new entrants, possibly with new technology, which might change the rules of the competitive game. The *relative power of buyers* also affects segment attractiveness. Buyers with strong bargaining power relative to sellers will try to force prices down, demand more services, and set competitors against one another – all the expense of seller profitability. Finally, a segment may be less attractive if the *bargaining power of suppliers* is strong as they are in a position to control prices or reduce the quality or quantity of ordered goods and services.

Having evaluated the relative attractiveness of different market segment the company is then in a position to select a **targeting strategy**. A company can select from three generic strategies with respect to targeting. These three strategies are **undifferentiated target marketing, differentiated target marketing, concentrated target marketing** and **micro marketing**, each of which shall be discussed now (Hollensen and Opresnik, 2015):

- Using an **undifferentiated marketing** or **mass marketing strategy**, a company decides to ignore market segment differences and go after the whole market with one offer. This strategy focuses on what is common in the needs of consumers rather than on what is different. The company designs a product and a marketing strategy that will appeal to the largest number of potential buyers. This is only feasible, if a market analysis will show now strong differences in customer characteristics that have implications for marketing strategy. Alternatively, the cost in developing a separate marketing mix for separate segments may outweigh the potential gains of meeting customer needs more accurately (Kotler, Armstrong and Opresnik, 2016).

- Using a **differentiated marketing** or **segmented marketing strategy**, a company decides to target several market segments and designs distinct offers for each. This is a powerful strategy when market segmentation reveals several potential targets and specific marketing mixes can be developed to appeal to all or some of the segments. For example, airlines design different marketing mixes for first-class and economy passengers, including varying prices, service levels, quality of food, in-cabin comfort and waiting areas at airports (Ellis-Chadwick and Jobber, 2016).

- A third market-coverage strategy, **concentrated marketing** or **niche marketing** or **focused marketing**, is especially viable when company resources are limited. Instead of going after a small share of a large market, the company goes after a large share of just one or a few segments or niches. Focused marketing allows research and development expenditure to be concentrated on meeting the needs of one set of customers, and managerial activities can be devoted to understanding their specific needs. Large organisations may not be interested in serving the needs of this one segment, or their energies may be so dispatched across the whole market that they pay insufficient attention to their requirements (Ellis-Chadwick and Jobber, 2016). An example of focused marketing in the consumer market is provided by Bang & Olufsen, the Danish audio electronics firm. It targets upmarket customers who value self-development and pleasure with its stylish television and music systems. The company places emphasis on distinctive design, good quality and simplicity of use (Gapper, 2005).

- **Customized Marketing:** In some markets the requirements of individual customers are unique and their purchasing power sufficient to make designing a separate marketing mix for each customer viable. Segmentation at this disaggregated level leads to the use of **customized marketing** (also labelled **individual marketing, one-to-one marketing, mass customization** and **markets-of-one marketing**). Many service providers, such as advertising and marketing research agencies, architects and solicitors, vary their offerings on a customer-to-customer basis. Customized marketing is often associated with close relationships between supplier and buyer because the value of the order justifies large marketing and sales efforts being focused on each customer. The move toward individual marketing mirrors the trend in consumer self-marketing which implies that individual customers are taking more responsibility for determining which products and brands to buy (Kotler, Armstrong and Opresnik, 2016).

3.2.6 Positioning Strategy

The final stages of the STP-process involve the development of positioning strategies together with an appropriate marketing mix. In their seminal work in this area, Ries and Trout (1981) suggested that positioning is essentially '**a battle for the mind**' of the customer. Consequently, successful positioning is often associated with products possessing favourable associations in the minds of customers. These add up to a differential advantage in the minds – and hearts – of the target customers of the company.

A useful tool for determining the position of a brand in the marketplace is the **perceptual map** (also called a **brand map** or **positioning map**). This is a visual representation of consumer perceptions of the brand and its competitors using attributes (dimensions) that are important to customers. The key steps in developing a perceptual map are as follows (Ellis-Chadwick and Jobber, 2016):

1.   Identify a set of competing brands
2.   Identify important attributes that consumers use when choosing between brands using qualitative research (e.g. group decisions)
3.   Conduct qualitative marketing research where consumers score each brand on all key attributes.
4.   Plot brand on a two-dimensional map

For example, suppose that a company seeks to enter the market for 'instant coffee', in which there are already competitors producing brands A, B, C, D, E, F and G. The company must establish what the customers believe to be the appropriate attributes when choosing between brands in this market and the perceived position of existing competitors with respect to these attributes. If we imagine that the important attributes have been found to be 'price' and 'flavour', a possible **positioning map** might be drawn as shown in Figure 3.8.

Figure 3.8: Hypothetical Positioning Map: Instant Coffee Market

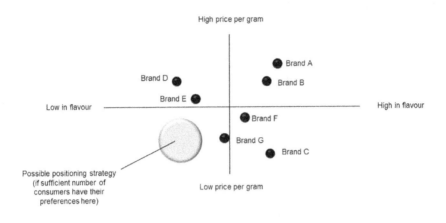

Source: Adapted from Hollensen and Opresnik, 2015, modified

With this information, the company must decide where to position its product within this specific market segment. Possibilities are contained within the box, the parameters of which are low to medium price per gram and low to medium in flavour. Perhaps a 'caffeine free' product could also be taken into consideration? Such a product would give the new brand distinctiveness, as opposed to positioning the brand next to another and fighting 'head on' for market share.

What is the most appropriate position for the new coffee brand depends on a number of factors. For example, as outlined earlier, we must assess the relative attractiveness of a particular position in a market for the new brand compared to the resources and competences of the company. Obviously, it is also important to consider if the number of customers in the chosen position is large enough to generate sufficient profit. Similarly, and related to this, we must assess the relative strengths of existing competitive brands in the market and whether we want to tackle this competition head on or not. Finally, we must consider what our objectives for the new product are, particularly with regard to brand image.

Once the company has assessed brand positioning in the market and determined where it wants to position its products and brands, the final step in the process of segmentation, targeting and positioning involves the design of marketing programmes, which will support the positional strategy in selected target markets. In the 'instant coffee' example above the company must therefore determine what price, flavour (product) distribution and promotional strategy will be necessary to achieve the selected position in the market (Hollensen, 2006).

4. Marketing Mix in the Marketing Planning Process

To this point, we have discussed the analysis, which is essential in the framework of the development of detailed marketing programmes designed to meet corporate and strategic marketing objectives. In this and the following chapters, we will consider strategic decisions concerned with planning and implementing elements of the marketing mix; i.e. product, price, promotion and place decisions. In this chapter, we will start with the product element of the marketing mix (Hollensen and Opresnik, 2015).

4.1 Product and Service Decisions

Essentially, a product can be defined as anything that can be offered to a customer for attention, acquisition, use, or consumption and that might satisfy a want or need. Product is a core element in the marketing mix as it provides the functional requirements sought by customers. Careful management of the product offering is essential if your company is to produce the desired responses from customers but the product is only part of the story. In an age of intense competition where it is of critical importance to differentiate one's offerings from competitors.

In creating an acceptable product offer for international markets, it is necessary to examine first what contributes to the 'total' product offer. In the product dimensions, we include not just the core physical properties, but also additional elements such as packaging, branding and after-sales service that make up the total package for the purchaser. We can look at three levels of a product (Hollensen and Opresnik, 2015):

- **Core product benefits**: Functional features, performance, perceived value, image and technology.

- **Product attributes**: Brand name, design, packaging, price, size, colour variants, country of origin.

- **Support services**: Delivery, installation, guarantees, after-sales service (repair and maintenance), spare part services.

In this respect, it is much easier to standardize the core product benefits (functional features, performance, etc.) than it is to standardize the support services, which often have to be tailored to the business culture and sometimes to individual customers.

4.1.1 Different Product Levels

Product differentiation seeks to increase the value of the product or service. Levitt (1986) has suggested that products and services can be seen on at least four main levels which we shall quickly summarize to add comprehensiveness in the framework of product policy. These levels are the core product, the expected product, the augmented product and the potential product. Figure 4.1 shows these levels.

Differentiation is possible in all these respects.

At the centre of the model is the core, or generic, product. This is the central product or service offered. The **core benefit** addresses the following question: What is the buyer really buying? When designing products, marketers must first define the core, problem-solving benefits or services that consumer want.

Beyond the generic product, however, is what customers expect in addition, the **expected product**. When buying petrol, for example, customers expect the possibility of paying by credit card, the availability of screen wash facilities, and so on. Since most petrol forecourts meet these expectations they do not serve to differentiate one supplier from another.

At the next level, Levitt identifies the **augmented product**. This constitutes all the additional features and services that exceed customer expectations to convey added value and hence serve to differentiate the offer from that of competitors. Product planners must build an augmented product around the core benefit and expected product by offering additional customer services and benefits. The petrol station where one attendant fills the car with petrol while another cleans the windscreen, headlamps and mirrors, is going beyond what is expected. Over time, however, these means of distinguishing can become copied, routine, and ultimately merely part of what is expected.

Finally, Levitt describes the **potential product** as all those further additional features and benefits that could be offered. At the petrol station these may include a free car wash with every fifth fill up. While the model shows the potential product bounded, in reality it is only bounded by the imagination and ingenuity of the supplier (Hollensen and Opresnik, 2015).

Figure 4.1: Different Product Levels

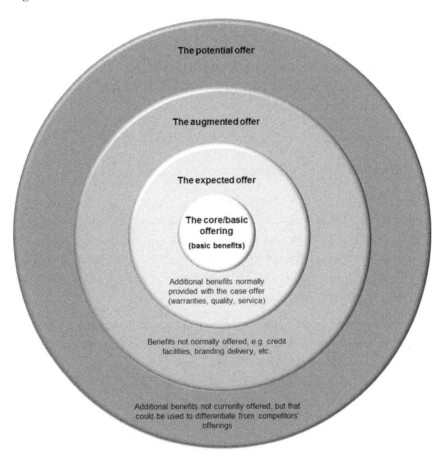

Source: Adapted from Hollensen and Opresnik, 2015, modified

In the past, suppliers have concentrated on attempts to differentiate their offerings on the basis of the core and expected product that convergence is occurring at this level in many markets. As quality control, assurance and management methods become more widely understood and practiced, delivering a performing, reliable, durable, conforming offer (a 'quality' product in the classic sense of the word) will no longer be adequate. In the future, there will be greater emphasis on the augmented and potential product as ways of adding value, creating customer delight and hence creating competitive advantage.

The key decisions in the development and marketing of individual products and services include **product attributes, branding, packaging, labelling** and **product support services**.

4.1.2 Product Line Decisions

Beyond decisions about individual products and services, product strategy also calls for building a product line. A **product line** is a group of products that are closely related because they function in a similar manner, are sold to the same customer groups, are marketed through the same types of outlets, or fall within given price ranges. For example, Nokia produces several lines of telecommunication products.

The major product line decision involves **product line length** – the number of items in the product line. The line is too short if the manager can enlarge profits by adding items and the line is too long if the marketer can increase profits by dropping items. Product line length is influenced by company objectives and resources. For example, one goal might be allowing for **upselling**. Thus, BMW wants to move customers up from its 3-series models to 5- and 7-series models. Another objective might be to allow **cross-selling**: Hewlett-Packard sells printers as well as cartridges.

A firm can lengthen the product line in two ways: by **line stretching** or by **line filling**. Product line stretching occurs when a company lengthens its product line beyond its current range. The firm can stretch its line downward, upward, or both ways. Mercedes-Benz, for example, stretched its Mercedes line downward because of the following reasons: Facing a slow-growth luxury car market and attacks by Japanese automakers on its high-end positioning, it successfully introduced its Mercedes C-Class cars.

Product line filling involves adding more items within the present range of the line. Reasons for this approach include reaching for extra profits, satisfying dealers, using excess capacity and being the leading full-line company. Sony, for example, filled its Walkman line by adding solar-powered and waterproof Walkmans, ultra-light models for exercises, and the Memory Stick Walkman. Line filling is overdone if it results in cannibalization and customer confusion (Kotler, Armstrong and Opresnik, 2016).

4.1.3 Product Mix Decisions

An organisation with several product lines has a product mix. A **product mix** (or **product assortment**) consist of all the product lines and items that a particular company markets.

A company's product mix has four important dimensions: width, length, depth, and consistency:

- **Product mix width** refers to the number of different product lines the company carries. For example, Procter & Gamble markets a wide product mix consisting of 250 brands organized into five major product lines: personal and beauty, house and home, health and wellness, baby and family, and pet nutrition and care products.
- **Product mix length** refers to the total number of items the firm carries within its product lines. P&G carries many brands within each line. For example, its house and home lines includes seven laundry detergents, six hand soaps, five shampoos, and four dishwashing detergents (Kotler, Armstrong and Opresnik, 2016).
- **Product line depth** refers to the number of versions offered for each product in the line. P&G's Crest toothpaste comes in 16 varieties.
- Finally, the **consistency** of the product mix refers to how closely related the various product lines are in end use, production requirements, distribution channels, or some other way. P&G's product lines are consistent insofar as they are consumer products that go

through the same distribution channels. The lines are less consistent insofar as they perform different functions for customers.

The hypothetical company in Figure 4.2 manufactures and markets three product lines (= product width). Product depth refers to the number of product items in each line – 3, 4 and 2 respectively – with the average being 3. By looking at Figure 4.2 a strategic assessment of a company's product offering can be made. For example, the product width could be extended by adding more product lines. The same could happen to the product depth. The depth of the product line depends upon the pattern of customer requirements, the product depth being offered by competitors, and company resources (Hollensen and Opresnik, 2015).

Figure 4.2: The Product Mix for a Hypothetical Company

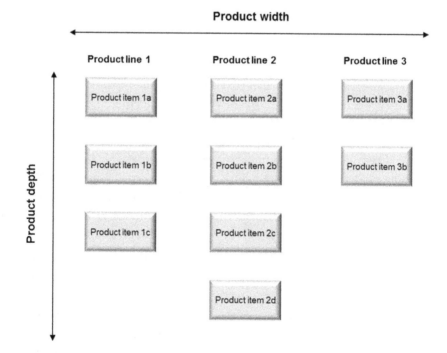

Source: Adapted from Hollensen and Opresnik, 2015, modified

4.1.4 Services Marketing

Services have grown dramatically in recent years. It is seen from the definition of a product that services often accompany products. Increasingly it is accepted that because buyers are concerned with benefits or satisfactions this is a combination of both tangible 'products', and intangible 'services'.

4.1.4.1 Characteristics of Services

Services are characterized by the following features (Hollensen, 2006):

- **Intangibility** means that services cannot be seen, tasted, felt, heard, or smelled before they are bought. For example, as services like air transportation or education cannot be touched or tested, the buyers or services cannot claim ownership or anything tangible in the conventional sense.

    Payment is for use or performance. Tangible elements of the service, such as food or drink on airlines, are used as part of the service in order to confirm the benefit provided and to enhance its perceived value.

    Against this background, a service marketing strategy consistently tries to **'make the intangible tangible'** and send the right signals about the quality. This is called **evidence management**, in which the service organisation presents its customers with organized, honest evidence of its capabilities.

- **Perishability** means that services cannot be stored for future usage – for example, unfilled airline seats are lost once the aircraft takes off. This characteristic causes considerable problems in planning and promotion in order to match supply and demand. To maintain service capacity constantly at levels necessary to satisfy peak demand will be very expensive.

    The marketer must therefore attempt to estimate demand levels in order optimise the use of capacity.

- **Heterogeneity** implies that services are rarely the same because they involve interactions between people. Furthermore, there is high customer involvement in the production of services.

  This can cause problems of maintaining quality, particularly in international markets where there are quite different attitudes towards customer service. For example, within a given Marriott hotel, one registration-desk employee may be cheerful and highly efficient, whereas another standing just a few feet away may be unpleasant and slow. Even the quality of a single Marriott employee's service varies according to his or her energy at the time of each customer encounter.

  Consequently, the management of staff is of supreme importance in the framework of service marketing.

- **Inseparability** means that services cannot be separated from their providers. The time of production is very close to or even simultaneous with the time of consumption. The service is provided at the point of sale. This means that economies of scale and experience curve benefits are difficult to achieve, and supplying the service to scattered markets can be expensive, particularly in the initial setting-up phase. If a service employee provides the service, then the employee is a part of the service.

  Because the customer is also present, **provider-customer-interaction** is a special feature of services marketing and both the provider and the customer affect the service outcome.

4.1.4.2 Categories of Service

All products, both goods and services, consist of a core element that is surrounded by an array of optional supplementary elements. If we look first at the core service products, we can assign them to one of three broad categories depending on their tangibility and the extent to which customers need to be physically present during service production. These categories are presented in Figure 4.3.

Figure 4.3: Categories of Service

Categories of service	Charactetistics	Examples
People processing	Customers become a part of the production process. The service needs to maintain local geographic presence	Education Healthcare Food service Hotel service
Possession processing	The object needs to be involved in the production process, but the owner of the object (the customer) does not. Involve tangible actions to physical objects to improve their value for the customers	Car repair
Information based services	Collecting, interpreting and transmitting data to create value to others. Minimal tangibility. Minimal customer involvement in the production process	Banking Internet services

Source: Adapted from Hollensen and Opresnik, 2015, modified

4.1.4.3 The 7Ps Model of Service Marketing

In the case of service organisations, the 4Ps marketing mix is felt to be insufficient. Some authors have suggested extending it to the so-called **7Ps**

approach which includes people, process and physical evidence. In services, people often *are* the service itself; the process of how the service is delivered to the customer is usually a key part of the service, and the physical evidence – the design of a shop, for example – is so critical to success that it should be considered as a separate element in the services marketing mix. Figure 4.4 contrasts the 4Ps and the 7Ps approach.

Figure 4.4: The 4Ps and 7Ps Model

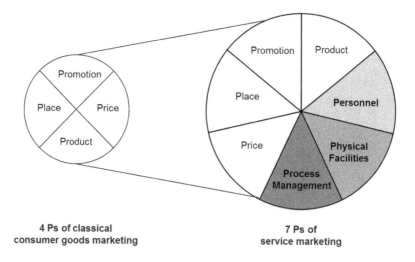

Source: Adapted from Hollensen and Opresnik, 2015, modified

Because of the specific characteristics described above, managing services enterprises involves specific challenges with the extended marketing mix. Therefore, we shall now briefly describe them:

- **Physical evidence:** Customers look for clues to the likely quality of a service by inspecting the tangible evidence of the service. For example, the ambience of a retail store is highly dependent on décor, and colour plays an important role in establishing mood.

- **People:** Because of the simultaneity of production and consumption in services, the firm's personnel occupy a key position in influencing customer perceptions of product quality. The term **service encounter** is used to describe an interaction between a service provider and a customer. These encounters may be short and quick such as when a customer picks up a newspaper at a newsstand or long and protracted involving multiple encounters such as receiving a university education.

- **Process:** The service process refers to the procedures, mechanisms and flow of activities by which a service is acquired. This process usually contains two elements, namely, that which is visible to the customer and where the service encounter takes place and that which is invisible to the customer but is still critical to service delivery. For example, waiting staff in a restaurant are a key part of the service encounter and they need to be well selected and well trained. How the treat customers is a key element of the service experience. But what happens in the kitchen, even though it is invisible to the customer is also critical to the experience. Both parts of the service process need to be carefully managed. Service process decisions usually involve some trade-off between levels of service quality (effectiveness) and service productivity (efficiency). For instance, if more people can be served (output) using the same number of staff (input), productivity per employee has risen. For example, a doctor who reduces consultation time per patient raises productivity at the risk of lowering service quality. Consequently, a balance must be struck between productivity and service quality.

Contrasting the 4Ps and the 7Ps model, there is no reason the – useful – extensions of the latter cannot be integrated within the 4Ps framework. People, process and physical evidence can be discussed under 'product', for example. The important issue is not to neglect them, whether the 4Ps approach or some other method is used to conceptualise the decision-making areas of marketing.

4.1.5 New Product Development (NPD)

Given the rapid changes in customer tastes, technology and competition, companies must develop a steady stream of new products and services (question marks in the terminology of the BCG matrix). A company can create new products in two ways. One is through acquisition – by buying another company, a patent or a license to produce someone else's product. The other is through **new product development (NPD)** in the company's own research-and-development (R&D) department.

The traditional new product development models involve the following stages in product development: idea generation, screening, concept development and testing, business analysis, product development and testing, test marketing, commercialization or launch (Baker and Hart, 1999).

An effective commercialization strategy relies upon marketing management making plain choices regarding the target market, and the development of a marketing strategy that provides a differential advantage.

A useful starting point for choosing a target market is an understanding of the **diffusion of innovation process** which explains how a new product spreads throughout a market over time. Figure 4.5 shows the diffusion of innovation curve which categorizes people or organisations according to how soon they are willing to adopt the innovation (Hollensen and Opresnik, 2015).

The graph shows that those actors (**innovators** and **early adopters**) who are willing to purchase the new product soon after launch are likely to from a minor part of the total number of actors who will eventually be willing to buy it. As the new product is accepted and approved by these customers, and the decision to purchase it becomes less risky, the customers that make up the bulk of the market, comprising the **early** and **late majority**, begin to try the product themselves. Finally, after the product has gained full acceptance, a group describes as the **laggards** adopt the new product.

Figure 4.5: The diffusion of innovation process

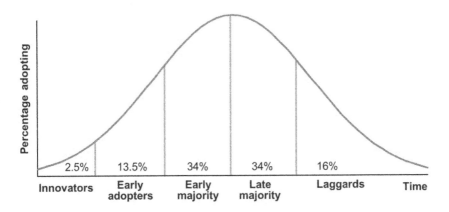

Source: Adapted from Hollensen and Opresnik, 2015, modified

4.1.6 The Product Life Cycle

The concept of the **product life cycle (PLC)** provides useful inputs into making product decisions and formulating product strategies. The product life cycle visualizes the course of a product's sales and profits over its lifetime. It involves four distinct stages: introduction, growth, maturity and decline (see Figure 4.6). Each stage is identified by its sales performance and characterized by different level of profitability, various degrees of competition and distinctive marketing programmes (Hollensen and Opresnik, 2015).

The four stages of the product life cycle can be briefly summarized as follows (Hollensen and Opresnik, 2015):

- **Introduction** is a period of slow sales as the product is introduced in the market. Profits are non-existent in this stage because of the large expenses of product introduction.
- **Growth** is a period of rapid market acceptance and increasing profits. Profits may begin to decline towards the latter stage of growth as new rivals enter the market, attracted by fast sales growth and high profit potential. The end of this stage is often associated with

competitive shakeout, whereby weaker suppliers terminate production.

- **Maturity** is a period of slowdown in sales growth because the product has achieved acceptance by most potential buyers. Saturation occurs, hastening competitive shakeout. The remaining companies are engaged in a fierce battle for market share by employing product improvements, advertising and sales promotional offers, and price cutting; the result is strain on profit margins. The need for successful brand building is increasingly recognized as brand leaders are in the strongest position to resist the pressure on profit margins (Doyle, 1989).

- **Decline** is the period when sales and profits fall as new technology or changes in consumer tastes work to reduce demand for the products and services. Suppliers may decide to end production completely or reduce product depth. Advertising may be used to defend against rivals and prevent the sales from falling further.

Figure 4.6: The Product Life Cycle

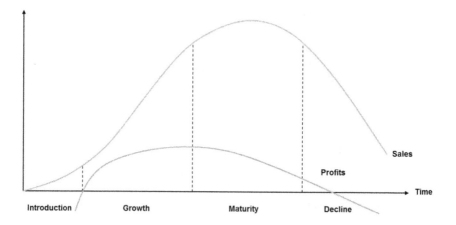

Source: Adapted from Hollensen and Opresnik, 2015, modified

4.1.7 Branding

Branding is the process by which companies distinguish their product offerings from the competition. By developing a distinctive name, packaging and design, a brand is produced. However, a brand name is more than a label employed to differentiate among the manufacturers of a product. It is a complex symbol that represents a variety of ideas and attributes. It tells the consumer numerous things by the body of associations it has built up and acquired as a public object over a period of time. The net result is the public image, the character or personality that may be more important for the customers. Essentially, a brand is a collection of perceptions in the eyes of the consumer influenced by values, communication, the marketing mix, and behaviour of staff.

The concept of the brand represents an acceptance of the fact that all purchasing decisions for both products and services involve a combination of *rational* and *emotional* criteria. The rational criteria are the physical components or factual elements of the product or service in question. The emotional criteria are the sum of the impressions, ideas, opinions and random associations that the potential purchaser has stored in their mind about the product or service. Rational and emotional elements combine to form a brand image. The word 'brand' is used to represent everything that people know about, think about or feel about anything. There are a number of implications of this definition.

Successful brand management necessitates the company innovating to stay abreast of constantly changing market conditions, ideally anticipating evolving tastes, and telling their brand stories to each new generation of consumers. The notion of **storytelling** is of key importance. Well-managed brands are continually telling stories about themselves, and updating these stories to take account of underlying change in society, though their core values usually remain constant. Astute management of brands also involves decisions about the service element that supports a brand and the extent to which a brand should embrace some higher order universal value. Charles Revson of *Revlon* stated early: 'In the factory, we make cosmetics; in the store we sell hope' (Hollensen and Opresnik, 2015).

4.1.7.1 Brand Equity

As stated above, brands represent customer's perceptions about a product and its performance. Finally, brands exist in the minds of consumers. Therefore, the real value of a strong brand is its power to capture consumer preference and loyalty. A powerful brand has high **brand equity**. Although the definition of brand equity is often debated, the term deals with the brand value, beyond the physical assets associated with its manufacture.

Aaker (1991), one of the leading authorities on brand equity, has defined the term as a set of brand assets and liabilities linked to the brand, its name and symbol that add to or subtract from the value provided by a product or service to a firm or to the firm's customers. Aaker has clustered those assets and liabilities into five categories:

- **Brand loyalty**. Encourages customers to buy a particular brand time after time and remain insensitive to competitors' offerings.
- **Brand awareness**. Brand names attract attention and convey images of familiarity. May be translated to: how a big percentage of the customers know the brand name.
- **Perceived quality**. 'Perceived' means that the customers decide upon the level of quality, not the company.
- **Brand associations**. The values and the personality linked to the brand.
- **Other proprietary brand assets**. Include trademarks, patents, and marketing channel relationships.

4.1.7.2 Brand Sponsorship

The basic purposes of branding are the same everywhere in the world. In general, the functions of branding are as follows (Hollensen and Opresnik, 2015):

- To distinguish a company's offering and differentiate one particular product from its competitors.
- To create identification and brand awareness.
- To guarantee a certain level of quality and satisfaction.

- To help with promotion of the product.

All these purposes have the same ultimate goals: to create new sales (market shares taken from competitors) or induce repeat sales (keep customers loyal).

Basically, a manufacturer has four brand sponsorship options (Kotler, Armstrong and Opresnik, 2016): The product may be launched as a **manufacturer's brand** (or **national brand**), as when IBM sells their output under their own brand names. Or the manufacturer may sell to resellers who give it a **private brand** (also called **store brand** or **distributor brand**). Another option is to market **licensed brands**. Finally, two companies can join forces and pursue a **co-branding** strategy (Hollensen and Opresnik, 2015).

4.1.7.3 Brand Development

Basically, a company has four options when it comes to developing brands (see Figure 4.7).

In the framework of brand development, an organisation can introduce **line extensions, brand extensions, multibrands**, or **new brands** (Kotler, Armstrong and Opresnik, 2016):

- **Line extensions** occur when a company introduces additional items in a given product category under the same brand name, such as new forms, sizes and flavours. A company might introduce line extensions as a low-cost, reduced-risk way to introduce 'new' products. Or it might want to meet customer desire for variety, to use excess capacity, or to claim more shelf space from resellers. However, an overextended brand name might potentially lose its specific meaning, or strongly extended brands can cause customer confusion. Another risk which has to be taken into account is that sales of an extension may come at the expense of other items in the line and increase cannibalisation.

Figure 4.7: Brand Development Strategies

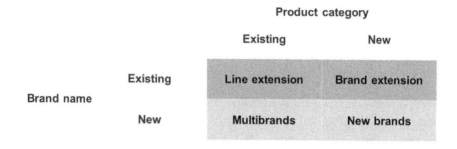

Source: Adapted from Hollensen and Opresnik, 2015, modified

- A **brand extension** strategy involves the use of a successful brand name to launch new or modified products in a new category. For example, Mattel has extended its enduring Barbie Doll brand into new categories ranging from Barbie home furnishings, Barbie cosmetics, and Barbie electronics to Barbie books and Barbie sporting goods. A brand extension is also referred to as **brand stretching** and can give a new product immediate recognition and quicker acceptance. It may also save the high advertising costs usually required to build a new brand name. On the other hand, brand extensions may confuse the image of the main brand as line extensions. And if brand extension fails, it may harm customer attitudes toward the other products carrying the same brand name. A major test of any brand extension opportunity is to ask if the new brand concept is compatible with the values inherent in the core brand to ensure a '**fluent fit**' between them. An example is the failure to extend the Levi's brand name to suits in the USA partly as a result of customers refusing to accept the casual, denim image of Levi's as being suitable for smart, exclusive clothing. Consequently, brand extensions are not viable when a new brand is being developed for a target group that holds different values and aspirations from those in the original market segment. When this occurs, the use of the brand extension strategy would detract from the new brand. The answer is to develop a separate brand name, as did Toyota with the Lexus, and Seiko with its Pulsar brand name developed for the lower-priced mass market for watches. Finally, management needs to guard against the loss of credibility if a brand name is extended too far, which can be called **brand overstretching**. The use of the Pierre Cardin name for such diverse products as clothing, toiletries and cosmetics has tarnished the brand name's credibility (Aaker, 1990).

- In the case of **multibrands**, new brand names are introduced in the same product category. A **single brand** or **family brand** (for a number of products) may be helpful in convincing consumers that each product is of the same quality or meets certain standards. In other words, when a single brand on a single market is marketed by the manufacturer, the brand is assured of receiving full attention for maximum impact. Conversely, the company may also choose to market several brands on a single market. This is based on the assumption that the market is heterogeneous and consists of several segments. For example, Procter & Gamble markets many different brands in each of its product categories.

- Within the framework of this brand development strategy a company might believe that the power of its existing brand name is waning and a **new brand** name is required. Alternatively, a company may create a new brand name when it enters a new product category for which none of the company's current brand names is appropriate. For example, Japan's Matsushita uses separate brand names for its different families of products: Technics, Panasonic National, and Quasar. As with multibranding, offering too many new brands can result in a company spreading its resources too thin. And in some industries, such as consumer packaged goods, customers and retailers have become concerned that there are already too many brands, with too few differences. Against this background, Procter & Gamble, Unilever, and other large consumer-product marketers are pursuing megabrand strategies – weeding out weaker brands and focusing their marketing spending primarily on brands that can achieve the number one or two market share positions in their categories.

4.2 Pricing Decisions

Pricing is one of the most important marketing mix decisions, price being the only marketing mix variable that generates revenues. Pricing is not a single concept, but a multi-dimensional one with different meanings and implications for the manufacturer, the middleman and the end-customer. Pricing strategy is of great importance because it affects both revenue and buyer behaviour. The whole pricing environment is therefore considered, first from the point of view of the company and its strategies and then from the aspect of the consumer (Hollensen and Opresnik, 2015).

4.2.1 A Pricing Framework

A company's pricing decisions are affected by both internal company factors and external environmental factors. It is important that firms recognize that the cost structures of product are very significant, but they should not be regarded as sole determinants when setting prices.

Figure 4.8 presents a general framework for pricing decisions. According to this model, factors affecting pricing can be broken down into two main groups (internal and external factors) which consist of various factors.

We shall now consider the most important elements in more detail.

4.2.1.1 Internal Factors Affecting Pricing Decisions

Internal factors affecting pricing include the firm's marketing objectives, marketing mix strategy, costs and organisational considerations (Nagle and Holden, 2001):

- **Marketing objectives:** Before determining the price, the company must decide on its strategy for the product. If the company has selected its target market and positioning, its marketing mix strategy will be straightforward. Pricing strategy is largely determined by decisions on market positioning. In addition, a company may seek other general or specific objectives. General objectives include survival, profit maximisation, market share leadership, and product quality leadership. At a specific level, a company may set prices low to prevent competition from entering the market. Thus, pricing plays an important role in helping to accomplish the company's objectives at many levels.

Figure 4.8: Factors Affecting Price Decisions

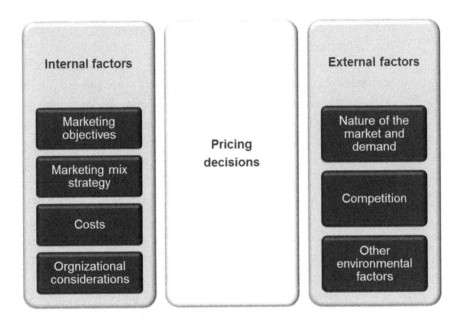

Source: Adapted from Hollensen and Opresnik, 2015, modified

- **Marketing mix strategy:** As price is only one element of the marketing mix price decisions must be coordinated with product design, distribution, and promotion decisions to form a coherent and effective marketing mix strategy. Decisions made for other marketing mix variables affect pricing decisions. For example, a decision to position the product on high-performance quality will suggest that the seller must charge a higher price to cover higher costs. Marketers must consider the complete marketing mix when setting

133

prices. If the product is positioned on on-price factors, then decisions about quality, promotion, and distribution will largely affect
price. If price is a crucial positioning factor, then price will strongly
affect decisions made about the other marketing mix elements.

- **Costs:** Costs set the baseline for the price that the company can
  charge. The firm wants to charge a price that both covers all its
  costs for producing, distributing, and selling the product and deliv-
  ers a fair rate of return. A company's costs are an important element in its pricing strategy. However, the company must consider
  costs alongside all of the other factors rather than in isolation. A
  company's costs take two forms, fixed and variable. **Fixed costs**
  (also known as **overhead**) are costs that do not vary with production or sales level. Examples include rent, interest, and executive
  salaries. **Variable costs** vary directly with the level of production.
  Each PC produced by Hewlett Packard, for example, involves a
  cost of computer chips, wires, packaging and other inputs. Finally,
  total costs are the sum of the fixed and the variable costs for any
  given level of production. Management wants to charge a price that
  will at least cover the total production costs at a given level of production.

- **Organisational considerations:** Management must decide who
  within the organisation should set prices. In small enterprises,
  prices are often set by top management rather than by the marketing or sales department. In large companies, pricing is typically handled by divisional or product line managers. In industries in which
  pricing is a key factor such as aerospace and oil, companies often
  have a pricing department to set the best prices. Others who have
  an influence on pricing include sales managers, production managers, finance managers, and accountants.

4.2.1.2 External Factors Affecting Pricing Decisions

The environmental factors are external to the firm and thus uncontrollable
variables in the foreign market. External factors affecting pricing include
the nature of the market and demand, competition, and other environmental elements (Hollensen and Opresnik, 2015).

The market and demand

One of the critical factors affecting pricing is the pressure of competitors. The firm has to offer a more competitive price if there are other sellers in the market. Thus, the **nature of competition** (e.g. oligopoly or monopoly) can significantly influence the firm's pricing strategy.

Under conditions approximating **pure competition**, price is set in the marketplace price and tends to be just enough above costs to keep marginal producers in business. Thus, from the point of view of the price setter, the most important factor is costs. The closer the substitutability of products, the more nearly identical the prices must be, and the greater the influence of costs in determining prices (assuming a large enough number of buyers and sellers).

Under conditions of **monopolistic or imperfect competition**, the seller has some discretion to vary the product quality, promotional efforts and channel politics in order to adapt the price of the total product to serve pre-selected market segments. Nevertheless, the freedom to set prices is still limited by what competitors charge, and any price differentials from competitors must be justified in the minds of customers on the basis of differential utility: that is, perceived value.

Whereas costs set the lower limit of prices, the market and demand set the upper limit. Both customers and industrial buyers balance the price of a product or service against the benefits of owning it. Thus, before setting prices, the marketer must comprehend the relationship between the price and demand for its product. Each price the company might charge will lead to a different level of demand. The relationship between the price charged and the resulting demand level is shown in the **price demand curve** in Figure 4.9.

The demand curve shows the number of units the market will buy in a given time period at different prices that might be charged. In the normal case, demand and price are inversely related; that it, the higher the price, the lower the demand and vice versa. Thus, the company would sell more if it lowered its price from P1 to P2. In the case of prestige goods, the demand curve sometimes sloes upward. Customers think that higher prices imply more quality. Marketers also need to know **price elasticity** – how responsive demand will be to a change in price. Consider the demand curve in Figure 4.9. The price decrease from P1 to P2 leads to a relatively small increase in demand from X1 to X2. If demand hardly changes with a small change in price, the demand is categorized as being **inelastic**. If demand changes greatly, the demand is **elastic**.

What determines the price elasticity of demand? Buyers are like to be less price sensitive when the product they are buying is unique or when it is high in quality, prestige, or exclusiveness. Consumers are also less price sensitive when substitute products are difficult to find or when they cannot easily compare the quality of substitute. Finally, buyers are less sensitive to price changes when the total expenditure for a product is low relative to their income or when the cost is shared by another party (Nagle and Holden, 2001).

Figure 4.9: The Price Demand Curve

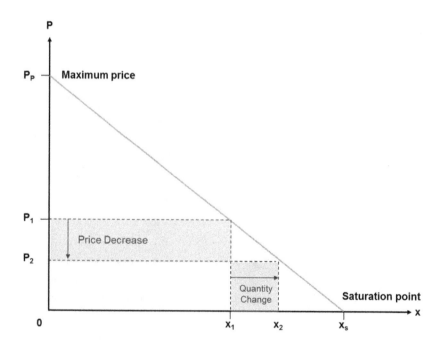

Source: Adapted from Hollensen and Opresnik, 2015, modified

Competition

In setting its prices, the company must carefully consider competitors' costs and prices and possible reactions to the company's own pricing moves. A consumer who is considering the purchase of a Sony digital camera, for example, will evaluate Sony's price and values against the prices and values of comparable products made by Canon, Olympus, and others. If a business lowers prices to gain share, and competitors follow, there is likely to be very little real share gain. And at reduced margins, with a limited increase in volume, total contribution is likely to go down. On the other hand, if a business raises prices to improve margins and competitors do not follow, the business could lose share and lower total contribution, even with higher margins (Hollensen and Opresnik, 2015).

Other external factors

When setting prices, the company also must consider a number of other factors in its external environment. **Economic conditions** can have a strong impact on the company's pricing strategies. Economic factors such as boom or recession, inflation, and interest rates affect pricing decisions because they affect both the costs of producing a product and customer perceptions of the product's price and value. The enterprise must also think about what impact its prices will have on other parties in its environment (e.g. resellers).

The **government** is another important external stakeholder in the framework of pricing decisions. For example, import controls are designed to limit imports in order to protect domestic producers or reduce the outflow of foreign exchange. Direct restrictions commonly take the form of tariffs, quotas and various non-tariff barriers. Tariffs directly increase the price of imports unless the exporter or importer is willing to absorb the tax and accept lower profit margins. Quotas have an indirect impact on prices. They restrict supply, thus causing the price of the import to increase. Since tariff levels vary from country to country, there is an incentive for exporters to vary the price somewhat from country to country (Hollensen, 2003).

In the following sections, we shall discuss the different available pricing strategies (Hollensen and Opresnik, 2015).

4.2.2 General Pricing Approaches

Companies set prices by selecting a general pricing approach. We will examine the following approaches in detail: the **cost-based approach** (**cost-plus pricing** and **break even analysis**), the **value-based pricing**, and the **competition-based pricing** (**going-rate pricing** and **sealed bid pricing**).

4.2.2.1 Cost-Based Pricing and Break-Even-Pricing

Companies often use **cost-oriented methods** when setting prices. The simplest pricing method is **cost-plus pricing** – adding a standard mark-up to the cost of the product. Construction companies, for example, submit project bids by estimating the total cost and adding a standard mar-up for profit. Cost-plus pricing can be best explained by using a simple example: suppose a watch manufacturer had the following costs and expected sales (Kotler, Armstrong and Opresnik, 2016):

- Variable cost   EUR 10
- Fixed costs   EUR 300.000
- Expected unit sales   50.000

Then the manufacturer's cost per watch/unit is given by:

- Unit Cost = Variable Cot + (Fixed Costs/Unit Sales) = 10 + (300.000/50.000) = EUR 16

Now, we shall suppose the manufacturer wants to earn a 20 per cent mark-up on sales. The manufacturer's mark-up price is given by:

- Mark-up Price = Unit Cost/(1-Desired Return on Sales) = 16/(1-0,2) = EUR 0,20

Consequently, the manufacturer would charge resellers EUR 20 a watch and make a profit of 20 per cent or EUR 4 per unit. The dealers, in turn, will mark up the watch. If resellers, for example want to earn 50 per cent on sales price, they will mark up the watch to EUR 40 (EUR 20 + 50 % of EUR 40). This number is equivalent to a mark-up on cost of 100 per cent (EUR 20/EUR 20).

The problem with this pricing approach is that it ignores demand and competitor prices and all other internal and external factors discussed above. In addition, the procedure is illogical because a sales estimate is made *before* a price is set. Furthermore, it focuses on internal costs rather than the customer's willingness to pay. Finally, there may be a technical problem in allocating overheads in multi-product companies (Christopher, 1982). Still, mark-up pricing remains popular for many reasons. First, manufacturers are more certain about costs than about demand. By tying the price to cost, sellers simplify pricing – they do not have to make regular adjustments as demand changes. Furthermore, this approach does give an indication of the minimum price necessary to make a profit. Another reason is that many stakeholders feel that cost-plus pricing is fairer to both buyers and sellers (Kotler, Armstrong and Opresnik, 2016).

Another cost-oriented pricing approach is **break even pricing.** This approach involves setting the price to break even on the costs of making and marketing a product; or setting the price to make a target profit. Break-even analysis is generally viewed as an accounting concept, but it is extremely useful in evaluation the profit potential and risk associated with a pricing strategy, or any marketing strategy. This section is to examine, from a marketing viewpoint, the usefulness of break-even volume. For a given price strategy and marketing effort, it is useful to determine the number of units that need to be sold in order to break even (produce a net profit equal to zero). The **break-even point** is normally represented as that level of output where the total revenue from sales of a product or service matches exactly the total costs of its production and marketing (break-even quantity). Such an analysis of cost-revenue relationships can be very useful to the pricing decision-maker. One use of break-even analysis is to compare the break-even volumes associated with different prices for a product. Break-even volume is the volume needed to cover the fixed cost on the basis of a particular contribution per unit. It can be estimated graphically using a break-even-chart, which shows the total cost and total revenue expected at different sales volume levels. Figure 4.10 shows a break-even chart for the watch manufacturer discussed above. Fixed costs are EUR 300.000 regardless of sales. Variable costs are added to fixed costs to form the total costs function, which rise with volume. The total revenue curve starts at zero and rises with each unit sold. The slope of the total revenue curve reflects the price of EUR 20 per unit. The total revenue and total cost curves cross at 30.000 units. This is the break-even volume. At EUR 20, the company must sell at least 30.000 units to break even; that is, for total revenue to cover total cost.

Figure 4.10: Break-Even Chart

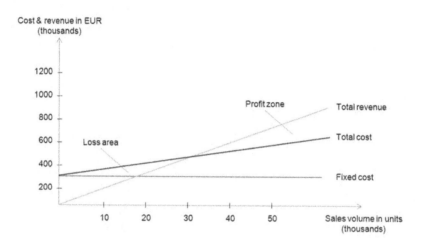

Source: Adapted from Hollensen and Opresnik, 2015, modified

Break-even volume can be computed using the following procedure:

- Contribution per Unit = Selling Price – Variable Cost per Unit
- Break-Even-Volume = Fixed Cost/(Price – Variable Costs) = 300.000/(20-10) = 30.000

If the enterprise wants to make a target profit, it must sell more than 30.000 units at EUR 20 each.

In summary, neither the cost-plus pricing model nor the break-even analysis is in itself a sufficient basis on which to determine prices. Nevertheless, taken together, they do point to a clear-cut and universal presumption for delineating pricing decisions which can be incorporated into a more realistic and marketing-oriented approach to pricing. This more market-oriented approach to pricing will be discussed in the following sections.

4.2.2.2 Value-Based Pricing

An increasing number of companies are basing their prices on the product's perceived value. Value-based pricing uses buyers' perceptions of value, not the seller's total costs, as the key to pricing. Value-based pricing implies that the marketer cannot design a product and marketing program and then set the price. Price in this context is considered along with the other marketing mix variables and other factors *before* the marketing program is determined.

Figure 4.11 compares cost-based pricing with value-based pricing. Cost-based pricing is product driven. The company designs what it considers to be a good product, totals the cost of making the product, and sets a price that covers costs plus a target profit. Once the price was set, the marketer's job was to convince customers that the product was worth it. If the marketer was not successful, then the price was lowered. If demand turned out to be higher than anticipated, then the price was raised.

An important point is that the customer was the last person to be considered in this chain of events (Kotler, Armstrong and Opresnik, 2016).

Figure 4.11: Cost-Based versus Value-Based Pricing

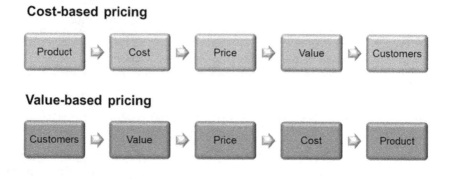

Source: Adapted from Hollensen and Opresnik, 2015, modified

Value-based pricing reverses this process and begins by understanding customers and the competitive marketplace. The first step is to look at the value customers perceive in owning the product and to examine their options for acquiring similar products and brands. The targeted value and price then drive decisions about product design and what costs can be incurred.

Although cost-based pricing is easier, it ignores the customer and the competition as already noted above. Marketers recognize that it is impossible to predict demand or competitors' actions simply by looking at their own costs. Consequently, cost-based pricing is becoming less popular (Hollensen and Opresnik, 2015).

4.2.2.3 Competition-Based Pricing

Consumers will base their judgements of a product's value on the prices that competitors charge for similar products. One form of competition-based pricing is **going-rate pricing**, in which a company bases its price largely on competitors' prices. Less attention is paid to its own costs or to demand. The enterprise might charge the same as, more than, or less than its competitors.

Competition-based pricing is also used when firms bid for jobs. Using **sealed-bid pricing**, a company bases its price on how it believes competitors will price rather than on its own costs or on the demand. The organisation wants to win a contract, and winning the contract requires piecing less than competitors. Yet the company cannot set its price below a certain level. It cannot price below cost without harming its competitive position (Kotler, Armstrong and Opresnik, 2016).

4.2.3 Pricing new Products

Pricing strategies usually change as the product passes through its life cycle. The introductory stage is especially challenging. Companies bringing out a new product face the challenge of setting prices for the first time. They can choose between two generic strategies: **market-skimming pricing and market-penetration pricing** (Hollensen and Opresnik, 2015).

Market-Skimming Pricing

Numerous companies that invent new products set high initial prices to 'skim' revenues layer by layer from the market. Market-skimming pricing involves setting a high price for a new product to skim maximum revenues from the segments willing to pay the high price. A skimming approach, appropriate for a distinctly new product, provides the firm with an opportunity to profitably reach market segments that are not sensitive to the high initial price. As a product ages, as competitors enter the market, and as organisational buyers become accustomed to evaluating and purchasing the product, demand becomes more price elastic.

Market skimming is appropriate under certain conditions. First, the product's quality and image must support its higher price, and a reasonable number of buyers must want the product at that price. Second, the costs of producing smaller volume cannot be so high that they cancel the advantage of charging more. Finally, competitors should not be able to enter the market quickly and easily and undercut the high price (Kotler, Armstrong and Opresnik, 2016).

Problems with skimming are as follows:

- Having a small market share makes the firm vulnerable to aggressive local competition
- Maintenance of a high-quality product requires a lot of resource (promotion, after-sales service) and a visible local presence, which may be difficult in distant markets.
- If the product is sold more cheaply at home or in another country, grey marketing (parallel importing) is possible.

Market-Penetration Pricing

Rather than setting a high initial price to skim off small but profitable market segments, companies might use market-penetration pricing. They set a low initial price in order to penetrate the market quickly and deeply – to attract a large number of buyers rapidly and win a large market share. The high sales volume results in falling costs, allowing the company to cut its price even further.

A penetration policy is appropriate when there is (1) high price elasticity of demand, (2) strong threat of imminent competition, and (3) opportunity for a substantial reduction in production costs as volume expands. Drawing upon the experience effect, a firm that can quickly gain substantial market share and experience can gain a strategic advantage over competitors. The viability of this strategy increases with the potential size of the future market. By taking a large share of new sales, experience can be gained when there is a large market growth rate. Of course, the value of additional market share differs between industries and often among products, markets, and competitors within a particular industry. Factors to be assessed in determining the value of additional market share include the investment requirements, potential benefits of experience, expected market trends, likely competitive reaction, and short- and long-term profit implications (Hollensen and Opresnik, 2015).

4.2.4 Price Bundling

Products can be bundled or unbundled for pricing purposes. Using **product bundling**, sellers often combine several of their products and offer the bundle at a reduced price. Many physical goods and services unite a care product with variety of supplementary products at a set price. This has become a popular marketing strategy. Food and beverage suppliers bundle ready-to-serve meals while computer vendors bundle a central processing unit, a monitor, a printer and software at a single price. Manufacturers of industrial goods, such as machine tools, electronic components and chemical substances, frequently offer their products at a system price in conjunction with an assortment of services. In the service sector, travel companies bundle flights, rent-a-cars, accommodations, and events into a one-price vacation package. Strategically this bundling activity is designed to benefit the consumer by reducing administration cost and consequently transaction costs.

Bundled prices offer a service firm a guaranteed revenue from each customer, while giving the latter a clear idea in advance of how much the bill will be. Unbundled pricing provides customers with flexibility in what they choose to acquire and pay for, but may also cause problems. For instance, customers may be put off by discovering that the ultimate price of what they want, is substantially higher than the advertised base price that attracted them in the first place (Hollensen, 2003).

4.3 Distribution Decisions

A product must be made accessible to the target market at an affordable price. Distribution decisions deal with the problems of moving products from points of origin to points of consumption. Often referred to as the **place element** in the marketing mix, distribution decisions are directed at ensuring that the right product is in the right place at the right time and in the right quantities. The creation of place, time, and possession utility for a select group of customers located in a specific geographic location provides the focus of the logistics manager's efforts. The distribution network is referred to as a **marketing channel** – a set of interdependent marketing institutions involved in the process of making a product or service available for use or consumption by the customer. Producers need to consider not

145

only the needs of their ultimate customer but also the requirement of **channel intermediaries**, those organizations that facilitate the distribution of products to customers.

Using an intermediary as opposed to selling direct to the customer can provide producers with a number of benefits. Channel intermediaries fill several valuable functions: reconciling the needs of producers and consumers by breaking bulk; improving distribution efficiency by reducing the number of transactions and creating bulk for transportation; improving accessibility between producer and consumer by reducing the location and time gap; and providing specialist services such as selling, servicing and installation to customers (Hollensen and Opresnik, 2015).

4.3.1 Types of Distribution Channel

Companies can design their distribution channels to make their products available to consumers in different ways. Each layer of marketing intermediaries that performs work in bringing the product closer to the final buyer is a **channel level**. The number of intermediary levels indicates the length of a channel.

Figure 4.12 shows several consumer distribution channels of various lengths.

The first channel at the top of the figure is called a **direct marketing channel** as it has no intermediary levels. In this case, the company sells directly to the customer. For example, Avon and Amway sell their products directly to their consumers. Cutting out distributor profit margin make this option attractive.

The elimination of a layer of intermediaries from a distribution channel is called **disintermediation**. For example, iTunes is displacing record shops in the distribution of music (Mills and Camek, 2004).

The remaining channels in Figure 4.12 are **indirect marketing channels**, containing one or more intermediaries.

Figure 4.12: Distribution Channels

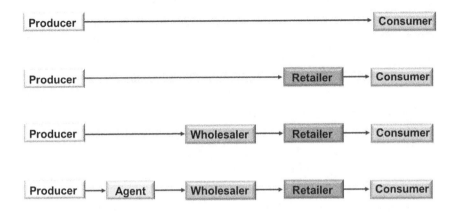

Source: Adapted from Hollensen and Opresnik, 2015, modified

4.3.2 Strategies for Market Coverage

The amount of market coverage that a channel member provides is important. Coverage is a bendable term. It can refer to geographical areas of a country (such as cities and major towns) or the number of retail outlets (as a percentage of all retail outlets). Regardless of the market coverage measure(s) used, the company has to create a distribution network (dealers, distributors and retailers) to meet its coverage goals (Hollensen and Opresnik, 2015).

As shown in Figure 4.13, three different approaches are available (Hollensen and Opresnik, 2015):

- **Intensive distribution.** This calls for distributing the product through the largest number of different types of intermediary and the largest number of individual intermediaries of each type. For example, many mass-market products, such as cigarettes, foods, toiletries, beer and newspapers, and other similar items are sold in millions of outlets to provide maximum brand exposure and consumer convenience.

- **Selective distribution.** This entails using more than one, but fewer than all, of the intermediaries who are willing to sell a company's products. Thus, a producer uses a limited number of outlets in a geographical area to sell its products. The advantages to the manufacturer are the opportunity to select only the best outlets to focus its effort to build close relationships and to train distributor staff on fewer outlets than with intensive distribution, and, if selling and distribution is direct, to reduce costs. Upmarket brands are often sold in carefully selected outlets. Retail outlets and industrial distributors like this arrangement since it reduces competition. Products such as audio and video equipment, cameras, personal computers and cosmetics are distributed in this manner. Selective distribution gives producers good market coverage with more control and less cost than does intensive distribution.

Figure 4.13: Strategies for Market Coverage

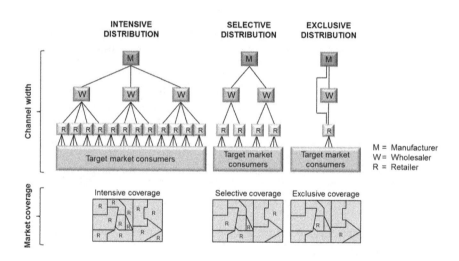

Source: Adapted from Hollensen and Opresnik, 2015, modified

- **Exclusive distribution.** This is an extreme form of selective distribution in which only one wholesaler, retailer or industrial distributor is used in a geographic area. Exclusive distribution is often found in the distribution of luxury automobiles. For example, Bentley dealers are few and far between – even large cities may only have one dealer. This reduces a purchaser's power to negotiate prices for the same product between dealers. It also allows very close cooperation between producer and retailer over servicing, pricing and promotion. Initially, Apple's iPhone was also subject to exclusive distribution in the UK through the mobile phone operator O2 and retailer the Carphone Warehouse. The right to exclusive distribution may be requested by distributors as a condition for stocking a manufacturer's product line (Ritson, 2008).

Channel coverage (width) can be identified along a continuum ranging from wide channels (intensive distribution) to narrow channels (exclusive distribution).

Regarding the types of intermediaries to be used at each level in the channel structure, this can vary quite extensively depending upon the industry in question.

4.3.3 Vertical Integration in the Distribution Channel

Channel integration is the process of incorporating all channel members into one channel system and uniting them under one leadership and one set of goals. Channel integration is relevant for the manufacturer to consider when high transaction costs occur between manufacturer and distributor, as a result channel conflicts and/or bad cooperation climate. There are two different types of integration (Hollensen and Opresnik, 2015):

- **Vertical integration**: seeking control of channel members at different levels of the channel.
- **Horizontal integration**: seeking control of channel members at the same level of the channel (i.e. competitors).

Integration is achieved either through acquisitions (ownership) or through tight cooperative relationships. Getting channel members to work together for their own mutual benefit can be a difficult task. However, today cooperative relationships are essential for efficient and effective channel operation.

Historically, conventional distribution channels have lacked such relationships and leadership, often resulting in damaging conflict and poor performance. One of the biggest channel developments over the years has been the emergence of **vertical marketing systems** (VMS) that provide channel leadership. Figure 4.13 contrasts conventional distribution channels and a vertical marketing system.

A **conventional distribution channel** consists of one or more independent producers, wholesaler, and retailers. Each is a separate stakeholder seeking to maximise its own profits, even at the expense of the system as a whole. No channel member has much control over the other members, and no formal means exists for assigning roles and resolving channel conflict.

In contrast, a **vertical marketing system (VMS)** consists of producers, wholesalers, and retailers acting as a unified system. One channel member owns the others, has contracts with them, or wields so much power that they must all cooperate. Vertical integration offers the promise of potential efficiencies gained from a reduction in management overhead, integration information systems, reduction or elimination of selling costs within the integrated channel, and better management and control of marketing campaigns and physical distribution logistics. It is sometimes the only way to introduce new technological advances into a channel. Integration enables unilateral decisions on who is going to do what and the more direct rewarding of key personnel down the channel for responding to the changes. It also gives the integrating firm more control over training and management succession. However, competitive market forces often make the use of independent channel agents more efficient, and vertical integration should be employed only when the market fails – when gross inefficiencies result from working with independent channel participants (Hollensen and Opresnik, 2015).

Figure 4.14 shows an example of vertical integration. The starting point is the conventional marketing channels (CMCs), where the channel composition consists of isolated and autonomous participating channel members.

Channel coordination is here achieved through arm's-length bargaining. At this point, the vertical integration can take two forms: forward and backward (Hollensen and Opresnik, 2015):

- The manufacturer can make **forward integration**, when it seeks control of businesses of the wholesale and retail levels of the channel.
- The retailer can make **backward integration**, seeking control of businesses at wholesale and manufacturer levels of the channel.
- The wholesaler has two possibilities: both forward and backward integration.

Figure 4.14: Vertical Integration

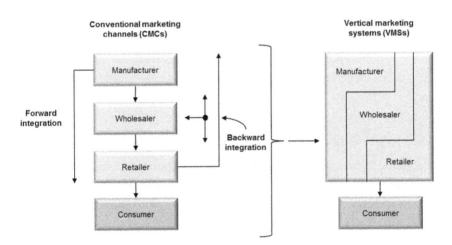

Source: Adapted from Hollensen and Opresnik, 2015, modified

The result of these manoeuvres is the vertical marketing system. Here the channel composition consists of integrated participating members, where channel stability is high due to assured member loyalty and long-term commitments.

4.3.4 Multichannel Distribution Systems

Distribution channels can be seen as sets of interdependent organisations involved in the process of making a product or service available for consumption or use. When making channel choices, companies can choose from a wide variety of alternatives. In the past, many companies used a single channel to sell to a single market or market segment. Today, more and more companies have adopted **multichannel distribution systems** – often called **hybrid marketing channels**. A multichannel distribution system (or hybrid marketing channel) occurs when a single company sets up two or more marketing channels to reach one or more customer segments.

The increasing popularity of this strategy results from the potential advantages provided: extended market coverage and increased sales volume; lower absolute or relative costs; better accommodation of customers' evolving needs; and more and better information. This strategy, however, can also produce potentially disruptive problems: consumer confusion; conflicts with intermediaries and/or internal distribution units; increased costs; loss of distinctiveness; and, eventually, an increased organisational complexity (Hollensen and Opresnik, 2015).

4.3.5 Marketing Logistics and Supply Chain Management

Marketing logistics – also called **physical distribution** – involves planning, implementing, and controlling the physical flow of goods, services, and related information from points of origin to points of consumption. In summary, it involves getting the right product to the right customer in the right place at the right time.

It is important to state that logistics is also a critical component of the firm's marketing capability. The right product, price and promotional mix are ineffective without dependable and timely product availability (place). Timely availability creates value by allowing customers to purchase products or services where desired and if appropriate arrange delivery when and where desired. For a customer, availability or timely availability is equally as important as price and assortment. Consequently, physical distribution and logistics effectiveness has a major impact on both customer satisfaction and company cost structures (Kotler, Armstrong and Opresnik, 2016).

While the role of logistics has not always been visible and well defined in commercial enterprises, transportation, inventory storage and customer service have always been performed. However, top management did not always fully appreciate the strategic importance and competitive impact of integrated logistics. Wide acceptance of enterprise operating philosophies such as just-in-time, total quality management, customer satisfaction and customer responsiveness served to enhance the role of logistics in achieving competitive advantage. A well-planned and executed logistics effort can achieve timely shipment arrival, undamaged product and satisfied customers at the lowest attainable total cost.

Logistics plays a major role in achieving customer expectations. The participants involved in logistical process management include wholesalers, distributors, retailers and third party service providers necessary to provide warehousing, transportation and a wide range of other value added services. The transportation service decision includes selection of transport modes and providers. The managerial aspect of logistics includes scheduling and execution of activities to respond to customers and facilitate shipments. Management or execution activities include order processing, selection and shipment. Measurement includes monitoring activities to ensure performance both satisfies customers and deploys firm resources effectively. Typical measures include customer service level, cost, productivity, asset utilization and quality (Hollensen, 2006).

4.3.6 Logistics Value Chain

Marketing logistics involves not solely **outbound distribution** (moving products from the factory to resellers and ultimately to customers) but also **inbound distribution** (moving products and materials from suppliers to the factory of the manufacturer) and **reverse distribution** (moving broken, unwanted, or excess products returned by consumers or resellers). Consequently, marketing logistics entails entire **supply chain management** – managing upstream and downstream flows of materials, final goods, and relating information among the stakeholders involved (Kotler, Armstrong and Opresnik, 2016).

The logistics value chain links all activities required to support profitable transactions as a single process linking business with customers. In some situations, the value chain is owned by a vertically integrated firm which controls all activities from raw material procurement to retail sales. Such vertical integration is found, for example, in the petroleum industry where firms control product value added from the drill to retail sales (Hollensen, 2006).

4.4 Communication Decisions

Communication is the remaining decision about the marketing programme. The role of communication is to communicate with customers and to provide information which buyers need to make purchasing decisions. Although the communication mix carries information of interest to the customer, in the end it is designed to persuade the customer to purchase a product. Communication involves sharing points of view and is at the heart of forming relationships. A company simply cannot connect with customers unless it – directly or indirectly – communicates with them.

Promotion is the process whereby marketers inform, educate, persuade, remind, and reinforce consumers through communication. It is designed to influence buyers and other stakeholders. Although most marketing communications are aimed at consumers, a significant number also address shareholders, employees, channel members, suppliers, and society. In addition, effective communication is a two-way road: Receiving messages is often as important as sending them.

Integrated marketing communication (IMC) is the coordination of advertising, sales promotion, personal selling, public relations, and sponsorships to reach consumers with a powerful unified effect. These five elements should not be considered separate entities. In fact, each element of the communication plan often has a multiplier effect on the other. For example, it implies that website visuals are consistent with the images portrayed in advertising and that the messages conveyed in a direct marketing campaign are in line with those developed by the public relations department (Hollensen and Opresnik, 2015).

4.4.1 Key Opinion Leader Management

Marketing communications reach customers directly and indirectly. In **one-step communication**, all members of the target audience are simultaneously exposed to the same message. **Multiple-step communication** uses influential members of the target audience, known as **opinion leaders**, to filter a message before it reaches other group members, modifying its effect positively or negatively for the rest of the group. Because of their important role, opinion leaders have often been called **gatekeepers** to indicate the control they have over ideas flowing into the group. Marketers interested in maximising communication effectiveness nearly always attempt to identify opinion leaders. This is called **Key Opinion Leader (KOL) Management**. Opinion leaders are open to communication from all sources and more inclined to be aware of information regarding a broad range of subjects. They read a lot, talk to salespeople and other people who have information about products. Opinion leaders can have a sort of **multiplier effect**, intensifying the strength of the message if they respond positively and pass it on to others, especially if it is going on through the mass media. Consequently, the resources used to gain support from opinion leaders are eventually well spent (Hollensen and Opresnik, 2015).

4.4.2 The Promotional Mix

To communicate with and influence customers, several tools are available. Advertising is usually the most visible component of the **promotional mix** and to many people advertising epitomizes marketing: it is what they believe marketing to be. Evidently, this is a restricted view as marketing concerns much broader issues than simply how to advertise. Nevertheless, advertising is an important element in the promotional mix. The entire range of techniques available to the marketer is the promotional mix and comprises seven key elements (Hollensen and Opresnik, 2015):

- **Advertising**: any paid form of non-personal communication of products in the prime media, i.e. television, the press, outdoor, cinema, and radio.
- **Sales promotion**: incentives to customers or the trade that are designed to stimulate purchase.

- **Public relations**: the communication of a product or business by placing information about it in the media.
- **Sponsorship**: the association of the company or its products with an individual, event or organisation.
- **Internet promotion**: the promotion of products to customers and businesses through internet technologies.
- **Direct marketing**: the distribution of products, information and promotional benefits to target customers through interactive communication in a way that allows response to be measured.
- **Personal selling**: oral communication with potential purchasers with the intention of making a sale.

In addition to these key tools, the marketer can also use other techniques, such as exhibitions, and product placement in movies, songs or video games. It is of paramount importance to stress that promotional mix decisions should not be made in isolation as all aspects of the marketing mix need to be consistently blended in order to achieve a sustainable competitive advantage. Consequently, the promotional mix must be aligned with the decisions made regarding product, pricing and distribution, in order to effectively communicate benefits to target customers.

In the following sections, we will now describe each of the tools in more detail (Hollensen and Opresnik, 2015).

4.4.3 Advertising

Advertising is one of the most visible forms of communication. Because of its wide use and its limitations as a one-way method of communication, advertising in international markets is subject to a number of difficulties. Advertising is often the most important part of the communications mix for consumer goods, where there are a large number of small-volume customers who can be reached through mass media. For most business-to-business markets, advertising is less important than the personal selling function. Of all the elements of the marketing mix, decisions involving advertising are those most often affected by cultural differences among country markets. Consumers respond in terms of their culture, style, feelings, value systems, attitudes, beliefs, and perceptions.

Because advertising's function is to interpret or translate the qualities of products and services in terms of consumer needs, wants, desires, and aspirations, the emotional appeals, symbols, persuasive approaches, and other characteristics of an advertisement must coincide with cultural norms if the ad is to be effective.

We shall revert to international communication strategies and its affecting factors later in this chapter (Hollensen and Opresnik, 2015).

4.4.3.1 Theories of How Advertising Works

For many years, there has been substantial debate about how advertising works. Researchers agree that there can be no single all-embracing theory that explains how all advertising works because it has varied tasks.

The basic competing views on how advertising works have been phrased the **strong theory of advertising** and the **weak theory of advertising** (Jones, 1991).

The strong theory is shown on the left-hand side of Figure 4.15. A person passes through the stages or awareness, interest, desire and action (**AIDA model**). According to this theory, advertising is powerful enough to increase people's knowledge and change their attitudes, and as a consequence is capable of persuading people who had not previously bought a product to buy it.

It is therefore a conversion theory of advertising: non-buyers are converted to become buyers. Advertising is assumed to have a powerful influence on consumers (Hollensen and Opresnik, 2015).

Figure 4.15: Strong and Weak Theories of How Advertising Works

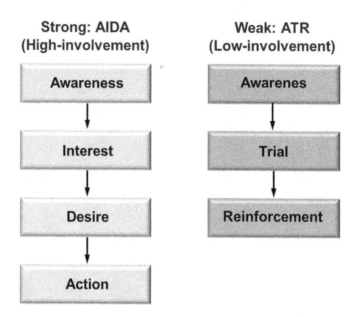

Source: Adapted from Hollensen and Opresnik, 2015, modified

This model has been criticized substantially as for many types of products there is little evidence that customers experience a strong desire before buying the brand. For example, in rather inexpensive product fields a brand may be bought on a trial basis without any strong conviction that it is superior to competing brands. Furthermore, the theory is criticized because it is limited to the conversion of a non-buyer to a buyer and ignores what happens after action (Ehrenberg, 1992).

The major opposing model is shown on the right-hand side of Figure 4.15. The stages in this model are awareness, trial and reinforcement (**ATR model**). The ATR model suggests that advertising has a much less powerful influence than the AIDA model would suggest. Ultimately, the target is existing buyers who presumably are well disposed to the brand, and advertising is designed to reinforce these favourable perceptions so they continue to buy it.

As already mentioned in earlier chapters, level of involvement plays a critical part in determining how people make purchasing decisions. Jones (1991) suggests that involvement may explain when the strong and weak theories apply. For high-involvement decisions such as the purchase of expensive consumer durables, the decision-making process is studied with many alternatives evaluated and an extensive information search undertaken. Therefore, advertising is more likely to follow the strong theory. However, for low-involvement purchase decisions such as low-cost packaged goods people are less likely to consider a wide range of brands thoroughly before purchase. Consequently, the weak theory of advertising is more probable to apply. Advertising is mainly intended to keep customers doing what they already do by providing reassurance and reinforcement (Hollensen and Opresnik, 2015).

4.4.3.2 Developing an Advertising Strategy

We now examine the different steps in developing an effective advertising strategy. The basic framework and concepts of international advertising are essentially the same wherever used.

Figure 4.16 shows the different steps and decisions, which are involved. It is worthwhile to state that each of the stages identified in Figure 4.16 is appropriate irrespective of whether the company is conducting an advertising campaign, a direct marketing or sales promotion campaign, all that changes is the detail involved.

In the following we examine some specific advertising issues (Hollensen and Opresnik, 2015).

Figure 4.16: Developing an Advertising Strategy

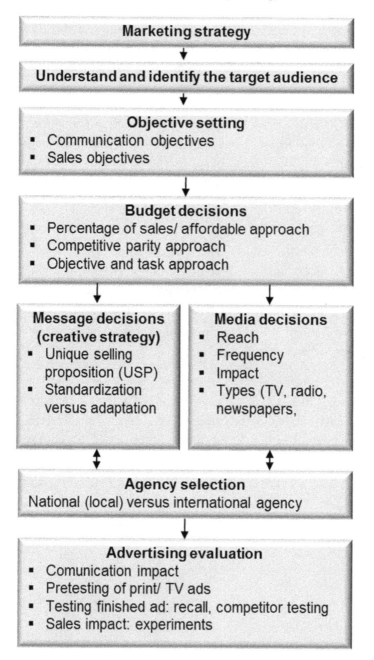

Source: Adapted from Hollensen and Opresnik, 2015, modified

Marketing Strategy

The foundation for developing an advertising strategy is a clear definition of the marketing strategy as advertising is only one element of the marketing mix and decisions should not be taken in isolation. The following questions are of central importance in this respect: what is the product's competitive position? What is the target market and what differential advantage does the product possess? Target market definition allows the target audience to be identified in rough terms and identification of the product's differential advantage points to the features and benefits of the product that should be highlighted in its advertising (Hollensen and Opresnik, 2015).

Identify and Understand the Target Audience

The target audience is the group of people at which the advertisement strategy is aimed. The audience may be potential buyers or current users, those who make the buying decision or those who strongly influence it. The audience may be individuals, groups, or the general public.

Once the target audience has been identified, it needs to be understood. Buyer motives and choice criteria need to be thoroughly analyzed. This process is vital as it has fundamental implications for message and media decisions and all later stages (Hollensen and Opresnik, 2015).

Objective Setting

Although, ultimately advertising is a means of stimulating sales and increasing profits, a clear understanding of its communication objectives is important. Major advertising objectives (and means) might include some of the following (Ellis-Chadwick and Jobber, 2016):

- **Create awareness**: Advertising can be used to create awareness of a brand, or a particular service. Awareness creation is of critical importance when a new product is being launched or when the company is entering a new market.

- **Stimulate trial**: In addition, advertising can be used to stimulate trial, such as car advertising encouraging motorists to take a test drive.

- **Position products in customers' mind**: Advertisement has a major role to play in positioning brands in the 'hearts and minds' of the target audience (Ries and Trout, 2001). Creative positioning involves the development or reinforcement of an image or set of associations for a brand, such as L'Oréal's repeated use of the slogan 'Because I'm worth it'.

- **Correct misconceptions**: Another objective of advertising might include the correction of misconceptions about a product or service, reminding customers of sales, special offer and specific benefits of the product.

- **Remind and reinforce**: Once a clear collection of perceptions in the minds of the target audience has been established, the objective of advertising might be to remind consumers of the product's existence, and to reinforce image. This strategic objective is especially appropriate for leading brands in mature markets, such as Coca-Cola and Nivea cosmetics. The goal of those companies is to maintain top-of-mind awareness and positive associations. Given their rather strong market position, a major advertising task is to defend against competitive products trying to gain market share.

Budget Decisions

The amount that is spent on advertising governs the achievement of communication objectives. Controversial aspects of advertising include determining a proper method for deciding the size of the promotional budget, and its allocation across markets and over time.

In general, there are four methods of setting advertising budgets (Lane et al., 2005):

- **Percentage-of-sales method**
  This approach bases advertising on a specific percentage of current or expected sales revenue. Alternatively, the company may budget a

percentage of the unit sales price. This method is easy to apply and makes management think about the relationships between promotion spending, selling price, and profit per unit. However, this approach fosters a decline in advertising expenditure when sales decline, a move that may encourage a further downward spiral of sales. In addition, it ignores market opportunities, which may suggest the need to spend more (or less) on advertising. Finally, the method fails to provide a means of determining the correct percentage to use.

- **Affordable method**
  This approach bases advertising expenditure on what level management regards as an amount that can be afforded. SMEs often use this method, reasoning that the company cannot spend more on advertising that it actually has. Problematically, this approach of setting budgets completely ignores the effects of promotion on sales. Its use as the sole criterion for budget neglects the communication objectives that are highly relevant for a firm's products and the market opportunities that may exist to grow sales and profits.

- **Competitive-parity method**
  Some firms use the competitive-parity method, setting their promotion budgets based upon matching expenditure to, or using a similar percentage of sales figure as their major competitors. However, matching expenditure assumes that the competition has arrived at the 'correct' level of budget, and ignores market opportunities and communication objectives. Using a similar percentage of sales ratio likewise lacks strategic vision and might only be justified if it can be shown to prevent costly advertising wars. Furthermore, the method does not recognize that the firm is in different situations in different markets. If the firm is new to a market, its relationships with customers are different from those of existing domestic companies. This should also be reflected in its promotion budget.

- **Objective-and-task method**
  The weaknesses of the above approaches have led some firms to follow this approach, which develops the promotion budget by defining specific objectives, determining the tasks that must be per-

formed to achieve those objectives, and estimating the costs of performing these tasks. The sum of these costs is the proposed promotion budget. The advantage of this approach is that it stimulates management to think about objectives, media exposure levels and the resulting costs. However, it is also the most difficult method to apply. Often, it is extremely complicated to figure out, which specific tasks will achieve a stated objective.

Message Decisions (creative strategy)

This step concerns decisions about what **unique selling proposition (USP)** needs to be communicated, and what the communication is intended to achieve in terms of consumer behaviour in the country concerned. These decisions have important implications for the choice of advertising medium, since certain media can better accommodate specific creative requirements (use of colour, written description, high definition, demonstration of the product, etc.) than others.

Before a message can be decided, a sound understanding of the advertising platform should be acquired. The advertising platform is the foundation on which advertising messages are built. The platform should be important to the target audience and communicate competitive advantages. This is why an understanding of the motives and choice criteria of the target audience is essential for effective advertising.

The advertising message translates the platform into words, symbols and illustrations that are attractive and meaningful to the target audience. As we shall see below, the choice of media available to the advertiser is vast, therefore one of the central challenges of message formulation is to keep the message succinct and adaptable across various media.

Most of those who look at a press advertisement read the headline but not the body copy. Because of this, some advertisers suggest that the company or brand name should appear in the headline otherwise the reader may not know the source of the advertisement. A variety of creative treatments can be used, from lifestyle, to humour, to shock advertising (Hollensen and Opresnik, 2015).

Media Decisions

The selection of the media to be used for advertising campaigns needs to be done simultaneously with the development of the message theme. A key question in media selection is whether to use a mass or target approach. The mass media (television, radio and newsprint) are effective when a significant percentage of the general public are potential customers. This percentage varies considerably by country for most products, depending on, for example, the distribution of incomes in different countries.

The selection of the media to be used in a particular campaign typically starts with some idea of the target market's demographic and psychological characteristics, regional strengths of the product, seasonality of sales, and so on. The media selected should be the result of a careful fit of local advertising objectives, media attributes and target market characteristics. Furthermore, media selection can be based on the following criteria (Hollensen and Opresnik, 2015):

- **Reach**. This is the total number of people in a target market exposed to at least one advertisement in a given time period ('opportunity to see', or OTS).
- **Frequency**. This is the average number of times within a given time period that each potential customer is exposed to the same advertisement.
- **Impact**. This depends on compatibility between the medium used and the message.

High reach is necessary when the firm enters a new market or introduces a new product so that information about, for example, a new product's availability is spread to the widest possible audience. A high level of frequency is appropriate when brand awareness already exists and the message is about informing the consumer that a campaign is under way. Sometimes a campaign should have both a high frequency and extensive reach, but limits on the advertising budget often create the need to trade off frequency against reach.

A media's **gross rating points (GRPs)** are the result of multiplying its reach by the frequency with which an advertisement appears within the media over a certain period. Hence it contains duplicated exposure, but indicates the critical mass of a media effort. GRPs may be estimated for individual vehicles, for entire classes of media or for a total campaign.

The cost of running a media campaign also has to be taken into consideration. Traditionally, media planning is based on a single measure, such as 'cost per thousand GRPs'.

The media planner faces the choice of using television, press, cinema, posters, radio or a combination of median classes. Each medium possesses its own set of creative qualities and restrictions. We shall now take a closer look at the main media types (Hollensen and Opresnik, 2015):

- **Television** is an expensive but commonly used medium in attempting to reach broad national markets. It can be used to demonstrate the product in action, or to use colour and sound to build an atmosphere around the product, thus enhancing its image. Although TV was traditionally one of the most powerful advertising mediums, concerns about fragmentation of the audience have led many advertisers to move away from it or reduce their spending accordingly. In addition, research has again questioned whether viewers actually watch ads when they are on, finding that people may spend as little as 23 per cent of the time the ads are on watching them, with the remainder spent talking, reading, surfing between channels or doing tasks such as cleaning, ironing of office work. However, television is still the largest advertising medium and it continues to play a significant role in brand building.

- **Newspaper** and press advertising is useful for providing factual information and offers an opportunity for consumers to re-examine the advertisement at a larger stage. In virtually all urban areas of the world, the population has access to daily newspapers. In fact, the problem for the advertiser is not having too few newspapers but too many. Most countries have one or more newspapers that can be said to have a truly national circulation. However, in many countries newspapers tend to be predominantly local or regional and, as such, serve as the primary medium for local advertisers. Attempting to use a series of local papers to reach a national market is considerably more complex and costly.

- **Magazines** have a narrower readership than newspapers and can be used to target particular markets. One growing sector is customer magazines, whereby leading brand such as Audi and Mercedes-Benz produce colour magazines of pictures and editorial about their products. For technical and industrial products, magazines can be quite effective. Technical business publications tend to be international in their coverage. These publications range from individual businesses (e.g. beverages, construction, textiles) to world-wide industrial magazines covering many industries. Marketers of international products have the option of using international magazines that have regional editions (e.g. Newsweek, Time and Business Week).

- **Radio** is limited to the use of sound and it therefore more likely to be useful in communicating factual information rather than building brand image. Radio is a lower-cost broadcasting activity than television. Commercial radio started several decades before commercial television in many countries. Radio is often transmitted on a local basis and therefore national campaigns have to be built up on an area-by-area basis.

- **Cinema** benefits from colour, movement and sound, as well as the presence of a captive audience. In countries where it is common to subsidize the cost of showing movies by running advertising commercials prior to the feature film, cinema advertising has become an important medium. India, for example, has a relatively high level of cinema attendance per capita (few have television at home). Therefore cinema advertisements play a much greater role in India than in, for example, the United States. Cinema is a particularly good but expensive medium for brands trying to reach young audiences.

- **Outdoor advertising** includes posters/billboards, shop signs and transit advertising. This medium shows the creative way in which space can be sold to customers. In the case of transit advertising, for example, a bus can be sold as an advertising medium. Outdoor posters/billboards can be used to develop the visual impact of advertising. In some countries, legal restrictions limit the poster space available. Outdoor advertising is believed to be effective for reminder advertising. Technology is helping outdoor advertising gain a bigger share of advertising in the prime media as backlit and scrolling sites are gradually replacing more traditionally glued posters.

- **Internet Advertising and Social Media Marketing** allow global reach to be achieved at relatively low cost. The number of website visits, clicks on advertisements and products purchased can be measured and interactivity between supplier and consumer is enabled. Google is market leader in so-called 'paid search' or 'pay-per-click' advertising. The disadvantages of Internet advertising are that it is impersonal and requires consumers to visit a website. This may require high expenditure in traditional media or the placing of sponsored links on search engines. Because of the growing significance of this tool, it is further dealt with in a separate section.

Agency Selection

Confronted with the many complex problems that international advertising involves, many businesses instinctively turn to an advertising agency for advice and practical assistance. Agencies employ or have instant access to expert copywriters, translators, photographers, film makers, package designers and media planners who are skilled and experienced in the international field. Only large multinational enterprises can afford to carry such people in-house.

Advertising Evaluation

Advertising evaluation and testing is the final stage in the advertising decision process. The key questions in advertising research are what, when and how to evaluate. What should be measured depends on whatever the advertising is trying to achieve. Measurement can take place before, during and after campaign execution. **Pre-testing** takes place before the campaign is executed and is part of the creative process. This is typically done with a fo-cus group, which is shown various alternative commercials and the mem-bers are asked to discuss their likes, dislikes and understanding of each other. **Post-testing** can be used to assess a campaign's effectiveness once it has run in order to provide necessary information to plan future campaigns. The major measures used in post-test television advertising research are im-age/attitude change, actual sales and usage, though other financial measures such as cash flow, shareholder value and return on investment are increas-ingly being used (Ellis-Chadwick and Jobber, 2016).

4.4.4 Sales Promotion

Sales promotions are marketing activities that stimulate consumer purchases and improve retailer or middlemen effectiveness and relationship. Sales pro-motion communicates via an array of promotions not encompassed by any of the definitions above, each aiming for exposure to a target audience and some furthermore offering an incentive to respond actively. Examples in-clude money off and free gifts (**consumer promotions**), price discounts (**trade promotions**) and sales force competitions (**business promotions**).

Sales promotions are short-term efforts directed to the customer or retailer to achieve such specific objectives as consumer-product trial or immediate purchase, consumer introduction to the store, gaining retail point-of-pur-chase displays, encouraging stores to stock the product, and supporting and augmenting advertising and personal sales efforts. In this sense, sales pro-motion may be regarded as a short-term tactical device. A typical sales pat-tern initially involves sales boost during the promotion period because of the incentive effect. This is followed by a fall in sales to below normal level because some consumers will have stocked up on the product during the promotion. The long-term sales effect of the promotion could be positive, neutral or negative. If the promotion has attracted new buyers, who find that they like the brand, repeat purchases from them may give rise to a posi-tive long-term effect. Alternatively, if the promotion has devalued the brand in the eyes of customers, the effect may be negative (Rothschild and Gaidis, 1981).

A vast amount of money is spent on sales promotion and many companies are engaging in joint promotions. Some of the key reasons for the growth in sales promotion include the following (Peattie and Peattie, 1983):

- **Increased impulse purchasing**: the rise in impulse purchasing favours promotions that take place at the point of purchase.
- **The rising cost of advertising and advertising clutter**: these factors erode advertising's cost-effectiveness.
- **Shortening time horizons**: the attraction of the fast sales boost of a sales promotion is raised by greater competition and shortening product life cycles.
- **Competitor activities**: in some markets, sales promotions are used so often that all competitors are simply forced to follow suit.
- **Measurability**: measuring the sales impact of sales promotions is relatively easy compared to advertising since its effect is more direct and, usually, short term.

4.4.4.1 Major Sales Promotion Tools

Sales promotion can be directed at the customer, the trade or the business. We shall now discuss the main consumer, trade, and business promotion tools (Kotler, Armstrong and Opresnik, 2016).

4.4.4.1.1 Consumer Promotion Tools

Consumer promotion tools include premiums, money off, free samples, coupons, prize promotions, bonus packs, and loyalty cards (Hollensen and Opresnik, 2015):

- **Premiums** are any merchandise offered free or at very low cost as an incentive to purchase a product. They can come in three forms: free in- or on-pack gifts, free in-the-mail offers and self-liquidating offers, where customers are asked to pay a sum of money to cover the costs of the merchandise. The key objective of premiums is in encouraging bulk purchasing and maintaining share.

- **Money off promotions** provide direct value to customer, and consequently an unambiguous incentive to purchase. Although they have proven track record of stimulating short-term sales increases they can easily be matched by competitors and if used frequently, can devalue brand image.

- **Free samples** of a brand may be delivered to the home or given out in a store and are used to stimulate trial. For new brands or brand extensions (for example, a new shampoo) this is an effective, if sometimes expensive, way of generating trial. There are a variety of methods of delivering samples including direct mail, inserts within publications or packages, or sampling points inside stores.

- **Coupons** are certificates that give buyers a saving when they purchase specified products. They can promote early trial of a new brand or stimulate sales of a mature brand. Coupons can be delivered by direct mail, in stores, as inserts in publications or on packages. The traditional disadvantages of couponing are in the logistical effort of the redemption handling process, and consumer resistance to the need to physically clip and carry coupons. New technology may overcome all of these problems with innovations such as barcode scanning for coupons, and 'smart cards' for consumers, which store information about coupon entitlements.

- **Prize promotions** can be competitions, draws and games. These are often used to attract attention or stimulate interest in a brand. Competitions require participants to exercise a certain degree of skill and judgement and entry is usually dependent or purchase at least. Draws make no demands on skill or judgement and the result depends on chance. A classic example of draw is when direct mail recipients are asked to return a card on which there is a set of numbers. These are then compared against a set of winning numbers. An example of game promotion is where a newspaper encloses a series of bingo cards and customers are told that, over a specified period of time, sets of bingo numbers will be published. If these numbers form a line or full house on a bingo card a prize is won. Such a game fosters repeat purchase of the newspaper.

- **Bonus packs** give added value by giving customers extra quantity at no additional cost and are often used in the drinks, confectionary and detergent markets. The promotion might be along the lines of

'Buy 10 and get 2 extra free'. Because the price is not lowered, this form of promotion is less risky concerning the devaluation of the brand image.

- **Loyalty cards** are becoming increasingly popular in retailing. Points are then gained every time money is spent at an outlet. Other loyalty schemes might involve the accrual of points that can be swapped for money-off vouchers to be used against purchases at the store or for bargain offers on other purchases such as theatre tickets. The goal is to attract customers back to the outlet. In addition, some schemes collect information on the customer including his or her name and address and, when it is swiped through the checkout machine detailed information on purchases is recorded. This implies that the purchasing behaviour of individual customers is better known to the retailer, which can then use this information to target tailored direct mail promotions at those who are likely to be responsive. Despite their growth, loyalty schemes have attracted their critics. Schemes may simply raise the cost of doing business and, if competitors respond with me-too offerings, the final outcome may be no more than a minor tactical advantage (Dowling and Uncles, 1997).

4.4.4.1.2 Trade Promotion Tools

The trade may be offered or may demand discounts in return for purchase, which may be part of a joint promotion whereby the retailer agrees to devote extra shelf space, buy larger quantities, engage in a joint competition and/or allow demonstrations in the outlet. Manufacturers may use several trade promotion tools. Many of the tools used for consumer promotions such as prize promotions and premiums can also be used as trade promotions. Major trade promotion tools include price discounts, free goods, and allowances (Hollensen and Opresnik, 2015):

- **Price discounts:** The trade may be offered a straight reduction in price on purchases during a stated period of time. The concentration of buying power into fewer trade outlets has placed increasing power with these institutions and this influence is often translated into discounts from manufacturers. Volume discounts are given to retailers that hit sales targets (Quilter, 2005).

- **Free goods:** An alternative to a price discount is to offer more merchandise at the same price.
- **Allowances:** A manufacturer may offer an allowance in return for retailers providing promotional facilities in store. For example, allowances would be needed to stimulate a supermarket to display cards on its shelves indicating that a brand was being sold at a special price.

4.4.4.1.3 Business Promotion Tools

Companies spend a vast amount of money every year on promotion to industrial customers. These business promotion tools are used to generate business leads, stimulate purchase, reward customers, and motivate sales people. Business promotion includes many of the same tools used for consumer or trade promotions. Here, we focus on two additional major tools – conventions and trade shows, and sales contests (Hollensen and Opresnik, 2015):

- **Conventions and trade shows:** Many enterprises and trade associations organize conventions and trade shows to promote their products and services. Companies selling to the industry show their products at the trade show. Vendors receive many benefits, such as opportunities to find new sales leads, contact customers, introduce innovative products, and inform customers with publications.
- **Sales contests:** A sales contest is a contest for sales people or dealers to motivate them to increase their sales efforts and ultimately performance over a given period. These contests motivate and recognize good company performers, who may receive trips, cash prizes, or other incentives.

4.4.4.2 Developing the Sales Promotion Program

The marketer must make several other decisions in order to define the complete sales promotion program. First, the marketer has to decide on the size of the incentive and set conditions for participation. Incentive might be offered to everyone or merely to specific groups. Hereafter, the marketer must decide how to promote and distribute the promotion program. In this respect, marketers are increasingly blending several media coherent campaign concept. Furthermore, the length of the promotion is also an important issue (Kotler, Armstrong and Opresnik, 2016). The final stage in a sales promotion program involves testing the promotion. As with advertising, both pre-testing and post-testing methods are available. The major pre-testing techniques include group discussions (testing ideas on groups of potential targets), hall tests (bringing a sample of customers to a room where alternative promotions are tested) and experimentation (where, for example, two groups of stores are selected and alternative promotions run in each). After the sales promotion has been implemented the results have to be monitored carefully. The company should thoroughly analyze sales before, during and after the promotion (Hollensen and Opresnik, 2015).

4.4.5 Public Relations

A company is dependent on many groups if it wishes to succeed. The marketing concept focuses on customers and distributors, but the needs and interests of other stakeholders (such as employees, shareholders, the local community, the media, government and pressure groups) are also of central importance and public relations is concerned with all of these groups. **Public relations** can be defined as building good relations with the company's various publics by obtaining favourable publicity, building a positive corporate image, and handling or heading off unfavourable rumours, stories, and events (Kotler, Armstrong and Opresnik, 2016).

Public relations can accomplish many objectives, as outlined below (Lesly, 1998):

- **Prestige and reputation**: It can foster prestige and reputation, which can help companies to sell products, attract and keep good employees, and promote favourable community and government relations.

- **Promotion of products**: the desire to buy a product can be supported by the unobtrusive things that people read and see in the press, radio and TV. Awareness and interest in products and companies can be stimulated.

- **Dealing with issues and opportunities**: the ability to handle social and environmental issues to the mutual benefit of all stakeholders involved.

- **Goodwill of customers**: ensuring that customers are presented with useful information, are treated with respect and have their complaints dealt with fairly and speedily.

- **Goodwill of employees**: promoting the sense of identification and satisfaction of employees with their company. Activities such as internal newsletters, recreation activities, and awards for service and achievement can be used.

- **Overcoming misconceptions**: managing misconceptions about a company and its products so that unfounded opinions do not severely damage its operations.

- **Goodwill of suppliers and distributors**: building a reputation as a good customer and a reliably supplier.

- **Goodwill of government**: influencing the opinions of public officials and politicians so that they feel the company operates in the public interest.

- **Dealing with unfavourable publicity**: responding rapidly, accurately and effectively to negative publicity.

Public relations firms' billings in the international arena have been growing at double digit rates for some years. Handling such international PR problems as global workplace standards is big business for companies serving corporate clients such as Mattel Toys, McDonald's, and Nike. Fast growth is also being fuelled by the expanding international communications industry. New companies need public relations consultation for 'building an international profile'.

Three major reasons for the growth in public relations are a recognition of the power and value of public relations, increased advertising costs leading to an exploration of more cost-effective communication routes, and improved understanding of the embracing role of public relations (Hollensen and Opresnik, 2015).

4.4.6 Sponsorship

Sponsorship can be defined as a business relationship between a provider of funds, resources or services and an individual, event or enterprise which offers in return some rights and association that may be used for commercial advantage (Sleight, 1989).

Companies have a wide range of entities and activities from which to choose, including sports, arts, community activities, teams, tournaments, music festivals, individual personalities or events, competitions, fairs and shows. Sport sponsorship is by far the most popular sponsorship medium as it usually offers high visibility through extensive television coverage, the ability to attract a broad cross-section of the community and to service specific niches (Ellis-Chadwick and Jobber, 2016).

4.4.6.1 Principle Sponsorship Objectives

Organisations should be clear about their reasons for spending money on sponsorship. The five principal objectives of sponsorship are to gain publicity, create entertainment opportunities, foster favourable brand and company associations, improve community relations and create promotional opportunities (Hollensen and Opresnik, 2015):

- **Gaining publicity:** Sponsorship provides multiple opportunities to create publicity in the media. With the advent of global media the possibilities for global sponsorships are opening up. Sponsoring soccer World Cup or the Olympic Games by plastering the brand name on the bleachers has helped global companies to establish a strong identity in the global marketplace.

- **Creating entertainment opportunities:** Another major objective of sponsorship is to create entertainment opportunities for customers and the trade. Sponsorship of music, the performing arts and sports events can be particularly effective.

- **Fostering favourable brand and company associations:** A further objective of sponsoring is to create favourable associations for a brand and company. For example, Red Bull's sponsorship of events such as 'Flugtag', at which amateur pilots launch handmade flying machines off a ramp, reinforces its 'weird' image and its energy associations (Clark, 2005).

- **Improving community relations:** Sponsorship of schools – for example, by providing low-cost personal computers – and supporting community programmes can foster a socially responsible, caring reputation for an organisation.

- **Creating promotional opportunities:** Sponsored events provide a perfect opportunity to promote company brands. Sweatshirts, bags, pens, etc., carrying the company logo and the name of the event can be sold to a captive audience.

4.4.6.2 Components of Assessing a Sponsorship Property

Selection of an event, programme or celebrity to sponsor should be undertaken by assessing the following components (Hollensen and Opresnik, 2015):

- **Cost of initial sponsorship outlay**
- **Budget needed for supporting marketing or public relations activity**
- **Time & resource implications for firm's staff:** the number of staff and the quantity of resources that are needed, so as the sponsorship opportunity can be fully leveraged.
- **Duration of relationship:** the benefits of a positive sponsorship association can take time to develop. Sponsors frequently seek out options to extend the contracts of their sponsorship relationship. If a sponsor can only avail of a short-term contract, with no options

for a contract extension then the sponsorship property, will prove unattractive for investment.

- **Targeted groups**: a variety of different stakeholders can be targeted by sponsorship campaigns. A firm must ensure there is a match between the audience of the sponsored property and their selected target market. The sponsor can associate itself with a certain lifestyle or consumer segment. The stronger the association between a sponsor's target audience and the sponsorship properties target audience, the better the strategic 'fit'.

- **Geographic scope**: how far reaching is the sponsorship property? Will it have an impact in foreign markets? For example, certain sports sponsorship properties have a far greater reach in global geographic markets (e.g. F1 car racing). Sponsorship properties that have good geographic reach are expensive and scarce in supply.

- **Strategic fit between sponsor and sponsorship property**: compatibility is needed between the two entities. Marketers can use the sponsorship association with a property to give a clear message about their product and what their company stands for.

- **Uniqueness to break through clutter**: companies strive for sponsorship opportunities that break through the sponsorship clutter that exists, gaining sufficient media coverage, and helps form positive brand associations. Specsavers, an optician chain, exploited a unique sponsorship opportunity by sponsoring referees for football games, creating a distinctive and powerful message – 'That referee needs glasses!'

- **Image of sponsored property**: a sponsor has to assess whether the sponsored property is seen in a positive or negative light. Likeability of the sponsored property can transfer through to likeability of the sponsor.

- **Estimated number of viewers, listeners, or attendees to the sponsored property**: the attendance at a sponsored event is a basic evaluation metric used. Similarly viewing or listener figures are used for broadcast sponsorship activities.

- **Estimated media coverage**: the sponsored property needs to acquire the right amount and right type of media coverage. The company should assess the newsworthiness of a sponsorship property.

- **Corporate hospitality potential**: some events are highly sought after for their potential to entertain clients. Sponsoring sports or entertainment events allow firms the opportunity to build and enhance relations with channel members and corporate accounts (e.g. Heineken sponsors European Club Rugby Championship, which provides Heineken the opportunity to provide corporate hospitality to publicans).

- **Leverage potential**: here the firm evaluates if there is any marketing, sales or sales promotion spin offs that may accrue from the sponsorship. In order for any sponsorship to work effectively to its full potential, it must be supported by other marketing communications activities. The sponsors must communicate the association between themselves and the sponsorship property.

- **Exclusivity on sponsorship property**: some sponsorship properties offer sponsors different tiers of sponsorship association, having multiple sponsors. This in turn may confuse the intended target as to who is sponsoring a particular property. If a sponsor has complete exclusivity over a sponsorship property, then they can leverage the relationship more effectively. For example, Coca-Cola and Pepsi used Beckham in campaigns causing confusion.

- **Legacy effects**: sponsors must assess whether past historical linkages with an incumbent sponsor may be broken. Otherwise sponsorship confusion may arise. Typically, firms who have strong past relationships with a sponsorship property, that may be have been built over numerous years, have stronger sponsorship legacy effects.

- **Potential for negative exposure**: firms should make risk assessment on whether a potential sponsorship may backfire in a blaze of negative publicity. For example, the Festina, watch brand was decimated when during the Tour de France, the cycling team they sponsored where found to be drug cheats. Similar examples include: Roy Keane & 7Up during the infamous Saipan World Cup incident, Michelle

4.4.6.3 Sponsorship Evaluation

Despite the phenomenal growth of sponsorship over the last decade, there still remains much ambiguity about sponsorship evaluation. There is no definitive framework for evaluating a sponsorship programme. Yet companies spend millions on sponsorships annually. To evaluate any sponsorship effectively they must first set measurable goals. Firms must utilize both quantitative and qualitative evaluation techniques to accurately measure the effects of sponsorship. We shall describe possible evaluation techniques in more detail now (Hollensen and Opresnik, 2015):

- **Exposure obtained**: an organisation could view the number of people who attended an event as an easy key performance indicator to use in the evaluation process. The amount of media exposure and quality of media coverage could be qualitatively assessed such as radio airplay or editorial space. For example a media clippings book could be generated, with all the media stories related to the event, documented for assessment. Media audits analysing the quantity and quality of coverage can be undertaken.

- **Communications results**: the firm could track recall levels amongst target audiences, to gauge any communications impact, from the sponsorship.

- **Increasing sales or market share**: companies could use bottom-line metrics as an indication of the success of a sponsorship programme. However this would be a naive metric to use in isolation, as sales may have been impacted due to an exogenous variable within the marketing environment, and may not be attributable directly to a sponsorship programme. Competitor activity, changing trends or changing economic conditions, may be the cause of sales changes, not sponsorship activity.

- **Feedback gained from participating groups**: a firm could gauge the reactions of stakeholders to the sponsored property. A firm could undertake surveys or in-depth interviews to gauge stakeholder reactions to these sponsorships.

4.4.7 Digital and Social Media Marketing

4.4.7.1 Evolution

The Internet has changed the way people, organizations and institutions communicate. Accordingly, media planning is undergoing a dramatic change from traditional ATL communication tools such as newspapers and magazines to non-traditional BTL tools such as mobile and Internet marketing. Figure 4.17 displays that mobile and desktop Internet adspend is already accounting for nearly 1/3 of the Global adspend market in 2016 (Hollensen, Kotler and Opresnik, 2017).

Figure 4.17: Global shares of total adspend by medium in % 2016

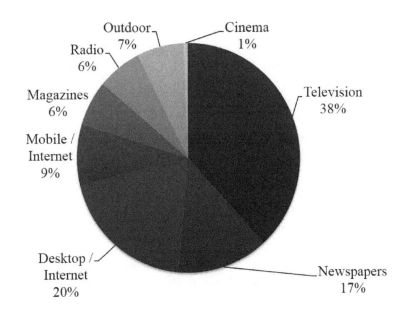

Source: Based on ZenithOptimedia research, www.zenithoptimedia, accessed 20th December 2016

A major strength of direct e-mail is its ability to qualify leads. Appropriate software allows the firm to track who is reading and responding along with the types of responses. This enables the firm to segment the audience accordingly, targeting future communications based on recipients' self-reported priorities.

A checklist for launching a successful e-mail marketing campaign includes the following aspects (Linkon, 2004):

- **Solid planning**. Companies are required to have clear and measurable objectives, and they must carefully plan their campaign.

- **Excellent content**. Standards are higher with e-mail, so firms have to make sure they are offering genuine value to the subscriber.

- **Appropriate and real 'from' field**. This is the first thing recipients look at when they are deciding whether to open an e-mail.

- **Strong 'subject' field**. The next place recipients look before deciding whether to open an e-mail is the subject field. Therefore, it needs to be compelling.

- **Right frequency and timing**. Organizations must not overwhelm their audience. They are not supposed to send e-mail Friday through Monday or outside of normal business hours.

- **Appropriate use of graphics**. Businesses should not get carried away. If graphics add real value and aren't too big, they could be used.

- **Lead with company's strength**. Companies should not bury the best content or offer. They need to ensure it is at the top or at the e-mail equivalent of 'above the fold'.

- **Shorter is better**. Nobody reads a lot these days, and they read less in e-mail than anywhere else.

- **Personalize**. Marketers should use just three or four elements of personalization, and response rates can potentially improve by 60 per cent. They should try to go beyond just the first name and learn about the subscribers.

- **Link to company's Web site**. This is where the richness of content and interactivity can really reside. Marketers should tease readers with the e-mail so they will link to the Web site. Advertising can also be incorporated, serving the same role as the initial e-mail: to create a desire in the audience for more information. The Web site catch page is crucial to this tactic and is often where many people falter when integrating traditional advertising with online promotions.

- **Measure and improve**. The ability to measure basics such as open and click-through rates is one of the main advantages of e-mail marketing, but companies should not stop there. They should also track sales or other conversions and learn from what works and make necessary adjustments.

Web 2.0 websites allow you to do more than just retrieve information, as this was mainly the case with Web 1.0. Web 2.0 transforms broadcast media monologues (one-to-many = Web 1.0) into social media dialogues (many-to-many). The term Web 2.0 was first used in 2004 to describe a new way software developers and end-users started to utilize the internet to create content and applications that were no longer created and published by individuals, but instead continuously modified by all users in a participatory and collaborative fashion. The popularity of the term Web 2.0, along with the increasing use of blogs, wikis, and social networking technologies, has led many in academia and business to work with these 'new' phenomena. For marketers, Web 2.0 offers an opportunity to engage consumers. A growing number of marketers are using Web 2.0 tools to collaborate with consumers on product development, service enhancement and promotion. Companies can use Web 2.0 tools to improve collaboration with both its business partners and consumers. Among other things, company employees have created wikis, which are Web sites that allow users to add, delete and edit content, and to list answers to frequently asked questions about each product, and consumers have added significant contributions. Another Web 2.0 marketing feature is to make sure consumers can use the online community to network among themselves on content that they choose themselves. Besides generating content, the Web 2.0 Internet user tends to proactively bring in a whole new perspective on established processes and approaches, so that the users create innovative ideas for the future development of companies (Hollensen and Opresnik, 2015).

With the creation of the World Wide Web and Web browsers in 1990s, the Internet was transformed from a mere communication platform into a certifiably revolutionary technology. For consumers, digital technologies have not only provided the means to search for and buy products while saving time and money, but also to socialize and be entertained. The emergence of social networking sites such as MySpace and Facebook has enabled consumers to spend time socializing, and the development of video streaming and music downloads means that they can be entertained as well. A major challenge for marketers is to tap in to the huge audiences using the net.

The Internet is a global channel of communication, but the advertising messages are often perceived in the local context by the potential customer. Herein lays the dilemma that often causes the results from internet promotion to be less than anticipated.

Traditional media have two capabilities – building brands and direct marketing. In general, most promotional forms are useful for one or the other. The internet however, has the characteristics of both broadcast mass media and direct response advertising.

In the conventional model of communications in the marketplace, there are clear distinctions between the sender, the message and the recipient, and control of the message is with the sender. In 'market space', control of the message is shared between sender and receiver because of the interactivity of the medium, its ability to carry a message back in reply to that sent, and the impact of the information technology on time, space and communication. The above stated impacts on the feedback loop are built into the Internet and on the aspects of interference. In general, interference is more likely to be from internet clutter and less from external sources.

The web represents a change away from a **push strategy** in international promotion, where a producer focuses on compelling an intermediate to represent the products or services or a distributor to stock its goods, towards a **pull strategy** in which the producer communicates directly with the customer. In this transition process, promotional costs and other transaction costs are reduced. The differentiating feature of the Internet from other promotional vehicles is that of interactivity. This results in the special feature that Internet combines the attributes of both selling and advertising. Interactivity facilitates a completely innovative approach to reaching potential customers. Unlike television, for example, where the consumer passively observes, with the web there is an active intent to go onto the Internet and more attention to content as a result. In the Internet, the potential customer has a high involvement approach to advertising. A continual stream of decisions is demanded from the user. Each click represents a decision and therefore the web is a very high involvement medium. In addition, unlike traditional media, the web is a medium by which the user can click through and obtain more information or purchase the product. Web advertisements can and are often targeted to a user profile that in turn affects the way the message will be received. Increasingly, the ads displayed on the web are specific to user interests and appear as these interests are revealed while the user navigates the web (Hollensen and Opresnik, 2015).

4.4.7.2 Definition of Social Media Marketing

Social media are Internet-based technologies that facilitate online conversations and encompass a wide range of online, word-of-mouth forums including social networking websites, blogs, company sponsored discussion boards and chat rooms, consumer-to-consumer e-mail, consumer product or service ratings websites and forums, Internet discussion boards and forums, and sites containing digital audio, images, movies, or photographs, to name a few. Since 2009, the official company and brand web sites have typically been losing audience. This decline is believed to be due to the emergence of social media marketing by the brands themselves, an increasingly pervasive marketing practice. For social media usage and development, the diversity of languages is creating communication challenges on a global basis. Facebook has 1,100 million weekly users, with more than 70% outside the United States. To effectively communicate with non-English users, Facebook has 70 translations available on its site made possible by a vast network of 300,000 volunteers and translators. Facebook and Twitter are mostly interactive social media on an intimate level. As such, these platforms offer direct selling companies means of communicating with key stakeholders (customers and distributors) in the industry. On the other hand, YouTube, with its more traditional one-way audience communication, appears to be used more effectively for recruiting consumers to become distributors of information or products.

Figure 4.18: Top 10 Visited Multi-Platform Social-Networking Websites & Forums, October 2016 by US Market Share of Visits (%)

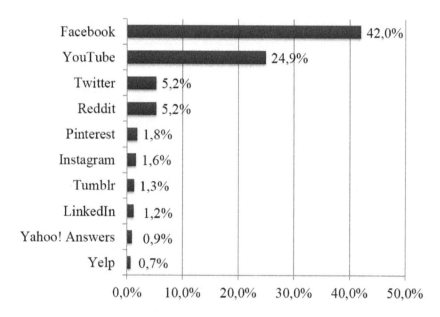

Source: www.marketingcharts.com, accessed 20th December 2016

One of the 'shooting stars' during the last years is LinkedIn, which is a social networking website for people in professional occupations. Launched in

2003, it is mainly used for professional networking. While Facebook, YouTube, and Twitter continue to dominate social media in the US and Europe some other countries, the global scene tells a different story. In Germany, Russia, China (see above) and Japan, the most visited social networking site is not Facebook but home-grown rivals.

By the end of 2016 the Top 10 Visited Multi-Platform Social-Networking Websites & Forums by US Market Share of Visits (%) browser-based (excluding in-app) visits across PC and mobile combined were the following (Hollensen, Kotler and Opresnik, 2015).

4.4.7.3 Extended Model of Social Media Marketing Communication

Integrated marketing communications (IMC) have traditionally been considered to be largely one-way in nature ('Bowling' – see below Figure 4.19). In the old paradigm, the organization and its agents developed the message and transmitted it to potential consumers, who may or may not have been willing participants in the communication process. The control over the dissemination of information was in the hands of the firm's marketing organization. The traditional elements of the promotion mix (advertising, personal selling, public relations and publicity, direct marketing and sales promotion) were the tools through which control was asserted.

The twenty-first century is witnessing an explosion of Internet-based messages transmitted through these media. They have become a major factor in influencing various aspects of consumer behaviour including awareness, information acquisition, opinions, attitudes, purchase behaviour and post-purchase communication and evaluation. Unfortunately, the popular business press and academic literature offers marketing managers very little guidance for incorporating social media into their IMC strategies (Hollensen and Opresnik, 2015).

Social networking as communication tools has two interrelated promotional roles:

- **Social networking should be consistent with the use of traditional IMC tools.** That is, companies should use social media to talk to their customers through such platforms as blogs, as well as Facebook and Twitter groups. These media may either be company-sponsored or sponsored by other individuals or organizations.

- **Social networking is enabling customers to talk to one another.** This is an extension of traditional word-of-mouth communication. While companies cannot directly control such consumer-to-consumer (C2C) messages, they do can influence the conversations that consumers have with one another. However, consumers' ability to communicate with one another limits the amount of control companies have over the content and dissemination of information. Consumers are in control; they have greater access to information and greater command over media consumption than ever before.

Marketing managers are seeking ways to incorporate social media into their IMC strategies. The traditional communications paradigm, which relied on the classic promotional mix to craft IMC strategies, must give way to a new paradigm that includes all forms of social media as potential tools in designing and implementing IMC strategies. Contemporary marketers cannot ignore the phenomenon of social media, where available market information is based on the experiences of individual consumers and is channeled through the traditional promotion mix. However, various social media platforms, many of which are completely independent of the producing/sponsoring organization or its agents, enhance consumers' ability to communicate with one another.

Although a little oversimplified, marketing in the pre-social media era was comparable to 'Bowling' (see Figure 4.19). A game of bowling shows how you may have traditionally communicated with your consumers, with the firm and the brand (the bowler) rolling a ball (the brand communication message) towards the pins (our target customers). Clearly this is a very direct one-way communication approach. This is the old traditional push model. Marketers targeted certain customer groups and sent out their advertising messages like precisely bowled bowling balls. They used traditional media to hit as many bowling pins as possible. One key characteristic of this bowling marketing game was the large amount of control the company retained over marketing communication because consumers were given only limited freedom of action.

Figure 4.19: The Bowling to Pinball model: Transition of market communication from 'Bowling' to 'Pinball'

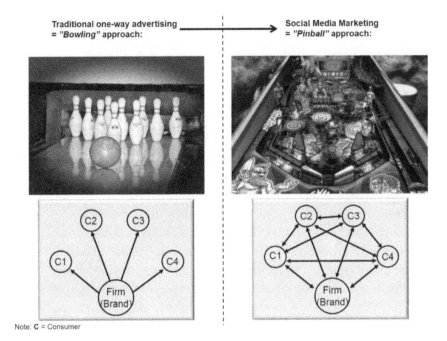

Source: Adapted from Hollensen and Opresnik (2015), modified

For many bigger companies a large TV-budget has been the ball that marketers rolled down the lane, trying to hit as many the pins as possible. Marketers were in control, happily counting how many 'pins' they had hit, and how often. Success in this game was clear-cut, and the metrics clear (Hennig-Thurau et. al., 2013).

In a social media marketing world, the bowling metaphor does not fit anymore. On this arena, marketing can be better described as playing 'Pinball': Companies serve up a 'marketing ball' (brands and brand-building messages) into a dynamic and chaotic market environment. The 'marketing ball' is then diverted and often accelerated by social media 'bumpers', which change the ball's course in chaotic ways. After the marketing ball is in play, marketing managers may continue to guide it with agile use of the 'flippers' but the ball does not always go where it is intended to.

Consequently, in the 'pinball' world, you cannot know outcomes in advance. Instead, marketers have to be prepared to respond in real time to the spin put on the ball by consumers. When mastered well, the pinball game can deliver big point multipliers, and if the company is very good, even more balls can be shot into the game. A reason for this may be that today consumers have a large audience to bring up new topics on the communication agenda. In the ideal situation, you are reaching networked influencers, advocates, and other high-value consumers, who may sustain and spread positive conversations about the brand across multiple channels.

Occasionally, the marketing ball will come back to the company. At this point, the firm (brand) has to use the flippers to interact and throw it back into the social media sphere. If the company or the brand do not feed the social marketing media sphere by flipping communications back, the ball will finally drop through the flippers and on longer term, the two-way relationship between consumers and the firm (brand) will die (Hollensen and Opresnik, 2015).

The 'Bowling to Pinball' model can be further elaborated into an extended model of interactive market communication (Hollensen and Opresnik, 2015).

Figure 4.20: The extended interactive market communication model'

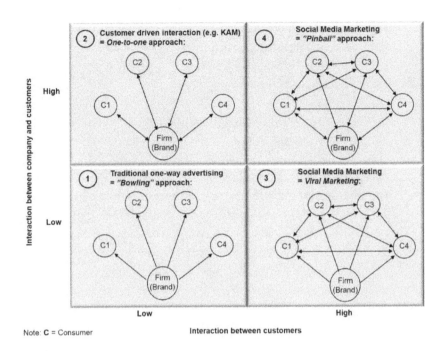

Source: Adapted from Hollensen and Opresnik (2015), modified

The four different communication styles, represented in Figure 4.20 are (Hollensen and Opresnik, 2015):

- **The Traditional one-way advertising** (mass media advertising like television advertising, newspaper / magazine advertising etc.) represents the 'Bowling' approach where the firm attempts to 'hit' as many customers with 'shotgun' mass media methods. Normally this approach is a one-way communication type.

- **Customer-driven interaction** represents a higher degree of interaction between the company and its different key customers. Often the company finds some Key Account managers, who have the responsibility of taking care of the one-to-one interaction between the firm and its key accounts (customers).

191

- **Viral Marketing** is representing the version 1.0 of Social Media Marketing, where the company e.g. uses an untraditional YouTube video to get attention and awareness about its brand. The interaction between the potential 'customers' is quite high (blogging sites etc.), but the feed-back to the company is relatively low (no double arrows back to the company).

- **Social Media Marketing** is representing the version 2.0 of Social Media Marketing, where there is also an extensive feed-back to the company itself (double arrows back to the company). Here the company proactively has chosen to be a co-player in the discussion and blogging on the different relevant social media sites (Facebook, Twitter etc.). This also means that the company here tries to strengthen the interaction with the customers in a positive direction, in order to influence the customer behavior. To do so, the company needs a back-up team of social media employees who can interact and communicate on-line with potential and actual customers. Consequently, this strategy is also very resource demanding.

4.4.7.4 The 6C Model of Social Media Marketing

The social media (e.g. Facebook or Twitter) are essentially vehicles for carrying content. This content – in form of words, text, pictures and videos – is generated by millions of potential customers around the world, and from your perspective (= company's perspective) this can indeed be an inspiration to create further value for these customers.

The following model of Hollensen and Opresnik (2015) mainly represents alternative 4 in Figure 4.20. If there had been no feed-back to the company in the model, it would have been more like alternative 3. Figure 4.21 defines six distinct, interrelated elements (Cs) that explain the creation and retention of consumer engagement, seen from a company perspective; however, the user-generated contents still plays an important role in the model (Hollensen and Opresnik, 2015):

- **Company and contents:** The 6C model begins with the company and the content it creates. Basically, the Internet remains a 'pull' medium, in the way that firms seek to pull viewers to its content, and finally to the company itself. However, before any 'pull' can happen, the content has to be pushed (seeded) forward in the chain. Content can take the form of e.g. a Facebook product or brand page, and/or a YouTube video pushed out to viewers. Consequently, content pushed into the social media sphere by a company acts as a catalyst for our model of engagement or participation.

Figure 4.21: The 6C model (Company, Contents, Control, Community, Consumers, Conversation)

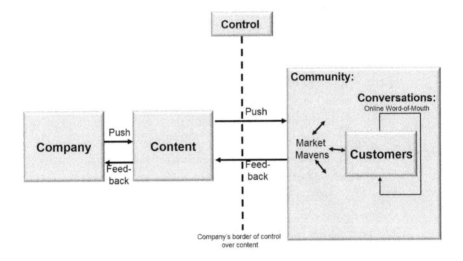

Source: Adapted from Hollensen and Opresnik (2015), modified

- **Control:** The dashed line denoting control in the 6C model (Figure 4.21) is intended to represent a wall beyond which the company let over control of its brand to the online community and the customers. To accelerate the viral uptake of its brand messaging, the company sometimes gives up the digital rights and blocks in order to encourage online community members to copy, modify, re-post, and forward the content. The content is intended to be copied and/or embedded into people's websites, blogs, and on Facebook walls. The key point to this stage in the process is that the company (the content creator) must be willing, and even embrace, the fact that they no longer have full control over the content: it is free to be taken, modified, commented on, and otherwise appropriated by the community of interest. This may challenge the conventional 'brand management' wisdom stating that managers must keep control of brand image and messaging.

- **Community:** The company creates content and pushes it over the symbolic border of control to the other side, where a community of interested consumers now takes it up. At this point, communication becomes bidirectional. The use of arrows in Figure 4.21 for push and pull, attempts to reflect the 'give-and-take' that goes on between a community and the company, represented by the content creators. In its simplest form, it is reflected in the art of commenting: posting reactions, on Facebook or YouTube, to the content. In some cases, the company can even lean about 'customer behaviour' in the market by following these online community discussions. In an ideal world, a series of reflexive conversations take place in the community, independent of any action by the company, which will often have a passive role as an observer.
  When transferring the 'content' into the online community, the company and the content providers often try to target the 'Market Mavens', which are defined as individuals who have access to a large amount of marketplace information, and proactively engage in discussions with other online community members and customers to diffuse and spread this content.
  Market mavens are typically the first to receive the message and transmit it to their immediate social networks. They function as connectors or bridges between different subcultures and their network of social hubs can facilitate immediate transmission of the content to thousands of online community members.

- **Customers and conversations:** The ultimate expression of engagement occurs when a multitude of online conversations circle around the phenomenon and content, as illustrated above and in

Figure 4.21. The 6C model distinguishes between the online community and potential customers, as the latter are usually a subset of the former. The online community may also include people who have heard of the Web-based initiative but not directly participated in it.

In general, there seems to be a growing escalation in participation on the part of customers; a willingness to engage with a brand that extends beyond just purchase decisions at the point of sale.

According to the 6C model, Social media further extend the conversations between marketers and consumers through a feedback loop, which might happen after some on-line conversation (blogging etc.) in the community. After some time of online conversation, the company may have chats with the online community in hopes of influencing purchase decisions. Moreover, social media initiatives provide marketers a glimpse into the world of customer-to-customer communication, which represents a significant extension of the more traditional advertising and word-of-mouth communication.

Furthermore, social media provide insights into the behavior of non-customers. Most social media marketers try to trigger buzz among prospective customers. This has led to social sharing whereby online community member broadcast their thoughts and activities to strangers all over the world. This social sharing has opened the lives of individual consumers that companies can then exploit to tailor their offerings to better match preferences (Hollensen and Opresnik, 2015).

4.4.7.5 Effective Online Advertising Strategy

Marketers can use online advertising to build their brands or to attract visitors to their Web sites. Online advertising can be described as advertising that appears while customers are surfing the Web, including banner and ticker ads, interstitials, skyscrapers, and other forms (Kotler, Armstrong and Opresnik, 2016).

An effective advertising strategy for online advertising aims at targeting the right advertisement message to the right person at the right time (Kumar and Shah, 2004).

4.4.7.5.1 Who to Advertise to?

Is online advertising for everyone? Knowledgeable marketers will state that advertisement design depends on the type of product or service being sold and the desired target segment. In this respect, it is instrumental to divide the desired target segment according to first-time visitors to the company's Web site, registered users, and general information seekers. There is bound to be some overlap across these segments. However, this form of segmentation can provide useful insights while designing online advertising. Based on the user segment, the Web site can be programmed to respond appropriately. For example, every first-time visitor to a Web site can be made to see the same advertisement. Visitors identified as information seekers may be shown useful content instead of products and services directly, and registered users may see a customized advertisement message based on their profiles. Technologically, it is feasible to identify the type of user by studying their browsing behaviour through clickstream data and by using 'cookie' files (Hollensen and Opresnik, 2015).

4.4.7.5.2 How to Advertise?

After identifying the user or the Web site visitor, the next step is determining how to advertise or what format to use for advertising. There are several different formats of Internet advertisements: **banner ads** (which move across the screen), **skyscrapers** (tall, skinny ads at the side of a Web page) and **interstitials** (ads that pop up between changes on a Web site).

Content sponsorships are another form of Internet promotion. Many companies achieve name exposure on the Internet by sponsoring special content on various Web sites, such as news or financial information. These sponsorships are best placed in carefully targeted sites where they can offer relevant information or service to the audience.

The type of advertisement chosen should be directed toward not only 'pushing' the message across but also 'pulling' the customer to click deeper into the Web site by designing ads that contribute to the overall Web site experience. For example, a Web site with too many pop-up ads on the first page runs the risk of driving the user away (Hollensen and Opresnik, 2015).

4.4.7.5.3 What to Advertise?

People use the Internet to seek information as well as products and services. Marketers can be creative and design advertisements that could just give out helpful information to the user. For example, a user browsing for a digital camera may be offered useful tips and pointers on how to get the best results from digital photography. Non-commercial advertising like this may not have a short-term financial gain but may contribute to superior browsing experience leading to customer loyalty and repeat visits from the user. If customer profile or history of purchase is known, it is possible to predict future purchase behaviour and companies can program buying information in the Web site code. The next time the company's Web site detects a particular user returning to the Web site, there will be an advertisement ready with an appropriate and tailored content. If deployed properly, this approach can help marketers cross-selling products through combinations of online advertisement messaging (Hollensen and Opresnik, 2015).

4.4.7.5.4 When to Advertise?

The first three dimensions of the advertising strategy discussed so far would be rendered ineffective if the timing is not right. In the case of offline media, one can proactively call up the customer or send him/her a direct mailer at a specific time with a customized advertising message. However, these rules do not apply online. In the case of the Internet, users may decide to go online and visit the Web site during work, in the middle of the night, or whenever they want to. Therefore, timing in the Internet context would refer to the time from the instance a user is detected online.

The question is when to activate the advertisement. As soon as the user comes online, after he/she has browsed for a while, or at the time of the first purchase? Studies conducted with Internet ad timings have indicated that generally response (click-through) to pop-ups is greater when the ad appears immediately after the user enters the site. However, the results could vary greatly depending on the user segment and the user's information-seeking purposes.

Amazon.com employs a subtle form of advertisement in real time. Basically, while performing a search for a particular book, the search also throws up a list on the side or bottom of the page of relevant books that may complement the book the user was originally considering purchasing. Amazon.com was first to use 'collaborative filtering' technology, which sifts through each customer's past purchases and the purchasing patterns of customers with similar profiles to come up with personalized site content. Furthermore, the site's 'Your Recommendations' feature prepares personalized product recommendations, and its 'New for You' feature links customers through to their own personalized home pages. In perfecting the art of online selling, Amazon.com has become one of the best-known names on the Web (Hollensen and Opresnik, 2015).

4.4.7.5.5 Where to Advertise?

It is crucial to make Internet ads visible at vantage points to maximize their hit-rate with the intended target segment. Unlike other forms of media, where one can pick a well-defined spot within a finite set of possibilities, cyberspace offers an infinite number of possibilities across thousands of portals, search engines, and online publishers, as well as multiple possibilities within the vendor's Web site. Finding the perfect spot may seem like finding a needle in a haystack.

There are two ways to tackle this. The first is the easy way out. Follow intuition and place advertisements at obvious locations, such as frequently visited portals and search engines. However, this is not a cost-effective solution. A more refined approach involves analyzing the browsing pattern of an Internet user on a company's Web site using the Web site's log files. Analysis of the log files can help model the browsing behaviour of a random visitor to the Web site. Based on this information, Internet ad displays may be placed at appropriate locations. Marketing managers can also leverage this model to sell complementary products to potential users. For example, a department store such as Marks & Spencer may advertise cosmetics on the page where a user is buying fragrances online. An electronics store like Best Buy may advertise the latest CD releases on the page listing different audio systems.

However, this form of analysis is limited to advertising within the company's Web site. A more advanced research approach involves modelling browsing behaviour at multiple Web sites using clickstream data. Information analyzed in this manner renders a total view of a customer's online habits before purchase consideration. Such information is invaluable to marketers who would be interested in knowing when and where they're most likely to find their potential customers and, based on that information, how they should place the Internet advertisements to pull the relevant customers to their site (Hollensen and Opresnik, 2015).

4.4.7.6 Online Performance Tracking

Having designed an online advertising strategy, the next critical step is to track its performance. Traditional offline media (radio, television, and print advertisements) have well-defined and well-researched metrics in place that can accurately measure ad effectiveness.

Some of the most commonly used measures include (Hollensen and Opresnik, 2015):

- **click-throughs:** the number of times that users click on an advertisement

- **cost per click:** the amount spent by the advertiser to generate one click-through

- **cost per action/lead (CPA/L):** the amount spent by the advertiser to generate one lead, one desired action, or simply information on one likely user. The advertiser pays an amount based upon the number of users who fulfil the desired action.

- **cost per sale (CPS):** the amount spent by the advertiser to generate one sale. Here, the advertiser pays an amount based upon how many users actually purchase something.

Increasingly, many marketers claim to be optimizing their online campaigns using the 'cost per sale' metric, but it is clear that they are looking at sales (through online advertisements) as strictly margin transactions. The problem with this approach is that, while each individual transaction may look profitable to start with, it may not necessarily hold true over the lifetime duration of the customer. Similarly, initial returns that seem to be unprofitable may translate into very profitable transactions when measured over the lifetime value of the customer.

Therefore, **Customer Lifetime Value (CLV)**, which may be defined as the measure of expected value of profit to a business derived from customer relationships from the current time to some future point, is maybe the most relevant of all metrics. It provides a direct linkage on a customer-by-customer basis to what is most important for any company-profits. Marketing spend and outcome of advertisements guided by lifetime value measures would yield the most superior decision support system for a marketer. As companies become increasingly customer-centric, a switch to a customer lifetime value metric and building of buyer loyalty will become inevitable (Hollensen, 2006).

4.4.7.7 Building Buyer Loyalty

Using the web as a vehicle for building loyalty on the part of international buyers involves several different stages (Fletcher et al., 2004):

- **Attract:** attracting clients to visit the web site. They do so on a voluntary basis and will not come simply because a site has been created. To create awareness of the site, it is necessary to use banner ads and links to other sites

- **Engage:** engaging visitor's attention. This is necessary to get the visitor to the site to participate and encourage interaction. Most sites fail as promotional mediums because they are boring and have poorly presented material. In this connection, the content of the site is most important.

- **Retain**: retain the visitor's interest in your site. This is important to ensure repeat visits to the site and the creation of a 'one-to-one 're-lationship between the firm and its potential overseas customer. One way of achieving this is by persuading the customer to provide information on their requirements so that the firm can customize its offering and thereby increase switching costs.

- **Learn**: learn about the client and their preferences. This is enabled by providing on the site a facility for easy feedback and comment. The use of cookies can assist.

- **Relate**: adopt a deliberate policy of building relationships with site visitors. This is achieved by providing value added content, by tai-loring the product/service to the needs of each customer and promising customized delivery.

4.4.7.8 Smartphone Marketing

Smartphone marketing, mobile marketing or **M-marketing** should be considered within the context of m-business and m-commerce. Emerging from recent developments in communications technology, m-business represents 'mobile' business and 'refers to the new communications and information delivery model created when telecommunications and the Internet converge'.

Together with the widespread adoption of 3G and 4G smartphones among consumers, mobile marketing has increasingly become an important tool in brands' international advertising and promotional efforts.

The next generation of the internet standard in mobile marketing (m-marketing) will allow programs to run through a web browser rather than a specific operating system. That means consumers will be able to access the same programs and cloud-based content from any device – personal computer, laptop, smartphone or tablet – because the browser is the common platform. This ability to work seamlessly anytime, anywhere, on any device could change consumer behaviour and shift the balance of power in the distribution systems towards the end of the distribution system – the end-buyer, who has cheaper and cheaper access to the new mobile devices. It will create opportunities for marketers to distribute goods and services more directly to the end-buyers and it will present increasing challenges for the intermediaries between the manufacturers and the end-buyers.

Rapidly emerging innovations have also delivered the possibility of smartphones able to use product bar codes to access product-related information and phones able to act as e-wallets, as either a prepaid card for small purchases or a fully functioning credit/debit card unit.

However, the mobile industry will also see a lot more enforcement on the mobile security and privacy in the coming years, as many questions have been raised regarding mobile payments, coupons and applications. Mobile commerce is on the rise, which means people are more comfortable with the idea of paying with their phones. However, there is still a critical view throughout the mobilized world regarding the safety of this kind of payment system (Hollensen and Opresnik, 2015).

4.4.7.9 App Marketing

By December 2016, there were 1.6 million Android apps and 1.4 million Apple apps available. On average, smartphone users have about 40 apps on their phones and regularly use about 15. For companies, apps provide ample revenue opportunities. Worldwide revenue from apps was approximately $12 billion in 2012 and is estimated to increase to over $60 billion in 2017.

As free apps become increasingly prevalent, paid app downloads are expected to decline, and advertising and in-app purchases are likely to become the main revenue streams in the coming years. With the rise in smartphones and tablets across the globe, the mobile app industry has been rapidly growing. Mobile advertising has seen triple-digit percentage growth each year since 2010.

Mobile apps can be classified into **mobile commerce** and **mobile value-added services (MVAS)**:

- **Mobile commerce:** Here the app mostly has the purpose of selling a product or a service. For example, the Domino's Pizza app is designed to generate sales and promote special deals to customers.

- **Mobile value-added services (MVAS):** Here the app offers services that are not directly tied to sales but are designed to help customers solve problems or make decisions. Such an app enriches the total customer experience of a product / service offering.

An example of an MVAS is an airline app that can be used to generate a mobile boarding pass (QR code) in a co-production process between the airline and the customer. Conceptually, the core service (the flight) and the MVAS (mobile boarding pass) need to be interrelated constructs building the final customer experience - flight from A to B.

On the spectrum from mobile commerce to mobile services (MVAS), many apps offer on-the-go services paired with location-based technology. Companies employ technology for both geocoding (based on location latitude and longitude) and reverse geocoding (translating coordinates into a street address) to deliver accurate locations. One example of a location-based app is the **Tinder** dating app, which is a social discovery application that facilitates communication between mutually interested users. The Tinder 'matchmaking' app is based on criteria like geographical location, number of mutual friends, and common interests. Based on these criteria the app then makes a list of geographical near-by potential candidates. The app then allows the user to anonymously like another user by swiping right or pass by swiping left on them. If two users like each other it then results in a 'match' and they are then able to chat within the app (Hollensen, Kotler and Opresnik, 2017).

Summing up, developing an effective mobile marketing program is much more challenging than developing a traditional program aimed at laptop and desktop users. The mobile program needs to be planned, implemented, and tested for multiple devices (smartphones, tablets, laptops, and desktops) and different operating systems, and should adjust for the limitations of mobile devices in terms of screen and traditional keyboard size. In addition, the immediacy, location, and personalization attributes of mobile devices increase the need to develop a portfolio of messages to reflect such attributes as weather conditions (immediacy), distance to a store (location), and a consumer's preferences and past purchase behavior (personalization).

4.4.8 Direct Marketing

Many of the marketing and promotion tools that we have discussed so far in previous sections were developed in the context of mass marketing: targeting broad markets with standardized messages and offers distributed through intermediaries. Today, however, with the trend toward more specifically targeted or one-to-one marketing, many companies are adopting **direct marketing**, either as a primary marketing approach or as an important supplement to other strategies.

Direct marketing consists of direct connections with thoroughly selected individual consumers to both obtain an immediate response and cultivate enduring customer relationships. Direct marketers communicate directly with customers, often on a one-to-one, interactive basis. Making use of detailed databases, they tailor their marketing offers and communications to the specific needs of narrowly defined segments or even individual buyers. Beyond brand image building, direct marketers typically seek a direct, immediate, and measurable consumer response (Kotler, Armstrong and Opresnik, 2016). Direct marketing is a more encompassing concept than direct sales, which simply refers to sales from the producer directly to the ultimate consumer, bypassing the channel middlemen. This approach is not so much a promotional tool as a new distribution channel, but it grew out of direct mail, which is a traditional advertising medium. The traditional direct mail promotions of various products often offered 'direct response' options, including requests for more information, redeemable cents-off coupons, and participation in contests and lottery drawings. It was only a small step to a completed sale, and especially since credit cards became common, direct mail has become an important promotion *and* sales channel (Hollensen, 2006).

4.4.8.1 Benefits of Direct Marketing

For customers, direct marketing is convenient, easy to use, and private. From the comfort of their homes or offices, they can browse mail catalogues or company Web sites at any time. Direct marketing gives clients immediate access to a variety of products and information 'at their fingertips'. In addition, direct marketing is immediate and interactive as buyers can interact with sellers by phone or on the seller's Web site to create the configuration of information, products, and services they desire, and then order them instantly.

For Sellers, direct marketing is a powerful tool for building customer relationships. With the use of databases, marketers can target narrow groups or individual consumers, tailor their offers to the specific needs and wants, and promote these offers through personalised communications. Direct marketing can also be timed to reach prospects at just the right moment. Furthermore, this tool enables sellers access to buyers that they could eventually not reach through other channels. Finally, direct marketing can offer sellers a low-cost, efficient alternative for reaching their markets (Kotler, Armstrong and Opresnik, 2016).

4.4.8.2 Major Direct Marketing Tools

The major forms of direct marketing include personal selling, telephone marketing, direct mail marketing, catalogue marketing, direct-response advertising, and online marketing. We shall look at personal selling later in this chapter and examined online marketing already above. Here, we examine some other tools within the framework of online marketing as well as the other direct marketing forms (Hollensen and Opresnik, 2015).

4.4.8.2.1 Direct Mail Marketing

Direct mail marketing involves sending an offer, announcement, reminder, or other material to a person at a particular address with the purpose of promoting a product and/or maintaining an ongoing relationship. Direct mail at its best allows close targeting of individual customers in a way not feasible using mass advertising media. Direct mail is well suited to direct, one-to-one communication. It permits high target market selectivity, can be personalised, is flexible, and allows easy tracking of results. Clearly, the effectiveness of direct mail relies heavily on the quality of the target customer data.

In summary, direct mail can be very cost-effective at targeting specific segments of the market, with easily measurable results. However, critics point to low response rates, the existence of junk mail, the fact that personal information can be sold to mailers without the knowledge of the subject, and the fact that some firms persist in sending mail even when they have been asked to stop. In addition, direct mail may work out more expensive than e-mail campaigns, which are becoming more attractive as access to broadband expands rapidly (Benady, 2005).

4.4.8.2.2 Telemarketing

Telephone marketing (also called telemarketing) involves using the telephone to sell directly to consumers and business customers. There are a number of reasons why telemarketing has grown substantially in recent years. First, it has lower costs per contact than a face-to-face salesperson visit. Second, it is less time consuming than personal visits. Third, the growth in telephone ownership has increased access to households, and the use of toll-free lines has reduced the cost of responding by phone. Finally, despite the reduced costs compared to a personal visit, the telephone retains the advantage of two-way communication.

However, telephone marketing suffers from a number of disadvantages. First, it lacks the visual impact of a personal visit and it is not possible to assess the mood or reactions of the buyer through observation of the body language. It is easier for a consumer to react negatively over the telephone and the number of rejections can be quite high as telephone selling can be considered intrusive. Finally, although cost per contact is less expensive than a personal sales call, it is more expensive than direct mail, media advertising or the Internet (Ellis-Chadwick and Jobber, 2016).

4.4.8.2.3 Catalogue Marketing

Catalogue marketing is the sale of products through catalogues distributed to agents and consumers, usually by mail or at stores. In addition, most print catalogues have added Web-based catalogues to their marketing offer, and a variety of new Web-only cataloguers have emerged.

When used effectively, catalogue marketing to customers provides a convenient way of selecting products at home that allow in-depth discussion and evaluation with family members in a relaxed atmosphere away from crowded shops. Especially for remote rural locations it provides a valuable service, preventing the necessity to travel long distances to town shopping areas. For catalogue marketers, the expense of high-street locations is removed and there is the opportunity to display a wider range of products than in a shop. Nevertheless, catalogues are quite expensive to produce and they require regular updating, particularly when selling fashion items. In addition, they do not allow goods to be tested (e.g. shaver) or tried on (e.g. clothing) before purchase (Ellis-Chadwick and Jobber, 2016).

4.4.8.2.4 Direct Response Advertising

Direct response advertising appears in the prime media, such as television, newspapers and magazines, but differs from standard advertising as it is designed to elicit a direct response such as an order, enquiry or request for a visit of a salesperson. Typically, a free contact number is included in the advertisement and a website address. This tool combines the ability of broad-cast media to reach large sections of the population with direct marketing techniques that allow a rapid response.

Direct response television (DRTV) generally entails telephone numbers to let viewers call for purchases. The advantage is that marketer can get direct response to a mass-market advertisement, but whether viewers will inter-rupt their programme viewing to surf the Internet for a listed Web site or calling a particular contact number is questionable (Murphy, 2001).

4.4.8.2.5 Online Marketing

For many, e-mail has virtually replaced traditional letters and even tele-phone calls as the choice for correspondence. Every day, billions of e-mail messages are sent out. This has also influenced the way of doing business. Prepared well, **e-mail marketing** can be one of the most cost-effective communications tools. It is fast, inexpensive, and effective, and its response rates are many times that of direct mail. However, the e-mail marketing landscape is beleaguered with examples of marketers getting labelled as spammers, annoying customers, violators of privacy laws and worse.

A major strength of direct e-mail is its ability to qualify leads. Appropriate software allows the firm to track who is reading and responding along with the types of responses. This enables the firm to segment the audience ac-cordingly, targeting future communications based on recipients' self-re-ported priorities (Hollensen and Opresnik, 2015).

4.4.9 Personal Selling

The final major element of the promotional mix is **personal selling**. This involves face-to-face contact with a consumer and, unlike advertising, pro-motion and other forms of non-personal communication, personal selling allows a direct interaction between buyer and seller. This process implies that the seller can identify the specific needs and wants of the buyer and tailor the sales approach and presentation accordingly. However, such flexibility is expensive as the cost of a car, travel expenses and sales office overheads can mean that the total annual investment for a salesperson is often twice the level of a salary (Hollensen and Opresnik, 2015).

4.4.9.1 Sales Management

Establishing the company's own sales force requires sophisticated planning and considerable resources. Sales force management can be defined as the analysis, planning, implementation, and control of sales force activities. The following steps are involved in structuring and managing a sales force (Cateora and Graham, 2004):

- **Designing Sales Force Strategy and Structure:** Based on analyses of current and potential customers, the selling environment, competition, and the firm's resources and capabilities, marketing managers face two critical design decisions. They need to determine the sales force size and organize the sales force. The most practical method for deciding the number of sales people required is the 'workload approach'. It is based on the calculation of the total annual calls required per year divided by the average calls per year that can be expected from one salesperson. A company can divide up sales responsibilities along any of several lines. There are three alternative approaches to organizing the sales force: Territorial, product and customer sales force structure (Talley, 1961).

- **Recruiting Salespeople:** At the heart of any successful sales force operation is the recruitment and selection of high-calibre salespeople as the performance difference between an average salesperson and a top salesperson can be quite substantial.

- **Selecting Salespeople:** To select personnel for marketing positions effectively, management must define precisely what is expected of its people. A formal job description can aid management in expressing long-range needs as well as current needs. In addition to descriptions for each marketing position, the criteria should include special requirements indigenous to various countries (Hollensen, 2006).

- **Training Salespeople:** New and experienced salespeople may spend anywhere from a few weeks or months to a year or more in training. Many companies send their new sales representatives into the field almost immediately upon hiring them, after only a cursory training program. The rationale is that time is best spent prospecting and meeting with customers, rather than sitting in a training centre (Crittenden and Crittenden, 2004). It is factual that detailed training can be costly and may result in lost opportunities when a seller is not in the field. Yet effective long-term sellers must not only have appropriate personal characteristics, they must also know and identify with the company and its products, understand customer buying motives, and be prepared to make an effective sales presentation, counter initial resistance, and close the sale. Moreover, to be successful, the seller has to know how to develop and maintain the records necessary to process orders, service customers, and cultivate repeat sales.

- **Motivating Salespeople:** Effective motivation is based on a deep understanding of salespeople as individuals, their personalities and value systems. According to Luthans (1997) the basic motivation process involves needs (deprivations) which set drives in motion (deprivations with direction) to accomplish goals (anything which alleviates a need and reduces a drive).

- **Designing Compensation Systems:** To attract good salespeople, a company must have an appealing compensation plan. Compensation is made up of several elements – a fixed amount, a variable amount, expenses, and fringe benefits. Developing an equitable and functional compensation plan that combines balance, consistent motivation, and flexibility is extremely challenging in international operations. Besides rewarding an individual's contribution to the firm, a compensation program can be used effectively to recruit, develop, motivate, or retain personnel.

- **Evaluating and Controlling Salespeople:** Sales force evaluation provides the information necessary to check if targets are being achieved, and provides the raw information to steer training and motivation. In evaluation and control of sales people, emphasis is often placed on individual performance, which can easily be measured by sales revenues generated (often compared with past performance, forecasts, or quotas).

4.4.9.2 The Personal Selling Process

The actual selling process consists of several steps that the salesperson must master. These stages focus on the goal of getting new customers and receiving orders from them. However, most salespeople spend a great deal of their time maintaining existing accounts and building long-term customer relationships. The selling process consists of seven steps (Kotler, Armstrong and Opresnik, 2016):

- **Prospecting and Qualifying:** The first step in the selling process is prospecting – identifying qualified potential consumers. Usually, the salesperson must often approach many prospects to get just a few sales. Although the company supplies some guidance, salespeople require skill in finding their own. They can ask current customers for referrals. They can cultivate referral sources, such as suppliers, dealers, and bankers. Or they can search for prospects in directories or on the Web and track down leads using the telephone and direct mail.

- **Pre-Approach:** The pre-approach is the step in the selling process in which the salesperson learns as much as possible about a prospective customer before making a sales call or visit. The preparation carried out prior to a sales visit can reap dividends by enhancing confidence and performance when the salesperson is face-to-face with the customer. Salespeople will benefit from gaining knowledge of their own and competitor's products, by understanding buyer behaviour and by having clear sales call objectives and by having planned their sales representation. This is because the success of the sales interview is customer-dependant.

- **Approach:** During the approach step, the salesperson should know how to create a favourable initial impression with customers as this can often affect later perceptions. This step involves the salesperson's appearance, opening lines, and the follow-up remarks.

Positive impressions can be gained by adopting a business-like approach, being friendly but not overly familiar, being attentive to detail, and observing common courtesies. As in all stages of the selling process, listening to the customer is crucial.

- **Presentation and Demonstration:** The presentation step of the selling process offers the opportunity for the salesperson to convince customers that they can supply the solution to their problem. Consequently, it should focus on customer benefits rather than product features. The salesperson should continue to ask questions during the presentation to ensure that the customer has understood what he or she has said, and to check that what the salesperson has talked about really is of importance to the consumer.

- **Handling Objections:** Customers almost always have abjections during the presentation or when asked to place an order. The problem can be either logical or psychological, and objections are often unspoken. Although objections can cause problems, they should not be regarded negatively per se since they highlight issues that are important to the customer. It is of paramount importance in handling objectives to touch both substantive and emotional aspects. Salespeople have to listen to the objection without interruption and should employ an 'agree and counter' technique, where they agree with the buyer but then put forward an alternative point of view with respect to the problem of the consumer.

- **Closing:** After handling the prospect's objections, the salesperson tries to close the sale. Salespeople should know how to recognize closing signals from the buyer, including physical actions, comments, and questions. They can use several closing techniques: they can simply ask for the order, review points of agreement and offer to help write up the order. In this context, the salesperson may offer the buyer special reasons to close, such as a lower price or an extra quantity at no charge.

- **Follow-Up:** Follow-up is the last step in the selling process. Right after closing, the salesperson should complete any details on delivery time, purchase conditions, and other subjects. The salesperson then should schedule a follow-up call when the initial order is received, to ensure there is proper installation, instruction, and servicing. This visit would eventually reveal any problems, assure the buyer of the salesperson's interest, and reduce any buyer concerns that might have arisen since the sale.

4.4.10 Product Placement

Product placement is the deliberate placing or products and/or their logos in movies and television, usually in return for money. While it has been giant business in some countries, like the United States, for some time, restrictions preventing product placement have only recently been relaxed in Europe. For example, Steven Spielberg's science-fiction film 'Minority Report' featured more than 15 major brands, including Gap, Nokia, Pepsi, Guinness, Lexus and Amex, with their logos appearing on video billboards throughout the film. These product placements earned DreamWorks and 20th Century Fox $ 25 million, which went some way towards reducing the $ 102 million production costs for the film (Ellis-Chadwick and Jobber, 2016).

Product placement has grown substantially in recent years for the following reasons (Hollensen and Opresnik, 2015):

- **Mass-market reach**: media fragmentation implies that it is increasingly difficult to reach mass markets; Movies can reach hundreds of millions of consumers world-wide, creating instant brand awareness.
- **Positive associations**: brands can benefit from positive images in a film or television programme. For example, James Bond to be seen driving an Aston Martin, imparts the Bond association of sophistication, masculinity and style to the car.
- **Credibility**: many consumers do not realize that brands have been product-placed. The brands are perceived being used rather than appearing in a paid-for advertisement. This can substantially add to the credibility of the associations sought.
- **Message repetition**: movies are often repeated on television and bought on video or DVD, creating opportunities for brand message repetition.

- **Avoidance of advertising bans**: with bans on advertising certain products, such as alcohol and cigarettes, in particular media, product placement is an opportunity to reach large audiences.

- **Targeting**: by choosing an appropriate film or television programme, specific market segments can be reached.

- **Branding opportunities**: new brands can be launched linked to the movie.

- **Promotional opportunities**: placements in films can provide promotional opportunities by creating related Web sites.

5. Implementation and Controlling in the Marketing Planning Process

5.1 Organizing and Implementing the Marketing Plan

We have described and analysed each of the ingredients of a typical marketing mix. In developing a marketing plan an organisation will need to give careful consideration to each of these elements, whilst at the same being cautious not to fall into the trap of viewing each ingredient in isolation. As already stated in the first chapter, marketing and the marketing tools must constantly be viewed as a collective whole and opportunities for synergy will only be exploited if it is regarded accordingly. Each ingredient of the mix should consistently reinforce the 'message' being conveyed by the others. To ensure that the plan does represent a coherent whole, it is of key importance that the organisation's approach to each of the marketing elements is presented in the plan in a clear and easy to read format. It should then become obvious whether ambiguities are present and corrective action can be taken (Hollensen and Opresnik, 2015).

5.1.1 The Process of Developing the International Marketing Plan

Basically, marketing planning is a rational sequence and a series of activities leading to the setting of marketing objectives and the formulation of plans for achieving them. Companies generally undergo a management process in developing marketing plans. In SMEs this process is usually informal. In larger, more diversified organisations, the process is often systematized (Hollensen and Opresnik, 2015).

5.1.2 Deciding on the International Marketing Mix

Companies that operate in one or more foreign markets have to decide how much, if at all, to adapt their marketing mixes to local conditions. At one extreme are international companies that use a **standardised marketing mix**, selling largely the same products and services and applying the same marketing approaches world-wide. At the other end is an **adapted market-ing mix**. In the latter case, the company adjusts the marketing mix elements to each target market, bearing more costs but aiming at a larger market share and return due to a more sophisticated and tailored marketing mix.

5.1.3 Writing the Marketing Plan Document

Marketing planning is widely adopted by organisations from all sectors. The process of marketing planning integrates all elements of marketing management: marketing analysis, development of strategy and the implementation of the marketing mix. Marketing planning can, therefore, be regarded as a systematic process for assessing marketing opportunities and matching them with own resources and competences. In this respect, the process aids businesses to effectively develop, coordinate and control marketing activities. Basically, the major functions of the marketing plan are to determine where the company is, where it wants to go, and how it can get there. Marketing planning is able to fulfil these functions by driving the business through three sorts of activities: (a) analyses of the internal and external situations, (b) development of marketing strategy, and (c) design and implementation of marketing programmes (Hollensen, 2006).

The marketing planning process is linked to planning in other functional areas and to overall corporate strategy. It takes place within the larger strategic marketing management process of the business. To survive and flourish, the business marketer must properly balance the firm's resources with the objectives and opportunities of the environment. Marketing planning is a continuous process that involves the active participation of other functional areas. The marketing plan itself is the written document that businesses develop to record the output of the marketing planning process. This document provides details of the analysis and strategic thinking that have been undertaken and outlines the marketing objectives, marketing mix and plan for execution and control. As such, the plan plays a key role in informing organisational members about the plan and any roles and responsibilities they possibly have within it. The plan also provides details of required resources and should highlight potential obstacles to the planning process, so that steps can be taken to overcome them. The marketing plan is a kind of road map, providing direction to help the business implement its strategies and achieve its objectives: the plan guides top management and all functional areas within the organisation.

Once the core marketing analyses are complete, the strategy development process follows. The key during this phase is to base any decisions on a detailed and objective view from the analyses. The most appropriate target markets will be identified, basis for competing and positioning strategies determined and detailed marketing objectives presented. As these choices will affect how the business proceeds in relation to its customers and competitors, there must be consistency with the company's general corporate strategy. The marketing strategy must also be realistic and sufficiently detailed to form the basis for the marketing programmes which follow.

The final stage of the marketing planning process involves the determination of marketing mix programs and their implementation. A detailed explanation is needed of precisely what marketing tasks must be undertaken, how, by whom and when. There needs to be a comprehensive rationale connecting these marketing mix recommendations with the analyses and strategy preceding them.

Assuming that appropriate attention has been devoted to the marketing analyses and marketing strategy that guide the marketing programs, managers must next ensure that adequate detail is provided to make the marketing mix genuinely implementable. This means that each component of the marketing program – product, price, promotion, distribution and people – must be discussed separately and the tasks required to action it are fully explored.

Those involved in planning will usually prepare some form of written marketing plan document in which to explain the outputs of the process. The marketing plan provides a useful framework for the analytical and strategic thinking undertaken, the detailed marketing objectives and marketing programs, their implementation and control. Managers are able to refer back to the document for guidance and should regularly update it to ensure that a full record of the marketing planning activities is available. The document helps focus the views of senior management and explain the required marketing activities and target market strategy to other functional areas within the business, such as operations and finance (Dibb, 2002).

The key components of the marketing plan are the following (Hollensen and Opresnik, 2015):

1. Title page

2. Table of contents

3. Executive summary

4. Introduction and problem statement

5. Situational analysis

6. Marketing objectives

7. Marketing strategies

8. Marketing programs and action plans

9. Budgets

10. Implementation and control

11. Conclusion.

We shall now examine each section of the marketing plan structure in further detail (Hollensen and Opresnik, 2015).

5.1.3.1 Title Page

The title page is an identification document that provides the reader with the following essential information:

- legal name of business
- name of document ('Marketing Plan for …')
- date of preparation or modification of the document
- name, address, e-mail and phone number of the business or contact person

- name, address, e-mail and phone number of the individual or business who prepared the plan
- the planning period.

5.1.3.2 Table of Contents

This is the list of subjects covered in the marketing plan and where to find them.

5.1.3.3 Executive Summary

This gives busy executives and managers a rapid overview, in form of a concise summary of the key points in the marketing plan. This section encompasses a one-page summary of the basic factors involving the marketing of the product or service along with the results expected from implementing the plan.

5.1.3.4 Introduction and Problem Statement

The identification and clear presentation of the problem(s) or issue(s) facing the company is the most critical part of the introduction. Only a problem properly defined can be addressed. The marketer should shortly address the main problem in the marketing plan. The marketer needs to be on alert for symptoms parading as key issues and underlying problems. Strategic marketing problems are long-term, involve large sums of money, and affect multiple aspects of the firm.

5.1.3.5 Situational Analysis

Based on a comprehensive audit of the market environment, competitors, the market, products, and the company itself, this section provides a condensed view of the market (size, structure, and dynamics), prior to a detailed analysis of individual market segments, which form the heart of the marketing plan.

The process is based upon market segmentation – that is, homogeneous groups of customers with characteristics that can be exploited in marketing terms. This approach is taken because it is the one that is most valuable for managers in developing their businesses. The alternative product-oriented approach is hardly ever appropriate, given the varying requirements of the different customer groups in the market in which most organisations compete.

It is necessary to summarize the unit's present position in its major markets, in the form of a SWOT analysis for each major market segment, product, or business group. The word SWOT derives from the initial letters of the words strengths, weaknesses, opportunities, and threats. The analysis includes the following issues (Hollensen and Opresnik, 2015):

The Firm and its Market

- Identification and evaluation of the competences in the company (key personnel, experience, skills and capabilities, and resources), in comparison with competitors.
- The structure of the marketing organisation (lines of authority, functions and responsibilities).
- Description of the total potential market (i.e. potential customers).
- How does the company's product/service satisfy the needs of the market?
- Description of the particular customers to be targeted.
- Size of (a) total potential market (number of potential customers), and (b) the target market. Estimates should be supported with factual data.
- Growth potential of (a) total potential market, and (b) the target market. The marketer needs to look at local, national and international markets. Estimates should be supported with factual data.
- The company's market share (firm's sales divided by the total market sales in per cent)

Competitive Environment

- Major competitors: name, location, and market share.
- Comparison of the company's product/service with that of the major competitors (brand name, quality, image, price, etc.).
- Comparison of the company with that of the major competitors (reputation, size, distribution channels, location, etc.).
- How easy is it for new competition to enter this market?
- What has the company learned from watching competition?
- Are competitors' sales increasing, decreasing, steady? Why?

Technological Environment

- How is technology affecting the product/service?
- How soon can it be expected to become obsolete?
- Is the company equipped to adapt quickly to changes?

Socio-Political Environment

- Description of the changing attitudes and trends. How flexible and responsive is the firm?
- New laws and regulations that may affect the business. What might be the financial impact?

From the SWOT analyses, key issues that must be addressed. Marketers should summarize the company's internal and external assessment in form of a SWOT-matrix with the key points from the situation analysis.

5.1.3.6 Marketing Objectives

Within this section, the marketing objectives in terms of sales volume, market share, return on investment, or other objectives or goals should be stated precisely (e.g. 'To obtain a sales volume of 3.000 units equal to an increase in market share from 10 per cent to 15 per cent of total market, by the by the end of the next fiscal year.').

5.1.3.7 Marketing Strategies

The question addressed within this part is how to reach the company's objectives and goals? Which strategic models should be used (new market penetration, penetration, market development, etc.).

5.1.3.8 Marketing Programs and Action Plans

Marketing programs are the actionable means of achieving desired ends. They outline what needs to be done, how it will be done, when it will be done, and who will do it.

- How will the company implement the above strategy?
- Product/service: quality, branding, packaging, modifications, location of service, etc.
- Pricing: How will the firm price its product/service so that it will be competitive, yet profitable?
- Promotion/advertising: How, where, when, etc.
- Selling methods: Personal selling, mail-order, etc. The marketer must also include number of salespersons, training required, etc.
- Distribution methods
- Servicing of product
- Other: the marketer is supposed to add any other relevant information

5.1.3.9 Budgets

Having detailed the steps that will be necessary to achieve the marketing objectives, the writer of the plan should then be in a position to cost the various proposals and to derive an overall marketing budget for the planning period. Of course, in reality, this is not uncomplicated. Cost will certainly have been in the minds of marketing planners even before they commenced the marketing planning process. At the very least, the development of a suitable budget is likely in practice to have been an iterative process, with proposals being re-evaluated in the light of budgetary constraint.

There are a variety of ways of determining the marketing budget. Irrespective of the method actually used, in practice it would be usual to specify how the eventual budget has been allocated and to include such a specification in the marketing plan itself. It would also be typical for an allowance to be made for contingencies in the event that monitoring by the organisation suggests that the objectives will not be met. Sufficient resources should then exist for some form of corrective action to be taken.

A budget of cash flows should also be prepared. It identifies whether a company will have enough money to meet its cash requirements on a monthly basis. Some sales will be made in cash while others may be made on credit. Because sales made on credit will not result in the receipt of cash until a later date, they must not be recorded until the month in which the cash will actually be received. Therefore, the percentage of sales to be made in cash and the percentage to be made on credit must be estimated. The percentage of credit sales should be further broken down according to the business' different collection periods (30 days, 60 days, etc.).

5.1.3.10 Implementation and Control

As soon as the plan has been implemented, the management will then have to take responsibility for monitoring the progress of the organisation towards the goals specified. Managers will also need to concern themselves with the costs that have been incurred at each stage of implementation and monitor these against the budget. Thus, control mechanisms need to be put into place to monitor:

- the actual sales achieved, against the budget
- the actual costs incurred against those budgeted
- the performance of individual services against budget

- the overall strategic direction that the organisation is taking – i.e. will the overall corporate objectives be achieved in a manner commensurate with the organisation's mission?

If variances are detected in any of these areas, corrective action should be initiated, if necessary by utilizing resources allocated for contingency in the budget.

5.1.3.11 Conclusion

This section briefly concludes the problems stated in the beginning of the report, based on the analysis in the marketing plan. The conclusion is not a summary. The executive summary will normally also include the key results of the market analysis.

5.1.4 Implementing the Marketing Plan

Marketing strategy concerns the issues and challenges of *what* should happen and *why* it should happen. Implementation focuses on actions: *who* is responsible for different activities, *how* precisely the strategy should be carried out, *where* things will happen and when action will occur. No matter how well conceived a strategy and marketing plan might be, it will definitely fail if people are incapable of carrying out the necessary tasks to make the strategy actually work in the market. Consequently, implementation capability is an integral part of strategy formulation.

The implementation of a new strategy potentially entails profound effects on people in organisations. Unfortunately, most people most of the time are not open to change. It represents risk, uncertainty and more effort than the regular day job. Therefore, the implementation of a strategic move is usually associated with the need for people to adapt to change. Therefore, the management of change is an essential ingredient in effective planning and implementation.

Even though the benefits of adopting marketing planning are well established, the effectiveness of the process is not definite. A range of barriers to successful marketing planning have been highlighted in the literature. Consequently, careful attention is essential to ensure that marketing planning is effectively implemented. The starting point should be an appreciation of the probable barriers, so that preventative and remedial action can be taken (Hollensen and Opresnik, 2015).

The recommendation is that marketers should use the following three solutions (Hollensen, 2006):

- **Solution 1**: provide the necessary infrastructure and resources for marketing planning activities
- **Solution 2**: use a robust analytical process that is objective and complete in terms of the inclusion of the essential ingredients of marketing planning
- **Solution 3**: devote managerial time and attention to the on-going management of the resulting plan's implementation

5.1.5 Deciding on the Marketing Organisation

Marketing organisation provides the framework in which marketing implementation takes place. The firm's organisational structure is a critical variable for the implementation of the company's marketing plans. The following summary highlights the main reasons for this (Hollensen, 2006):

- There may be difficulties in coordinating and controlling operating units of different sizes and levels of complexity.
- Personnel in different markets will have diverse abilities and expectations, and organizing such a heterogeneous group can be challenging.
- There may be excessive head-office control.

Effective marketing planning only comes about when the marketing strategy and organisational structure correspond. The elementary question 'Do we have the right organisation for our strategy?' is one that all chief executives should be asking. This question can be broken down into four 'basic' parts, the first two of which are concerned with the division of responsibilities amongst the labour force, whilst the remaining questions focus on co-ordination and control:

- What tasks are required to put the strategies into operation?
- To whom should these tasks be assigned?
- How interdependent are these tasks?
- How can the organisation be sure that the tasks assigned will be performed?

There is nothing like *the* correct answers, and consequently there are accurate structures for all organisations, but successful firms are those that tend to have organisational structures that fluently fit their specific needs in terms of corporate objectives, strategies, corporate culture, etc.

There are many ways in which a multinational company and marketing can be organised. The most relevant are the following organisational structure archetypes (Ellis-Chadwick and Jobber, 2016):

- no marketing department
- functional structure
- international division structure
- product-based structure
- geographic structure
- matrix structure

5.2 Budgeting and Control

An organisation needs to budget in order to ensure that its expenditure does not exceed its planned income. Marketing control is an essential element of the marketing planning process because it provides a review of how well marketing objectives have been achieved. Consequently, this section will outline the need for a control system to supervise the marketing operations of the company (Hollensen and Opresnik, 2015).

5.2.1 Marketing Productivity and Economic Results

The **productivity** of an operation is related to how effectively input resources in a process are transformed into economic results for the service provider and value for its customers. The traditional productivity conception has been developed for manufacturers of physical goods as a production efficiency concept. Existing productivity models and measurement instruments are also geared to the context of manufacturers. Moreover, they are based on assumptions that production and consumption are separate processes and that customers do not participate in the production process (Hollensen, 2006).

High productivity is commonly assumed to be a primary goal in so much as a productive operation is more likely to have lower costs. It is the close connection with the cost performance of an operation of process that accounts for the interest in understanding and measuring productivity. Although the definition of productivity appears straightforward, productivity can be difficult to deal with for different reasons, but first of first of all the outputs are usually expressed in different forms to the inputs. Outputs are often measured in physical terms such as units (e.g. cars produced), tonnes (of paper), kilowatts (of electricity), or value (Euros), for example. However, the inputs are usually physically different and include measures of people (numbers, skills, hours worked or costs), cost of input resources or marketing actions (Johnston and Jones, 2004).

Especially, the intangible nature of many services means that it is difficult to define and measure the service outputs being provided. The measurement and management of inputs and outputs is also complicated because of the simultaneous production and consumption of many services, as well as their perishability and heterogeneity, as service encounters are experienced differently by different people or even by the same people in different circumstances.

Because the service (production) process and service consumption are usually simultaneous processes, where customers participate actively, the resources or inputs used to produce services cannot be standardized more than to a certain level. It is difficult to relate a given number of inputs, in volume or value terms, to a given amount of outputs. Frequently, it is even difficult to define 'one unit of service.' According to the traditional manufacturing-related productivity concept, productivity is defined as the ratio between outputs produced and inputs used, given that the quality of the outputs is kept constant (the constant quality assumption).

Only if the quality of the production output is constant and there is no significant variation in the ratio between inputs used and outputs produced with these inputs, productivity can be measured with traditional methods.

Productivity cannot be understood without taking into account the interrelationship between the use of inputs or production resources and the perceived quality of the output produced with these resources. The interrelationship between internal efficiency and external efficiency is crucial for understanding and managing service productivity.

Marketing actions, such as advertising, service improvements, or new product launches, can help build long-term assets (e.g., brand equity, customer equity). These assets can be leveraged to deliver short-term profitability (Rust et al., 2004). Thus, marketing actions both create and leverage market-based assets. In this context, it is important to distinguish between the 'effectiveness' and the 'efficiency' of marketing actions. For example, price promotions can be efficient in that they deliver short-term revenues and cash flows. However, to the extent that they invite competitive actions and destroy long-term profitability and brand equity, they may not be effective. Consequently, a company needs to examine both tactical and strategic marketing actions and their implications (Hollensen, 2006).

Financial benefits from a specific marketing action can be evaluated in several ways. **Return on investment (ROI)** is a traditional approach to evaluating return relative to the expenditure required to obtain the return. Commonly used retrospectively to measure short-term return, ROI is controversial in the context of marketing effectiveness. Because many market-

ing expenditures play out over the long run, short-term ROI is often preju-
dicial against marketing expenditures. The correct usage of ROI measures
in marketing requires an analysis of future cash flows.

Other financial impact measures include the internal rate of return, which is
the discount rate that would make the discounted return exactly equal to the
discounted expenditure; the net present value, which is the discounted return minus the net present value of the expenditure; and the economic
value-added (EVA), which is the net operating profit minus the cost of capital.

Except for the non-financial metrics such as awareness, in each case the
measures of financial impact weigh the return generated by the marketing
action against the expenditure required to produce that return. The financial
impact affects the financial position of the firm, as measured by profits,
cash flow, and other measures of financial health.

5.2.2 Marketing Budgeting

The purpose of a **marketing budget** is to pull all the revenues and costs
involved in marketing together into one comprehensive document. This is
an important managerial tool that balances what is needed to be spent
against what can be afforded and aids in the framework of prioritisation. It
is then used in monitoring the performance in practice.

Budgeting is also an organisation process that involves making forecasts
based on the proposed marketing strategy. The forecasts then are used to
construct a budgeted profit-and-loss statement (i.e. profitability). An important aspect of budgeting is deciding how to allocate the proposed investments across all of the anticipated programs within the marketing plan.

The marketing plans and the annual budget are interlinked in several ways –
the sales forecast, the pricing policy, the marketing expenditure budget and
the allocation of resources. A budget is a detailed plan outlining the acquisition and use of financial and other resources over some given time period.
The **annual budget** is commonly referred to as the '**master budget**'. Usually, it has three principal parts: the operating budget, the cash budget and
the capital expenditure budget. It is driven by the sales forecast. The budget

plays a key role in an organisation by moving the organisation from an informal reaction method of management to a formal controlled system of management. It addition, it might act as a motivator and communicator, as well as for functional coordination and performance evaluation (Hollensen, 2006).

It is evident that the annual budget and the marketing plan are interwoven and should be part of the same process in organisations. The management implications are significant. An organisation works effectively when there is clear communication and coordination across functional lines. For effective implementation of an organisation's strategy, the firm must serve customers better than the competition. This implies that all management policies and systems should be continuously reviewed.

Regardless of the organisational level, control involves some form of profitability analysis as already mentioned above when discussing various marketing metrics. In brief, **profitability analysis** requires that analysts determine the costs associated with specific marketing activities to find out the profitability of such units as different market segments, products customer accounts, and distribution channels (intermediaries).

An array of measures (often referred to as **marketing metrics**) is available to marketing managers who wish to measure the effectiveness of their activities. However, it is often difficult to determine the exact contribution of marketing efforts because outcomes are usually dependent on multiple factors. For example, higher sales may be caused by increased and/or better advertising, a more motivated sales force, weaker competition, and so on. This makes it difficult to justify, for example, increased advertising expenditure, because it is difficult to quantify the effects of advertising.

Despite these issues, marketing is requested to become accountable for its activities. In order to assess performance of marketing activities, marketing managers are using marketing metrics, which are quantitative measures of the outcomes of marketing activities and expenditures (Hollensen and Opresnik, 2015).

5.2.3 Controlling the Marketing Programme

At this point in the marketing planning process, the marketing plan is almost complete. The final step is to plan how the company will control the plan's implementation. Marketing control keeps both employees and activities on track so the organisation continues in the direction outlined in the marketing plan. However, some employees in the organisation often view 'control' as being negative because they tend to fear that the control process will be used to assess their performance and ultimately as a basis for 'punishment'.

In preparing a marketing plan, marketers have to plan for three types of marketing control: annual control, profitability control, and strategic control (Hollensen, 2006):

- **Annual control:** Because marketers generally formulate new marketing plans every year, they require annual plan control to assess the progress of the current year's marketing plan. This includes broad performance measures (e.g. sales results, market share results) to evaluate the company's overall effectiveness. If a company fails to achieve this year's marketing plan objectives, it will have difficulty achieving its long-term goals and mission. Although e.g. 'market share measures' are driven by sales performance, they reflect relative competitive standing. These measures aid senior managers gauge their organisation's competitive strength and situation over time.

- **Profitability control:** This assesses the organisation's progress and performance based on key profitability measures. The precise measures differ from company to company, but they frequently include ROI, contribution margin and net profit margins. Various companies measure the monthly and yearly profit-and-loss results of each product, line, and category, as well as each market or segment and each channel. By comparing profitability results over time, marketers can identify significant strengths and weaknesses and recognize problems and opportunities early. Closely related to profitability control, productivity control is measuring the efficiency of the e.g. the sales force, channels and logistics, and product management. The purpose is to measure profitability improvements through reduced costs or higher yield. As productivity is vital to the bottom line some companies appoint marketing controllers to establish marketing productivity standards. Noticeably, productivity control is connected not only with profitability but with customer relationships as well.

- **Strategic control:** This considers the organisation's effectiveness in managing the marketing function, in managing customer relationships, and in managing social responsibility and ethics issues. Whereas profitability control are applied monthly or more often, strategic control may be applied once or twice a year, or as needed to give top management a clearer picture of the organisation's performance in these strategic areas.

6. Conclusion

In the framework of a holistic and integrative approach to marketing to-day's marketers have to work closely with a variety of marketing partners when it comes to creating customer lifetime value and building strong customer relationships. In addition to being just excellent at customer relationship management, marketers must also be skilled at **partner relationship management**, which implies working closely with partners in other company departments and outside the organisation to jointly bring greater value to customers:

- **Partners inside the company:** Traditionally, marketers have been charged with understanding consumers and representing customer needs to different company departments. The old perception was – and surprisingly still is in numerous organisations – that marketing is done only by marketing, sales, and customer support people. However, in today's increasingly connected world, marketing no longer has sole ownership of customer interactions. Every functional area can interact with customers. The new and holistic approach is that every employee must be customer focused. David Packard, co-founder of Hewlett-Packard, wisely said, 'Marketing is far too important to be left only to the marketing department'.

  It is of paramount importance, that organisations are linking all departments in the cause of creating customer value. Rather than assigning merely sales and marketing people to customers, they should form cross-functional teams.

- **Marketing partners outside the company:** Changes are also occurring in how marketers connect with their suppliers, channel partners, and even competitors. Most enterprises today are networked companies, relying heavily on partnerships with other firms. In this respect, supply chain management enables companies to strengthen their connections with partners all along the supply chain. Success at building customer relationships also rests on how well the entire supply chain and, more generally, value net is managed. Companies adapting this integrative approach do not just treat suppliers as vendors and distributors as customers. They treat both as partners in delivering customer value.

As outlined throughout the book, we suggest to pursue an integrative marketing management approach which implies to direct each and every activity towards the customer, making formerly product-focused companies fully customer-centric. Companies must rethink marketing and develop a more inclusive approach directing all departments, functions and staff towards the customer.

References

Aaker, D. A. (1990) Brand extensions: The good, the Bad and the Ugly, Sloan Management Review, Summer, pp- 47-56

Aaker, D. A. (1991) Managing Brand Equity, The Free Press, New York, NY

Aaker, D. A. (1996) 'Measuring brand equity across products and markets', California Management Review, vol. 38, no. 3, pp. 102-20

Aaron, J. (2013) 'How to incorporate Reddit into your Marketing Strategy in 5 easy steps, https://www.inboundnow.com/how-to-incorporate-reddit-into-your-marketing-strategy-in-5-easy-steps/, accessed 24th February 2017

Adcock, A. (2000) Marketing strategies for competitive advantage, Wiley

Agrawal, AJ (2017) 5 Tips To Improve Your YouTube Marketing Strategy, https://www.forbes.com/sites/ajagrawal/2017/01/12/5-tips-to-improve-your-youtube-marketing-strategy/#3210aac3494f, accessed 7th March 2017

Anderson, J. C. and Narus, J. A. (2004) Business Market Management: Understanding, Creating and Delivering Value, Prentice Hall, New Jersey

Andreasen, A. R. (1994) Social marketing: Its definition and domain. Journal of Public Policy and Marketing 13 (1), pp. 108-14.

Ansoff, H. I. (1965) Corporate Strategy: An Analytical Approach to Business Policy for Growth and Expansion, McGraw-Hill, New York

Bagozzi, R. P. (1974) Marketing as an Organized Behavioural System of Exchanges, Journal of Marketing, Vol. 38, October, pp. 77-81

Bainbridge, J. (2005) Third Dimension, Marketing, 8, June, p. 36

Baker, M. and Hart, S. (1999) Product Strategy and Management, Pearson: Education, Prentice Hall

Barger, V.A. and Labrecque, L.I. (2013) An Integrated Marketing Communications Perspective on Social Media Metrics. International Journal of Integrated Marketing Communications, Spring, pp. 64-76

Barnes, J. G. (1994) Close to the Customer: but is it really a relationship?, Journal of Marketing Management, 10, pp. 561-570

Barnes, J. G. and Howlett, D. M. (1998) Predictors of equity in relationships between service providers and retail customers, International Journal of Bank Marketing, 16 (1), pp. 5-23

Bartlett, C. and Ghoshal, S. (1989) Managing Across Borders: The transnational solution, Harvard University Press, Boston, MA.

Berman, B. (2016) Planning and implementing effective mobile marketing programs, Business Horizons, Vol. 59, July–August 2016, pp. 431–439

Berry, L. L. (1983) Relationship Marketing, in Berry, L.L., Shostack, G.L., Upah, G.D. (Eds.) Emerging Perspectives on Service Marketing, Chicago, IL: American Marketing Association, pp. 25-28

Berry, L. L. (1995) Relationship Marketing of Services Growing Interest, Emerging Perspectives, Journal of the Academy of Marketing Science, 23 (Fall), pp. 236-45

Berry, L. L. (2000) Relationship Marketing of services: growing interest, emerging perspectives, in Shet, J. N. and Parvakiyar, A. (eds) Handbook of Relationship Marketing, Thousand Oaks, pp. 149-170

Best, R. J. (2000) Market-Based Management, 2nd edition, prentice Hall, Inc

Bickhoff, N., Hollensen, S. and Opresnik, M. O. (2014) The Quintessence of Marketing: What You Really Need to Know to Manage Your Marketing Activities, Heidelberg

Bitner, M. J. (1995) Building Service Relationships: It's All about Promises, Journal of the Academy of Marketing Science, 23 (Fall), pp. 246-51

Brennan, R. (1997) Buyer/supplier partnering in British industry: the automotive and telecommunications sectors, Journal of Marketing Management, 13 (8), pp. 758-776

Brodie, R. J., Coviello, N. E., Brookes, R. W. and Little, V. (1997) Towards a paradigm shift in marketing: an examination of current marketing practices, Journal of Marketing Management, 13 (5), pp. 367-382

Buttle, F. B. (1996) Relationship Marketing: Theory and Practice, Paul Chapman, London

Cannie, J. K., and Caplin, D. (1991) Keeping Customers for Life. American Management Association, New York.

Carlzon, J. (1985) Moments Of Truth, Albert Bonniers Förlag Ab, Stockholm

Carroll, A. B. and Buchholtz, A. K. (2000) Business and society: ethics and stakeholder management, South-Western College, Cincinnati

Chandy, R. K. and Tellis, G. J. (1998) Organizing for Radical Product Innovation, MSI Report, No. 98-102

Chaney, P. (2015) How to Use Yelp for Local Marketing, http://www.practicalecommerce.com/articles/114853-how-to-use-yelp-for-local-marketing, accessed 27t February 217

Charter, M. K., Peattie, K., Ottman, J. and Polonsky, M. J. (2002) Marketing and Sustainability, BRASS, Cardiff

Chartered Institute of Marketing (2005) Marketing and the 7Ps, Cookham, Chartered Institute of Marketing

Chaston, I. (1998) Evolving 'new marketing' philosophies by merging existing concepts: application of process within small high-technology firms, Journal of Marketing Management, 14, pp. 273-291

Christopher, M., Payne, A. and Ballantyne, D. (1991) Relationship Marketing, Butterworth Heinemann, London

Churchill, H. L. (1942) How to Measure Brand Loyalty, *Advertising and Selling*. Vol. 35, pp. 24ff

Collins, J. and Porras, J. I. (2002) Built to last – Successful habits of visionary companies, HarperCollins, New York

Croft, M. (2003) Mind your language, Marketing, June 19, pp. 48-49

Crosby, L. A. and Stephens, N. (1987) Effects of Relationship Marketing on Satisfaction, Retention, and Prices in the Life Insurance Industry, Journal of Marketing Research. Vol. 24, November, pp. 404-411

Daley, R. (2015) The Ultimate Pinterest Marketing Guide: How to Improve Your Reach and Promote Your Brand, https://blog.kissmetrics.com/ultimate-pinterest-marketing-guide/, accessed 15th February 2017

D'Andrea, M. (2012) The Marketer's Guide To SlideShare, https://blog.kissmetrics.com/marketers-guide-to-slideshare/, accessed 17th February 2017

Daneshkhu, S. (2014) 'Make-up enters age of selfie', Financial Times Europe, 29th July, p. 8

Davenport, H. (2001) How do they know their customers so well?, MIT Sloan Management Review, Winter, pp. 63-73

Davis, S. (2000) Brand asset management: Driving profitable growth through your brands, Jossey-Bass, San Francisco

Deloitte (2016), e-Sports: Bigger and smaller than you think, Deloitte Global www2.deloitte.com/global/en/pages/technology-media-and-telecommunications/articles/tmt-pred16-media-esports-bigger-smaller-than-you-think.html

DeMers, J. (2014): Your Guide To Using Snapchat For Marketing, http://www.forbes.com/sites/jaysondemers/2014/08/04/your-guide-to-using-snapchat-for-marketing/#635635c60f82

Dewsnap, B. and Jobber, D. (2002) A social psychological model of relations between marketing and sales, European Journal of Marketing, 36(7/8), pp. 874-894

Dibb, S. (2002) 'Marketing Planning best practices', The Marketing Review, No. 2, pp. 441-59

Dibb, S. and Simkin, L. (2001) Market Segmentation – Diagnosing and Treating the Barriers. Industrial Marketing Management, 30, 609-625

Douglas, S. P. and Craig, C. S. (2006) Collaborative and iterative translation: an alternative approach to back translation, Journal of International Marketing, 15(1): 30–43.

Doyle, P. (1989) Building successful brands: The strategic options, Journal of Marketing Management, 5(1), pp. 77-95

Doyle, P. (1995) Marketing in the new millennium, European Journal of Marketing, 29 (12), pp. 23-41

Drucker, P. F. (1993) Management Tasks, Responsibilities, Practices, Harper and Row, New York

Dube, A. and Helkkula, A., (2015) Service experiences beyond the direct use: indirect customer use experiences of smartphone apps", Journal of Service Management, Vol. 26 Iss 2 pp. 224 - 248

Duermyer, R. (2016) Blog Marketing: What It Is and How to Do It, https://www.thebalance.com/blog-marketing-1794404, accessed 20th February 2017

Dwyer, F. R., Schurr, P. H. and Oh, S. (1987) Developing buyer-seller relationships, Journal of Marketing, 51, pp. 11-27

Egan, J. (2008) Relationship Marketing, Pearson Education, Harlow

Ehrenberg, A. S. C. (1992) Comments on how advertisement works, Marketing and Research Today, August, pp. 167-169

Ehrenberg, A. S. C. and Goodhart, G. J. (1980) How advertising works, J. Walter Thompson/MRCA

Ellis-Chadwick, F. and Jobber, D. (2016) Principles and Practice of Marketing, 8th ed., Berkshire

Emiliani, M. L. (2000) 'Business-to-Business online auctions. Key issues for purchasing process improvement'. Supply Chain Management: An International Journal. Vol. 5, No. 4, pp. 176-186

Evans, P. B. and Wurster, T. S. (1999) 'Getting Real About Virtual Commerce', Harvard Business Review, Vol. 77, No. 6, (November-December), pp. 85-94

Evans, P. B. and Wurster, T. S. (2000) Blown to Bits: How the new economics of information transforms strategy, Boston, Harvard Business School Press

Fanning, J. (1999) Tell me a story: The future of branding. Irish Marketing Review, vol. 12, no. 2, pp. 3-15

Faris, P. W., Bendle, N. T., Pfeifer, P. E. and Reibstein, D. J. (2006) Key Marketing Metrics, Pearson, Harlow

Fletcher, R., Bell, J. and McNaughton, R. (2004) International e-Business Marketing, Thomson Learning

Fontein, D. (2016) Pinterest for Business: The Definitive Marketing Guide, https://blog.hootsuite.com/how-to-use-pinterest-for-business/, accessed 15th February 2017

Francis, T. (2000) Divine Intervention, Marketing Business, May, pp. 20-22

Frazier, G. L., Spekman, R. E., and O'Neal, C.R. (1988) Just-In-Time Exchange Relationships in Industrial Markets, Journal of Marketing, Vol. 52, October, pp. 52-67

Gilmore, A., Carsons, D. and Grant, K. (2001) SME Marketing In Practice, Marketing Intelligence & Planning, 19 (1), Pp. 6-11

Go, G. (2016) Steps to Successful Forum Marketing, https://www.the-balance.com/successful-forum-marketing-2531792, accessed 17th February 2017

Gobe, M. (2001) Emotional branding, Allworth Press, New York

Gordon, I. H. (1998) Relationship Marketing, Etobicoke, John Wiley & Sons

Gotte, A. (2016) A Step-by-Step Guide to Pinterest Marketing, https://adespresso.com/academy/blog/step-step-guide-pinterest-marketing/, accessed 15th February 2017

Griffin, T. (1993) International Marketing Communications, Butterworth Heinemann, Oxford

Grönroos, C. (1990) Relationship approach to the marketing function in service contexts: the marketing and organization behaviour interface, Journal of Business Research, 20, pp. 3-11

Grönroos, C. (1994) From marketing mix to relationship marketing: towards a paradigm shift in marketing, Management Decisions, 32, pp. 4-20

Grönroos, C. (1995) Relationship marketing: the strategy continuum, Journal of Marketing Science, 23 (4), pp. 252-254

Grossmann, R. P. (1998) Developing and managing effective customer relationships, Journal of Product and Brand Management, 7 (1), pp. 27-40

Grossnickle, J. and Raskin, O. (2001) What's ahead on the Internet: new tools, sampling methods, and applications help simplify Web research, Market Research, Summer: 9–13

Habibi, M.R., Davidson, A. and Michel Laroche (2017) 'What managers should know about the sharing economy', Business Horizons, Vol 60, January-February, pp. 113—121

Hall, E. T. (1976) Beyond culture, Garden City, NY: Anchor

Harridge-March, S. and Qinton, S. (2009): Virtual snakes and ladders: social networks and the relationship marketing loyalty ladder, The Marketing Review, 2009, Vol 9, No. 2, pp. 171-181

Hart, S., Smith, A., Sparks, L. and Tzokas, N. (1999) Are loyalty schemes a manifestation of relationship marketing, Journal of Marketing Management, 15, pp. 541-562

Hastings, G. (2003) 'Relational Paradigms in Social Marketing', Journal of Macromarketing, Vol. 23, No. 1, June pp. 6-15.

Hennig-Thurau, T. and Klee, A. (1997) The Impact of Customer Satisfaction and Relationship Quality on Customer Retention—A Critical Reassessment and Model Development, Psychology & Marketing, 14 (December), pp. 737-65

Hennig-Thurau, T., Hofacker, C.F. and Bloching, B. (2013) 'Marketing the Pinball Way: Understanding how Social Media change the generation of value for consumers and companies', Journal of Interactive Marketing, Issue 4, pp. 237-241

Hines, K. (2013) How to Improve Your Social Media Marketing With Blogging, http://www.socialmediaexaminer.com/how-to-improve-your-social-media-marketing-with-blogging/, accessed 20th February 2017

Hite, R. E. and Frazer, C. (1988) 'International advertising strategies of multinational corporations', Journal of Advertising Research, vol. 28, August - September, pp. 9-17

Hofacker, C.F., Ruyter, K.D., Lurie, N.H., Manchanda, P. and Donaldson, J. (2016), Gamification and Mobile Marketing Effectiveness, Journal of Interactive Marketing, Vol. 34, pp. 25–36

Hollensen, S. (2003) Marketing Management, Financial Times/Prentice Hall, London

Hollensen, S. (2006) Marketing Planning: A global perspective, McGraw-Hill, Berkshire

Hollensen, S. (2017) Global Marketing, 7th ed., Pearson Education Limited, Harlow, UK

Hollensen, S. (2015) Marketing Management, 3rd edition, Pearson Education Limited, Harlow, UK

Hollensen, S. (2014) Global Marketing, 6th ed., Pearson Education, Harlow, UK

Hollensen, S. and Opresnik, M. (2015) Marketing – A Relationship Perspective, 2nd ed., Vahlen, München

Hollensen, S., Kotler, P. and Opresnik, M. O. (2017) Social Media Marketing. A Practitioner Guide, Opresnik Management Consulting, Lübeck

Hooley, G., Saunders, J. and Piercy, N. (2004) Marketing strategy and competitive positioning, 3rd ed., Financial Times/Prentice Hall

Houston, F. S., Gassenheimer, J.B., and Maskulka, J. (1992) Marketing Exchange Transactions and Relationships. Quorum Books, Westport, CT.

Howard, J. A., and Sheth, J. N. (1969) The Theory of Buyer Behaviour. John Wiley & Sons, Inc., New York

Ilieva, J., Baron, S. and Healey, N.M. (2002) Online surveys in marketing research: pros and cons, International Journal of Market Research, 44(3): 361–76.

Jain, S. (1996) International Marketing Management (5th ed), South-Western College Publishing, Cincinnati, OH

Javalgi, R. and Moberg, C. (1997) Service loyalty: implications for service providers, Journal of Services Marketing, 11 (3), pp. 165-179

Jaworski, B., Kohli, A. and Sahay, A. (2000) Market-Driven Versus Driving Markets, Journal of Academy of Marketing Science, 28 (1), pp. 45-54

Johnston, A. (2016) How to Create an Instagram Marketing Strategy, http://sproutsocial.com/insights/instagram-marketing-strategy-guide/, accessed 14th February 2017

Jones, J. P. (1991) Over-promise and under-delivery, Marketing and Research Today, November, pp. 195-203

Jones, T. O. and Sasser, W. E. (1995) Why satisfied customers defect, Harvard Business Review, November/December, pp. 88-99

Kandampully, J. and Duddy, R. (1999) Relationship marketing: a concept beyond the primary relationship, Marketing Intelligence and Planning, 17 (7), pp. 315-323

Kanter, R. M. (1994) Collaborative advantage, Harvard Business Review, July/August, pp. 96-108

Kawasaki, G. and Fitzpatrick, P. (2014) The art of social media, Random House.

Keegan, W. J. (2002) Global Marketing Management, 7th ed., Prentice-Hall, Upper Saddle River, New Jersey

Keller, K. L. (1993) 'Conceptualizing, measuring, and managing customer-based brand equity', Journal of Marketing, vol. 57, no. 1, pp. 1-22

Kinard, B. R. and Capella, M. L. (2006) Relationship Marketing: the influence of consumer involvement on perceived service benefits, Journal of Service Marketing, 21 (6), pp. 359-368

Kissmetrics Blog (2017) Facebook Marketing: A Comprehensive Guide for Beginners, https://blog.kissmetrics.com/facebook-marketing/

Klompmaker, J. E., Rodgers, W. H. and Nygren, A. E. (2003) 'Value, not volume', Marketing Management, June, pp. 45-48

Kohli, A. K. and Jaworski, B. J. (1990) Market orientation: the construct, research propositions and managerial implications, Journal of Marketing, 54, pp. 1-18

Kohli, C., Suri, R. and Kapoor, A. (2015) Will Social Media kill branding, Business Horizons, Vol. 58, pp. 35-44

Kolowich, L. (2017) 10 of the Best Brands on Twitter, https://blog.hubspot.com/marketing/twitter-best-brands, accessed 11th February 2017

Kolowich, L. (2017) 10 of the Best Brands on Snapchat right now, https://blog.hubspot.com/marketing/snapchat-best-brands, accessed 14th February 2017

Komter, A. E. (2004) Gratitude and gift exchange, The Psychology of Gratitude, Robert A. Emmons and Michael E. McCullough, eds., pp. 195-213

Korporaal, G. (2015) 'The Changing Face of Cosmetics', The Deal, 20th March, pp. 28-21

Kotler, P. (1972) A Generic Concept of Marketing, Journal of Marketing, Vol. 36 April, pp. 46-54

Kotler, P. (1992) Marketing's new paradigm: what's really happening out there?, Planning Review, 20 (5), pp. 50-52

Kotler, P. (1994) Marketing Management: Analysis, Planning, Implementation, and Control. Prentice-Hall, Inc., Englewood Cliffs, New Jersey

Kotler, P. (1997) Marketing Management: Analysis, planning, implementation and control (9th ed), Prentice Hall, Englewood Cliffs, NJ.

Kotler, P. (1997) Method for the millennium, Marketing Business, February, pp. 26-27

Kotler, P. (1999) Kotler on Marketing, Free Press, New York

Kotler, P. (2000) Marketing Management, 10th edition, Prentice Hall, Englewood Cliffs, NJ

Kotler, P., Armstrong, G. and Opresnik, M. O. (2016) Marketing: An Introduction, 13th ed., Pearson, New Jersey

Kotler, P., Keller, K. L. and Opresnik, M. O. (2017) Marketing Management, 15th ed., Pearson, Hallbergmoos

Kotter, J. P. and Schlesinger, L. A. (1979) Choosing strategies for change, Harvard Business Review, March-April, pp. 106-111

Kumar, N. (1999) 'Internet distribution strategies: Dilemmas for the incumbent', Mastering Information Management, Part 7, Electronic Commerce, Financial Times, 15 March

Kumar, N., Scheer, S. and Kotler, P. (2000) From Market Driven to Market Driving, European Management Journal, 18 (2), pp. 129-141

Kumar, V. and Shah, D. (2004) Pushing and Pulling on the Internet, Marketing Research, Spring2004, Vol. 16, Issue 1, pp. 28-33

Lambin, J. (1976) Advertising, Competition and Market Conduct in Oligopoly Over Time Amsterdam: North Holland-Elsevier

Lancaster, G. and Massingham, L. (2001) Marketing Management, 3rd ed., McGraw-Hill

Lane, W. R., King, K. W. and J. T. Russell (2005) Kleppner's advertising procedure, 16th ed., Prentice Hall, Upper Saddle River, New Jersey

Lannon, J. (1991) Developing brand strategies across borders, Marketing and Research Today, August, pp. 160-168

Lassar, W., Mittal, B. and Sharma, A. (1995) 'Measuring customer-based brand equity', Journal of Consumer Marketing, vol. 12, pp. 11-19

Lauterborn, R. (1990) New Marketing Litany: 4P's Passe: C-Words take over, Advertising Age, October 1, pp. 25-27

Lee, S.F., LO, K.K., Leung, R.F. and Ko, A.S.O. (2000) Strategy formulation framework for vocational education: integrating SWOT analysis, balanced scorecard, QFD methodology and MBNQA education criteria, Managerial Auditing Journal, 15/8, pp. 407-23

Lenskold, J. D. (2004) Customer-centric marketing ROI; Harvard Business Review, January/February, pp. 26-31

Lesly, P. (1998) The handbook of public relations and communications, McGraw-Hill, Maidenhead

Levitt, T. (1983) After the Sale is Over…, Harvard Business Review, 16, pp. 87-93

Levitt, T. (1986) The Marketing Imagination, New York, New York: Free Press

Linkon, N. (2004) Using e-mail marketing to build business, TACTICS, November, p. 16

Linton, I. (1995) Database marketing: Know what you customer wants, Pitman, London

Little, R. W. (1970) The Marketing Channel: Who Should Lead This Extra-corporate Organisation, *Journal of Marketing*, Vol. 34, January, pp. 31-38.

Luthans, F. (1997) Organisational behaviour, McGraw-Hill, New York

Maignan, I. and Ferrell, O. C. (2004) Corporate social responsibility and marketing: an integrated framework, Journal of the Academy of Marketing Science, 32(1), pp. 3-19

McGoldrick, P. J. and Davies, G. (1995) International Retailing: Trends and strategies, Pitman, London

McGorty, C. (2017) 4 Reasons Why Google Plus Marketing is Still Relevant, http://fatguymedia.com/4-reasons-why-google-plus-marketing-is-still-relevant/, accessed 14th February 2017

McKenna, R. (1991) Relationship Marketing: Successful Strategies for the Age of the Customer. Addison-Wesley Publishing Co., Reading, MA.

Meenaghan, T. (1996) 'Ambush marketing – a threat to corporate sponsorship', Sloan Management Review, Fall, pp. 103 – 13

Meyer, C. (2001) While Customers wait, add value, Harvard Business Review, Vol 79, No 7, pp. 24-25

Michaelidou, N. and Dibb, S. (2006) Using email questionnaires for research: Good practice in tackling non-response, Journal of Targeting, Measurement and Analysis for Marketing, 14(4): 289–96.

Middleton, T. (2002) Sending out the winning message, Marketing Week, 16 May, pp. 43-45

Mills, J. F. and Camek, V. (2004) The risks, threats and opportunities of disintermediation: A distributor's view, International Journal of Physical Distribution and Logistics Management, 34(9), pp. 714-727

Mintz, O. and Currim, I. S. (2013) What drives Managerial Use of Marketing and Financial Metrics and Does Metric Use Affect Performance of Marketing-Mix Activities. Journal of Marketing, 77(March): 17-40

Morgan, R. M. (2000) Relationship marketing and marketing, in Shet, J. N. and Parvakiyar, A. (eds) Handbook of Relationship Marketing, Thousand Oaks, pp. 481-504

Morgan, R. M. and Hunt, S. D. (1994) The commitment-trust theory of relationship marketing, Journal of Marketing, 58 (3), pp. 20-38

Mort, G.S. and Drennan, J. (2002), Mobile digital technology: Emerging issues for Marketing, Journal of Database Marketing & Customer Strategy Management, Vol. 10, 1, September, pp. 9-23

Mueller, B. (1996) International Advertising: Communicating across cultures, Wadsworth, Belmont, CA

Mullane, J. V. (2002) The mission statement is a strategic tool: when used properly, Management Decision, Vol. 40, No. 5, pp. 448-455

Murphy, D. (2001) Dare to be digital, Marketing Business, December/January, pp. 3-5

Nagle, T. and Holden, R. (2001) The strategy and the tactics of pricing, 3rd ed., Prentice-Hall, Englewood Cliffs, New Jersey

Narver, J. C. and Slater, S. F. (1990) The effect of market orientation on business profitability, Journal of Marketing, 54, pp. 20-35.

Nørmark, P. (1994) 'Co-promotion in growth', Markedsføring (Danish marketing magazine), no. 14, p. 14

O'brian, S. and Ford, R. (1988) Can we at last say goodbye to social class?, Journal of the Market Research Society, 30(3), pp. 289-332

Ottesen, O. (1995) 'Buyer initiative: ignored, but imperative for marketing management – towards a new view of market communication', Tidsvise Skrifter, no. 15, avdeling for Ákonomi, Kultur og Samfunnsfag ved Høgskolen i Stavanger

Owen, J. (2009) How to manage: the art of making things happen, 2nd ed., Pearson Prentice-Hall, Harlow

Palmatier, R. W., Dant, R. P., Grewal, D. and Evans, K. R. (2006) Factors influencing the effectiveness of relationship marketing: a meta-analysis, Journal of Marketing, 70 (October), pp. 136-153

Palmatier, R. W., Jarvis, C. B., Bechkoff, J. R. and Kardes, F. R. (2009) The Role Of Customer Gratitude In Relationship Marketing, Journal of Marketing, Vol 73 (September 2009), pp. 1-18

Patterson, B. (2016) 5 Yelp Facts Business Owners Should Know (But Most Don't), http://marketingland.com/5-yelp-facts-business-owners-should-know-163054, accessed 27th February 2017

Paul, P. (1996) 'Marketing on the Internet', Journal of Consumer Marketing, vol. 13, no. 4, pp. 27-39

Payne, A., Christopher, M. and Peck, H. (eds) (1995) Relationship Marketing for Competitive Advantage: Winning and Keeping Customers, Oxford, Butterworth Heinemann

Peattie, K. and Peattie, S. (1993) Sales Promotion: Playing to win?, Journal of Marketing Management, 9, pp. 255-269

Pels, J. (1999) Exchange relationships in consumer markets?, European Journal of Marketing, 33 (1/2), pp. 19-37

Pitt, L. F., Ewing, M. T. and Berthon, P. (2000) Turning Competitive Advantages into Customer Equity, Business Horizons, September-October, pp. 11-18.

Pitta, D. A. (1998), marketing one-to-one and its dependence on knowledge discovery in databases, Journal of Consumer Marketing, Vol. 15 No. 5, pp. 468-480

Porter, M. (1980), Competitive strategy, Free Press, New York, NY

Porter, M. E. (1985) Competitive Advantage, The Free Press, New York.

Prahalad, C. K. and Hamel, G. (1990) The Core Competence of the Corporation, Harvard Business Review, May-June, pp. 79-91

Pressey, A. D. and Mathews, B. P. (1998) Relationship marketing and retailing: comfortable bedfellows?, Customer Relationship Management, 1 (1), pp. 39-53

Ratten, V. (2015) 'International Consumer Attitudes Toward Cloud Computing: A Social Cognitive Theory and Technology Acceptance Model Perspective', Thunderbird International Business Review, Vol. 57, No. 3, May/June, pp. 217-228.

Reichheld, F. F. (1996) The Loyalty Effect: The Hidden Force Behind Growth, Profits and Lasting Value, Boston, Harvard Business School Press

Reichheld, F. F. (2003) The one number you need, Harvard Business Review, December, pp. 46-54

Ries, A. and Trout, J. (1981) Positioning: The battle for your mind, McGraw-Hill, New York

Robbins, S. P and Coulter, M. (2005) Management, 8th ed., Prentice Hall, New Jersey

Rogers, R. M. (2003) Diffusion of innovations, Free Press, New York

Rosenberg, L. J. and Cziepiel, J. A. (1984) A Marketing Approach to Customer Retention, Journal of Consumer Marketing, Vol. 1, Spring, pp.45-51.

Rothschild, M. L. (1978) Advertising strategies for high and low involvement situations, American Marketing Association Educator's Proceedings, Chicago, pp. 150-162

Rothschild, M. L. and Gaidis, W. C. (1981) Behavioural Learning Theory: Its relevance to marketing and promotions, Journal of Marketing, 45, Spring, pp. 70-78

Rust, R. T. and Zahorik, A. J. (1993) Customer Satisfaction, Customer Retention, and Market Share, Journal of Retailing, 69 (Summer), pp. 193-215.

Rust, R. T., Moorman, C. and Bhalla, G. (2010) Rethinking Marketing, Harvard Business Review, January-February 2010, pp. 94-101

Rust, R., Lemon, K. and Zeithaml, V. (2004) Return on Marketing: Using customer equity to focus marketing strategy, Journal of Marketing, January, p. 109

Rust, T. M., Ambler, T., Carpenter, G. C., Kumar, V. and Srivastava, R. K. (2004) 'Measuring Marketing Productivity: Current knowledge and Future directions', Journal of Marketing Vol. 68, October, pp. 76–89

Sampson, P. (1992) People are people the world over: The case for psychological market segmentation, European Journal of Marketing, 28(10), pp. 236-244

Sanyal, R.N. and Samanta, S.K. (2004), 'Determinants of Bribery in International Business', Thunderbird International Business Review, Vol. 46, March-April, pp. 133-148

Saunders, J. (2016) 'Should companies be creators on YouTube?', Market Leader, Quarter 2, pp. 36-39

Schögel, M. and Mrkwicka, K. (2011) 'Communication shift, Chancen und Herausforderungen aus Marketingsicht, Marketing Review St. Gallen, No. 5, pp. 6-10

Scott D. M. (2015) The New Rules of Marketing & PR, 5th ed., John Wiley & Sons, Inc, New York

Shapiro, B. P. and Wyman, J. (1981) New Ways to Reach Your Customer, Harvard Business Review, (July-August), pp. 103-110

Shelly, B. (1995) 'Cool customer', Unilever Magazine, no. 2, pp. 13-17

Sheth, J. N. and Parvatiyar, A. (1995) The evolution of relationship marketing, International Business Review, 4 (4), pp. 397-418

Sheth, J. N. and Sisodia, R. S. (1999) Revisiting marketing's law like generalizations, Journal of the Academy of Marketing Sciences, 17 (1), pp. 71-87

Sheth, J. N., Gardner, D. M. and Garett, D. E. (1988) Marketing Theory: Evolution and Evaluation. John Wiley & Sons, Inc, New York

Siu, E. (2016) 10 Ways to Use Snapchat for Business, http://www.socialmediaexaminer.com/10-ways-to-use-snapchat-for-business/, accessed 14th February 2017

Sloane, G. (2014) General Electric's First Snapchat Is One Small Step for Brand Kind, http://www.adweek.com/digital/general-electrics-first-snapchat-one-small-step-brand-kind-158921/, accessed 14th February 2017

Shrivastava, P. and Souder, W. E. (1987) The strategic management of technical innovation: A review and a model, Journal of Management Studies, 24(1), pp. 24-41

Silverman, G. (2005) Is 'it' the future of advertising?, Financial Times, 24 January, p. 11

Simms, J. (2001) The value of disclosure, Marketing, 2 August, pp. 26-27

Simon, C. J. and Sullivan, M. W. (1990) 'The measurement and determinants of brand equity: a financial approach', working paper, Graduate School of Business, University of Chicago, Chicago, Ill

Singleton, D. and Zyman, S. (2004) Segmenting opportunity, Brand Strategy, June, pp. 52-53

Singca, R. (2016) Tumblr Marketing Tips for Your Business, http://blog.swat.io/2016/12/13/tumblr-marketing-tips-for-your-business/, accessed 14th February 2017

Siu, E. (2016) 4 Tips to Improve Your YouTube Marketing, http://www.socialmediaexaminer.com/4-tips-to-improve-your-youtube-marketing/, accessed 7th March 2017

Slater, S. F. and Narver, J. C. (1996) Competitive strategy in the market-focused business, Journal of Market-Focused Management, Vol. 1, pp. 159-74

Smith, P. R. and Taylor, J. (2004) Marketing Communications: An integrated approach, Kogan Page, London

Smith, M. (2010) 'Facebook 101 for Business: Your Complete Guide.' Social Media Examiner (August

10). http://www.socialmediaexaminer.com/facebook-101-business-guide/, accessed 25th January 2017

Stone, M. (2002) Multichannel customer management: The benefits and challenges, Journal of Database Marketing, Vol. 10, pp. 39-52

Stone, M., Davis, D. and Bond, A. (1995) Direct hit: Direct Marketing with a winning edge, Pitman, London

Storbacka, K., Strandvik, T. and Grönroos, C. (1994) Managing customer relations for profit: the dynamics of relationship quality, International Journal of Service Industry, Management, 5, pp. 21-38

Straker, K. and Wrigley, C. (2016), Emotionally engaging customers in the digital age: the case study of 'Burberry Love', Journal of Fashion Marketing and Management, Vol. 20, No. 3, 276-299

Strebel, P. (1996) Why do employees resist change?, Harvard Business Review, May-June, pp. 86-92

Stroud, D. (2008) Social networking: an age-neutral commodity – Social networking becomes a mature web application, Journal of Direct, Data and Digital Marketing Practice, Vol. 9, No. 3, pp. 278-292

Swaminathan, V., Fox, R. J. and Reddy, S. K. (2001) The impact of brand extension introduction on choice, Journal of Marketing, October, pp. 1-15

Szigin, I., Canning, L., Rappel, A. (2005) Online community: enhancing the relationship marketing concept through customer bonding, International Journal of Service Industry Management, Vol. 16, No. 5, pp. 480-496

Toyne, B. and Walters, P. G. P. (1993) Global Marketing Management: A strategic perspective (2nd ed), Allyn and Bacon, Needham Heights, MA

Treacy, M. and Wiersema, F. (1993) Customer intimacy and other Value Disciplines, Harvard Business Review, January-February, pp. 84-93

Tuten, T.L. and Solomon, M.R. (2015), Social Media Marketing, 2nd ed., Sage Publications Ltd.

Valentine, M. (2009) It's all in the mind, Marketing Week, 2 April, p. 29

Varadarajan, P. R. and Cunningham, M. H. (2000) Strategic alliances: a synthesis of conceptual foundations, in Shet, J. N. and Parvatiyar, A. (Eds) Handbook of Relationship Marketing, Thousand Oaks, CA: Sage, pp. 271-302

Webb, T. (2008) Apple's Guru Calls a New Tune, Observer, 15 June, p. 6

Webster, F. E. and Wind, Y. (1972) Organisational Buying Behaviour, Prentice-Hall, New Jersey

Webster, F. E., Jr. (1992) The Changing Role of Marketing in the Corporation, Journal of Marketing, Vol. 56, No. 4 (October), pp. 1-17

Young, Steve P. (2013) The 2013 YouTube Marketing Guide, https://blog.kissmetrics.com/2013-youtube-marketing-guide/, accessed 7th March 2017

Zarella, D. (2010) The social media marketing book, O'Reilly, California

About the authors

Svend Hollensen (svend@sam.sdu.dk) is an Associate Professor of International Marketing at University of Southern Denmark (Sønderborg) and a visiting professor at London Metropolitan University and University of Naples Federico II.

He is the author of globally published textbooks, including the best seller 'Global Marketing', 7th Edition (Pearson) which was published in 2017 and is no. 1 in sales outside United States, and no. 2 worldwide (in the segment 'International Marketing' textbooks). Indian and Spanish editions have been developed in co-operation with co-authors. The textbook Global Marketing has also been translated into Chinese, Russian, Spanish and Dutch.

His 'Marketing Management – A Relationship Approach', 3rd edition (Pearson) was published in 2015. He has been publishing articles in well-recognized journals like California Management Review, Journal of Business Strategy, Journal of Family Business Strategy and Marketing Intelligence & Planning.

Through his company, Hollensen ApS (CVR 25548299), Svend has also worked as a business consultant for several multinational companies, as well as global organizations like the World Bank.

Marc Oliver Opresnik (www.opresnik-management-consulting.de) is a
Professor of Marketing and Management and Member of the Board of Di-
rectors at SGMI St. Gallen Management Institute, a leading international
business school. He is also a Professor of Business Administration at the
Technische Hochschule Lübeck, as well as a visiting professor to international universities such as Regent's University London and East China University of Science and Technology in Shanghai. He has 10 years of experience working in senior management and marketing positions for Shell International Petroleum Co. Ltd. Along with Kevin Keller and Phil Kotler, he
is co-author of the German edition of 'Marketing Management' the 'Bible
of Marketing'. Dr. Opresnik also is the co-author with Phil Kotler and Gary
Armstrong of the Global Edition of 'Marketing: An Introduction', which is
one of the world's most widely used marketing text books. In addition, he is
co-editor and member of the editorial board of several international journals such as 'Transnational Marketing', 'Journal of World Marketing Sum-
mit Group' and 'International Journal of New Technologies in Science and
Engineering'.

In March 2014, Dr. Opresnik was appointed 'Chief Research Officer' at
'Kotler Impact Inc.', Phil Kotler's internationally operating company. In addition, he was appointed 'Chief Executive Officer' of the Kotler Business
Program, an initiative to enhance marketing education worldwide via online
and offline learning with Pearson as global educational partner.

As president of his firm 'Opresnik Management Consulting'
(http://bit.ly/Opresnik-Management-Consulting; https://www.face-
book.com/MarcOliverOpresnik; www.opresnik-management-consult-
ing.de) he works for numerous institutions, governments and international

corporations including Google, Coca-Cola, McDonald's, SAP, Shell International Petroleum Co Ltd., Procter & Gamble, Unilever, L'Oréal, Bayer, BASF and adidas. More than ¼ million people have benefited from his work as a coach in seminars on marketing, sales and negotiation and as a speaker at conferences all over the world, at locations such as St. Gallen, Berlin, Houston, Moscow, Kuala Lumpur, London, Paris, Dubai and Tokyo.

With his many years of international experience as a coach, keynote speaker and consultant, Marc Opresnik is one of the world's most renowned marketing, management and negotiation experts.

Index

6

6C model 192, 193, 195

A

Account 191
adidas 257
Amazon 198
Android 202
App Marketing 202
Apple 202, 253
ATL communication 181

B

banner ads 196, 200
blog 238, 239, 240, 241, 244, 252
Blogging 242
Bottom-up planning 27
BTL communication 181
Business mission statement 75
Business vision statement 75

C

Cannibalization 83
Cash cows 91
Coca-Cola 256
Content sponsorships 196
Conversion strategies 21
cost per action 199
cost per click 199
cost per sale 200
cross-functional teams 233
Customer Lifetime Value (CLV) 200
Customized marketing 109

D

decision support system (DDS) 200
Deloitte 238
Demographic variables 100
Diversification strategies 84
Dogs 92

E

e-mail marketing 182, 183, 246
environmental scanning 46

F

Facebook 184, 185, 187, 188, 192,
    193, 194, 244, 252
Five forces model 108
Forum, Internet Forums 240

G

General Electric 251
Geographic variables 102
Goals-down-plans-up-planning 27
Google 247, 256
Google Plus 247

H

Hollensen, Svend 2, 3, 8, 189, 191,
    192, 193, 242
Horizontal diversification 84

I

Instagram 243
Integrated marketing communications
    (IMC) 187

Internet marketing 181
interstitials 195, 196

K

Kotler, Philip 2, 8, 243, 244, 245, 256

L

L'Oréal 256
Lateral diversification 84
Lifestyle characteristics 103
LinkedIn 186
Loyalty 200, 237, 250

M

Macro level 56
magazines 181
Market Attractiveness-Competitive
    Position model (MA-CP) 93
Market development strategies 82
Market entry barriers (MEB) 82
Market penetration 82
Market segmentation 95
Marketing budget 25
Marketing budget 229
marketing management 7, 60, 77, 124,
    216
Marketing metrics 230
Marketing opportunity 71
Marketing Research 238, 245
Matching strategies 22
Maxi-Maxi (S/O) 73
Maxi-Mini (S/T) 73
McDonald's 256
metrics 189, 199, 200
Micro level 56
Mini-Maxi (W/O) 73
Mini-Mini (W/T) 73
Mission 16
M-marketing 201
Mobile commerce 202, 203

Mobile value-added services (MVAS)
    203
MySpace 184

N

newspapers 181

O

online advertising 195, 196, 199
Online Performance Tracking 199
Opportunities 70
Opresnik, Marc Oliver 2, 3, 8, 189,
    191, 192, 193, 242, 243, 245, 256

P

Partner relationship management 233
Personality characteristics 103
PEST analysis 57, 58
Pinterest 238, 240, 241
Planning gap 78
Positioning 23
Positioning strategy 110
Problem diagnosis 79
Procter & Gamble 256
Product development strategies 83
Profile segmentation 100, 101, 102,
    104, 106
Profiling 96
pull strategy 185
Purchase behaviour 105, 106
Purchase occasion 104
push strategy 185

Q

Question marks 90

R

recommendations 198

Reddit 235
relationship marketing 7, 241, 247,
   248, 251, 253
ROI 246

S

SAP 256
Segmentation 22
Segmentation, Targeting and
   Positioning (STP) 97
skyscrapers 195, 196
SlideShare 238
Smartphone marketing 201
Snapchat 238, 244, 251
Social Media Marketing 2, 3, 181, 185,
   192, 242, 253
Social networking 187, 188, 253
Socio-demographic variables 102
Stars 90
Stone, Biz 252
Strategic business unit 87
Strategic business unit (SBU) 20
Strategic fit 69
Strategic planning 74
Strengths 70
Stuck-in the-middle position 87
supply chain management 59, 153,
   233
SWOT analysis 19

T

Target marketing 107
Targeting 23
Targeting strategy 108
Television (TV) 189
Threats 70
Tinder 203
Top-down planning 27
Tumblr 252
Twitter 186, 187, 188, 192, 244

U

Unilever 251, 256

V

Value net 56
Vertical integration 58, 84
videos 192
Viral Marketing 192

W

Weaknesses 70
Web 2.0 183

Y

Yelp 237, 249
YouTube 186, 187, 192, 193, 194

CPSIA information can be obtained
at www.ICGtesting.com
Printed in the USA
LVHW091743301019
635835LV00005B/781/P